T0327953

LOUIS MARKOS
author of *Lewis Agonistes*

FROM ACHILLES TO CHRIST

Why Christians Should
Read the Pagan Classics

IVP Academic

An imprint of InterVarsity Press
Downers Grove, Illinois

InterVarsity Press
P.O. Box 1400, Downers Grove, IL 60515-1426
World Wide Web: www.ivpress.com
E-mail: email@ivpress.com

InterVarsity Press® is the book-publishing division of InterVarsity Christian Fellowship/USA®, a student movement active on campus at hundreds of universities, colleges and schools of nursing in the United States of America, and a member movement of the International Fellowship of Evangelical Students. For information about local and regional activities, write Public Relations Dept., InterVarsity Christian Fellowship/USA, 6400 Schroeder Rd., P.O. Box 7895, Madison, WI 53707-7895, or visit the IVCF website at <www.intervarsity.org>.

All Scripture quotations, unless otherwise indicated, are from the King James Version *of the Bible.*

Interior illustrations by Jennifer Barton
Design: Cindy Kiple .
Images: statue and cross with Christ: iStockphoto
Achilles: Yiannis Veslemes/iStockphoto

ISBN 978-0-8308-2593-6

Printed in the United States of America ∞

Library of Congress Cataloging-in-Publication Data

Markos, Louis.

  From Achilles to Christ: why Christians should read the pagan
  classics/Louis Markos.
    p. cm.
  Includes bibliographical references and index.
  ISBN 978-0-8308-2593-6 (pbk.: alk. paper)
  1. Christianity and other religions—Greek. 2. Christianity and
  other religions—Roman. 3. Christianity and literature. 4.
  Classical literature—Appreciation. I. Title.
    BR128.G8M34 2007
    261.5'8—dc22

                2007016680

P   20   19   18   17   16   15   14   13   12   11

Y   23   22

To my parents,

Tom and Angie Markos,

for keeping the legacy alive

CONTENTS

INTRODUCTION

The Only Complete Truth

TERTULLIAN, THAT TOUGHEST AND MOST uncompromising of early church fathers, asked a question that is still with us today: What has Athens to do with Jerusalem? That is to say, is there—indeed, should there be—a meeting ground between the Judeo-Christian strain that proceeds out of Jerusalem and the humanistic Greco-Roman strain that proceeds out of Athens? For Tertullian, the answer to his question was simple: nothing.

Despite Tertullian's scornful dismissal of Athens, Christian thinkers for the past two millennia have continued to ponder his question. Can the basic tenets and chief embodiments of both Christianity and humanism be combined in a way that pays homage both to the glory of God and the dignity of man,[1] the truths of Christ and the wisdom of the ancients? What business does a Christian have devoting time and energy to works written by pagans who lacked the light of the Christian, or even the Jewish, reve-

---

[1]True to the legacy of the great literature that I will be discussing in this book, I will be using traditional English grammar throughout. That is to say, I will use *he* and *his* as gender-inclusive pronouns and *man, men* and *mankind* to refer collectively to the human race.

lation? Are not all the really important answers to be found in the Bible and the sacred tradition? Have not the pagan writers of the ancient world been so superseded by Christianity as to be irrelevant as sources of wisdom in the life of the believer?

Many Christians, particularly evangelicals like myself, are prone to claim that the Bible is the ultimate source of truth. But that is not technically true. Christ, not the Bible, is the ultimate source of truth; the Bible is but the most perfect and reliable embodiment of that truth which resides in Christ alone. Indeed, in the Gospel of John, Christ tells his disciples that he is the truth (14:6). The distinction here is vital. If it is the living Messiah and not a single book that is the source of truth, then it is possible for that truth (albeit in a lesser, fragmented form) to appear throughout the imaginative literature of the ancient pre-Christian world.

We have all been programmed by our Creator with a desire to seek and yearn after the God who is truth. If it is true, as Paul teaches in Acts 17:26-28, that we were all made in his image, that he is not far from us, that in him we live and move and have our being, then it must also be true that those timeless works of ancient Greece and Rome that record the musings of humanity's greatest seekers and yearners will contain traces, remnants and intimations of that wisdom which made us.

Truth is limited neither to the Scriptures nor to the sacred tradition; the Bible, though it tells us all we need to know to find salvation in and through Jesus Christ, does not attempt or purport to be an encyclopedia of all knowledge and wisdom. It can lead us to Christ and can instruct us in the rudiments of our faith, but it cannot answer all our questions nor can it satisfy all our deepest desires and yearnings for truth, beauty and understanding. God speaks to us in many other ways and through many other media. Though the Scriptures must ever act as the touchstone against which all such communications are to be measured, we must not allow puritan suspicion of the moral value and doctrinal status of humanistic pursuits to prevent us from accessing these messages from our Creator.

CHRIST OVER CULTURE

There was a time when many of Christendom's wisest philosophers and theologians were eager to access such messages. In the heyday of medieval

Catholicism, lovers of Christ such as Thomas Aquinas could move smoothly, almost effortlessly, from the ethics and metaphysics of the pagan Aristotle to the spiritual revelations of Christ and the church. For Aquinas, Aristotle was more than just an authority to be acknowledged; he was a source of human truth and even (to a lesser extent) divine wisdom. The Greco-Roman understanding of virtue was, in its purest form, not antithetical to but prophetic of the biblical Christian virtues of faith, hope and love. As H. Richard Niebuhr has shown in his illuminating study *Christ and Culture* (1951), the Roman Catholic church has a strong tradition of viewing Christ and Christianity as representing the culmination and fulfillment of both the Old Testament law and the highest wisdom of the ancients—Christ over culture, to use Niebuhr's memorable phrase.

Unfortunately, the Catholic synthesis of Christianity and pagan humanism did not survive well the Protestant Reformation. Indeed, I would argue that much Christian (especially evangelical) suspicion surrounding the study of the Greeks and Romans can be traced back to the father of Reformed theology: Martin Luther.

Let me begin with a caveat. The debt of gratitude we owe Luther is immense, and we deviate from him at our peril. He helped to restore theology to its biblical Pauline roots and to render the gospel of salvation by grace through faith more accessible and vital than it had been for some time. Still, Luther also helped set in motion an attitude toward pre-Christian thought that led in part to the dissolution of the Thomistic synthesis.

In his well-known debate with Erasmus (one of Niebuhr's prime exemplars of Christ over culture) on the freedom of the will, Luther demonstrated a resistance to learning anything of spiritual and theological value from pagan philosophy and mythology. Holding fast to an extreme version of the doctrine of total depravity, Luther denies to unregenerate pagan man any ability to apprehend portions of Christ's truth or even to seek after those portions:

> The whole world, human reason itself, indeed free choice itself, is obliged to confess that it never knew Christ nor heard of him before the gospel came into the world. And if it did not know him, much less did it seek after him, or even could seek after him or make any endeavor to come to him. Yet Christ is the way, the truth, the life, and salvation. . . . Furthermore, when

Christ is called the way, the truth, and the life, and that antithetically, so that whatever is not Christ is not the way but error, not the truth but a lie, not the life but death, then it necessarily follows that free choice, since it is neither Christ nor in Christ, is included in the error, the lie, and the death. . . . Outside of Christ there is nothing but Satan, apart from grace nothing but wrath, apart from light only darkness, apart from the way only error, apart from the truth only a lie, apart from life only death.[2]

Though I heartily acknowledge that Christ is the only way and that no one could have invented by his own reason the full glory of the gospel, it does not necessarily follow that the pagans were totally incapable of seeking after that way (Acts 17:27, as I suggested above, states just the opposite: that the pagans *did* seek and groan). Yes, Christ alone is truth, but this does not mean that all non-Christian religions and philosophies are totally devoid of truth. Yes, Christ is the light of the world, but does that imply that outside that light all is utter darkness? Were we not all created in God's image, and though we are all fallen from our original state, does not a spark of divine fire remain in each of us?

I would surmise that most believers, evangelical or otherwise, would answer yes to that last question and would grant the possibility that pre-Christian and non-Christian pagans are capable of perceiving, at least in embryonic form, some of the truths revealed in Christ. Perhaps even Luther himself would admit it if pressed. In terms of his education and knowledge, we must remember, Luther was a classical humanist; *The Bondage of the Will* boasts no less than two dozen carefully chosen and subtly used references from such pagan writers as Cicero, Horace, Virgil, Cato, Ovid and Homer. Still, the mindset and the worldview that underlie the passage quoted above persist with many believers; there is an itch to label darkness and light clearly and to put them in eternally opposing camps.

Of course, to be fair to Luther, the dualistic mindset demonstrated in the passage above was by no means invented by the father of the Reformation. Tertullian would have applauded a theological paradigm that sharply distinguished darkness from light, truth from error, grace from wrath.

---

[2]Martin Luther, *The Bondage of the Will,* vol. 33 of Luther's Works, ed. Philip Watson (Minneapolis: Fortress, 1972), pp. 281-82.

Saint Jerome, who gave us the Vulgate, would also have praised this approach and would have resisted the notion that the pagan writers could teach Christians anything of spiritual value. Even Augustine himself—who, before his conversion, was a follower of the dualistic Manicheans—would most likely have positioned himself closer to Luther than Aquinas—despite the fact that he, like Luther, was an accomplished classicist and for several years a Neoplatonist.

Throughout the Middle Ages many schools of monasticism, especially those of an ascetic or anti-intellectual bent, carried on Tertullian's suspicion of all things pagan and his desire for a "pure" Christianity purged of classical elements. In many ways, this tradition is best summed up in a late medieval work, the *Imitation of Christ* (1426), which profoundly influenced Catholics and Reformers alike. Its author is generally considered to have been Thomas à Kempis, who, like Luther after him, was a strict Augustinian monk of a somewhat legalistic bent. The dualistic elements we often encounter in Luther are not, therefore, to be attributed solely to the Reformation but also to a certain strain of medieval Catholicism that Luther, the ex-Augustinian monk, was never quite able to shake off.

What then shall we say if we would restore the medieval bridge from Homer, Plato and Virgil to Christ, the Bible and the church? Shall we say that Christianity is not the only truth? Certainly not! But let us also not say that Christianity is the only truth. Let us say instead that Christianity is the only *complete* truth. The distinction here is vital. By saying that Christianity is the only complete truth, we leave open the possibility that other philosophies, religions and cultures have hit on certain aspects of the truth. The Christian need not reject the poetry of Homer, the teachings of Plato, or the myths of the pagans as one hundred percent false, as an amalgamation of darkness and lies (as Luther strongly suggests), but may affirm those moments when Plato and Homer leap past their human limitations and catch a glimpse of the true glory of the triune God.

I reject the all-or-nothing, darkness-or-light dualism that Luther at times embraced. But I also reject the modern relativist position that truth is like a hill and there are many ways around it. Yes, truth is like a hill, but the truth that stands atop that hill is Christ and him crucified. To arrive at the truth of Christ, the people of the world have pursued many, many dif-

ferent routes. Some have only scaled the bottom rim of the hill; others have
made it halfway. But many have reached the top and experienced the un-
speakable joy that comes only when the truth they have sought all their
lives is revealed to them.

Such is the case with the Magi. The Magi were not Jews, and they were
obviously not Christians. Most likely they were Zoroastrians whose main
vehicle for discovering God's nature and uncovering his plans was the
stars. These astrologers, bereft of the Old Testament, ignorant of the Law
and the Prophets, were yet able to identify the divine significance of the
star of Bethlehem. They sought after God—the true God—with all that
was available to them, and they opened their hearts to the possibility that
their journey would draw them to a higher truth than the one in which
they were raised. They did not know what that truth would be, and yet as
they were (like Cornelius and the Ethiopian eunuch) God-fearing men
with a sensitivity to God's spirit, they knew that when they finally encoun-
tered it, they would recognize it. The path they trod to Bethlehem may
have led them geographically west, but their journey's true spiritual direction was north, up the hill of truth. At the top they found Christ, the goal
not only of their Yuletide journey, but of their lifelong yearning for God.

It is to such pagan seekers that Paul refers, I believe, in the second chapter of Romans:

> For when the Gentiles, which have not the law, do by nature the things con-
> tained in the law, these, having not the law, are a law unto themselves:

> Which shew the work of the law written in their hearts, their conscience
> also bearing witness, and their thoughts the mean while accusing or else ex-
> cusing one another. (Romans 2:14-15)

If we are to accept these verses in a manner that is in any way literal, we
must confess that unregenerate pagans have an inborn capacity for grasping light and truth that was not totally depraved by the Fall. Indeed,
though the pagan poets and philosophers of Greece and Rome did not
have all the answers (they couldn't, as they lacked the special revelation
found only in Jesus), they knew how to ask the right questions—questions
that build within the readers of their works a desire to know the higher
truths about themselves and their Creator. Such is the case with Virgil,

whose *Aeneid* was so Christian in its themes and virtues that Virgil was considered by many medieval theologians and laymen to be a proto-Christian. Even more, his Fourth Eclogue, with its Isaiah-like celebration of the coming of a divine child who would bring peace and order to the earth, was interpreted by most as a pagan prophecy of Christ.

Thus, in the twenty-second canto of the *Purgatorio*, Dante introduces us to Statius, a first-century pagan poet whom he portrays as having converted to Christianity late in life. Statius ascribes both his early yearnings for Christ and his final conversion not to the Christian martyrs and theologians, but to Virgil. In an ecstatic, magic moment in which pagan past reaches out to Christian present and the two embrace, Statius exclaims:

> You [Virgil] were the lamp that led me from that night.
>   You led me forth to drink Parnassian waters;
>   then on the road to God you shed your light.
> When you declared [in the Fourth Eclogue], "A new birth has been given.
>   Justice returns, and the first age of man.
>   And a new progeny descends from Heaven"—
> you were as one who leads through the dark track
>   holding the light behind—useless to you,
>   precious to those who followed at your back.
> Through you I flowered to song and to belief.[3]

Statius goes on to say that when he first heard the gospel preached, he hearkened to it immediately, for it agreed so well with what he had read in Virgil.

The passage is a famous one, and it demonstrates as well as any illustration how man, though he cannot save himself, can of his own free will move himself and others toward God. In the lovely testimony of Statius, Virgil emerges as almost a Christ figure, one who sacrifices himself for others and devotes his life to uncovering truths that are useless to him but will provide light and guidance for those who come after. He is a bearer of good news, not of the full gospel of Christ, but of a lesser gospel that yet points to the greater: a candle that directs our eye to the moon, a moon that directs our soul to the sun. Cannot such a man be included, even if only

---

[3]Dante, *The Purgatorio*, trans. John Ciardi (New York: Mentor, 1957), pp. 226-27.

partially, in Isaiah's messianic blessing: "How beautiful upon the mountains are the feet of him that bringeth good tidings, that publisheth peace" (Isaiah 52:7).

THE UNKNOWN GOD MADE KNOWN

All well and good, the critic might say, but why should we take Dante's word on this? Where is the biblical precedent for such an embrace of the pagan and the mythic as a potential starting point for the journey toward Christian faith? I have already highlighted the Magi as a case study and also mentioned Cornelius (Acts 10) and the Ethiopian Eunuch (Acts 8)— all pagans who actively sought God and truth long before he revealed to them his way of salvation. To these examples we might add Paul's speech before the Areopagus in Athens (Acts 17). In this thrilling, bridge-building speech, Paul begins his proclamation of Christ's resurrection—the heart of the gospel as it is taught and disseminated in Acts—by complimenting the Athenians on their building of an altar to an unknown god. Rather than expose their pagan idolatry as a simple species of darkness and depravity, Paul exhorts his audience of stoics and epicureans to follow their limited light to its ultimate source in the resurrected Christ: "Whom therefore ye ignorantly worship, him declare I unto you" (Acts 17:23).

The God of the universe, Paul teaches the Athenians, created the heavens and the earth. More than that, he

> hath made of one blood all nations of men for to dwell on all the face of the earth, and hath determined the times before appointed, and the bounds of their habitation;
>
> That they should seek the Lord, if haply they might feel after him, and find him, though he be not far from every one of us:
>
> For in him we live, and move, and have our being; as certain also of your own poets have said, For we are also his offspring. (Acts 17:26-28)

Both the phrases "for we are also his offspring" and "in him we live and move and have our being" are quoted by Paul from the works of two pagan poets: Aratus and Epimenides, respectively. Paul is not merely using a clever advertising ploy to catch the attention of potential customers. The way he integrates these two pagan passages, which he clearly had memorized, into his sermon strongly suggests that he regarded them as pagan glimpses of truth into a mystery that would not be revealed fully until Christ. Indeed, Paul's use of these pagan verses, along with the line of continuity he draws from the altar to the unknown God to the God known in Christ, parallels his treatment of Old Testament characters, events and verses as types of a greater revelation to come. Certainly his discovery of a Christian teaching on law and grace in the juxtaposition of Hagar-Ishmael-Mount Sinai-Jerusalem and Sarah-Isaac-heavenly Jerusalem (Galatians 4:21-31) is no less strange and wonderful than his discovery of a premonition of God's intimate closeness in Christ in the poetry of two "lawless" Gentiles.

But Paul is not our only authority for believing that pagan myths and poetry can contain real seeds of Christian truth; there is also Christ himself. In the twelfth chapter of John's Gospel, Christ is informed shortly before the Last Supper by Andrew and Philip that some Greeks had come to Jerusalem for the feast and wished to speak with him. Jesus responds to their request by saying:

> The hour is come, that the Son of man should be glorified.
>
> Verily, verily, I say unto you, Except a corn of wheat fall into the ground and die, it abideth alone: but if it die, it bringeth forth much fruit.
>
> He that loveth his life shall lose it; and he that hateth his life in this world shall keep it unto life eternal.
>
> If any man serve me, let him follow me; and where I am, there shall also my servant be: if any man serve me, him will my Father honor. (John 12:23-26)

These words were surely meant by Jesus to be carried by Andrew and Philip back to the Greeks. The matter of the Greeks is not mentioned again in the Gospel; thus, if these words were not meant as a direct reply to the inquiring Greeks, then we must conclude: (1) that Jesus, though he certainly heard his disciples' request, is ignoring them and thus snubbing the Greeks; (2) that John has lost narrative control of his Gospel or shares with Jesus in the snub. Neither of these conclusions is satisfactory, and I conclude that the passage quoted above is meant in some way to be a message to the Greeks.

But who are these Greeks? Though I cannot prove it, I suspect that these Greeks, who are obviously interested in both the religious rites of the Jews and in the teachings and person of Jesus, are initiates of the Eleusinian mysteries. For as long as a thousand years before Christ, the city of Eleusis near Athens had harbored one of the oldest religious cults in Greece, a cult that practiced rites so secret that to this day we know little of what went on at their ceremonies. Still, nearly all scholars agree that their worship was centered at least in part around the myth of Persephone, the daughter of the earth goddess Demeter, and her abduction by Hades. According to the myth, Persephone was eventually reunited with her mother, but at a high cost: the girl could spend only two-thirds of the year with her mother; the other third she would live with Hades in the underworld. The etiological upshot of this ancient "deal" was the seasonal cycle of the year. When Persephone returned to Hades, Demeter became desolate and the crops began to die; during the winter months they lay buried like Persephone in the cold earth. In the spring, however, when Persephone returned to her mother, all of nature was reborn. At Eleusis they tended the shrine of Demeter, and it is believed that part of their ceremony included the viewing of a ripe ear of corn or grain. At the heart, therefore, of the Eleusinian mysteries was a faith in the rebirth of spring, a firm hope that life could spring out of death and that we, perhaps, could share in that new life.

If I am right and the Greeks of John's Gospel were members of this ancient cult—a cult well known throughout the Near East—then Jesus' reply would have carried special significance for them. This mini-parable of the grain of wheat is a unique one in the Gospels; it has no parallel in Christ's other parables or in his predictions of his death and resurrection. To me it is clear that Jesus constructed this brief but provocative parable specifically for these Greeks as an attempt to communicate with them directly, to build a bridge from myth to doctrine. It is possible that Jesus is doing here the same thing Paul does in his speech before the Areopagus: proclaiming himself as the embodiment of what they have until now worshiped in ignorance. By means of their own rational and emotional yearnings, these Greeks, along with the other initiates of Eleusis, had achieved a higher spiritual understanding: namely, that life can come only through death and that salvation consists somehow in sharing this divine surrendering and re-capturing of life. Having come this far, the Greeks needed only to be nudged by Jesus into a saving knowledge of the one who is more than a dying god or goddess: one who is, in fact, God dying.

I admit that this is all conjecture, but I find it telling that Jesus would express the central truth of his mission on earth—the crucifixion and resurrection—in the form of a parable that sums up so succinctly the heart of the Eleusinian mysteries. In the same way, John's discussion of the Logos in his prologue, regardless of whether it was inspired by Greek or Hebrew thought, is a representation of God, Christ and the universe that would speak strongly to a Platonist who was seeking after God. Just so, I would argue that Augustine's movement from Platonic philosopher to Christian bishop (documented so movingly in his Confessions) involved not a rejection of Plato but a growth from him: not a breach but an expansion. I imagine Augustine studying diligently all night, his books lit by a small candle that served him well until day broke—when the sunlight streamed in and the candle faded in the glory.

SEARCHING THE CLASSICS

Three centuries after Luther engaged in his titanic struggle with Erasmus, a British Anglican named John Henry Newman ended his own internal spiritual struggle by converting to Catholicism and in the process embracing Aquinas's Christ-over-culture ethos. That he did so was a great blessing for educators like myself who yearn to glean wisdom of both temporal and eternal worth from the works of Greece and Rome. In Dublin in 1852, Newman delivered a series of nine discourses intended to set the tone for a proposed Catholic university in Ireland. These discourses represent, to my mind, the finest modern attempt to unite the twin legacies of Athens and Jerusalem. Though the university was never built, the discourses were published as *The Idea of a University*, and in this form they continue to beckon believers in the Christian revelation to consider the legacy of the ancients.

In his third discourse, Newman takes us on a vivid whirlwind tour through a slightly scattered, intensely concentrated catalogue of the many ways the triune God of the Bible has revealed himself to mankind. "As in

the human frame," he asserts, "there is a living principle, acting upon it and
through it by means of volition, so, behind the veil of the visible universe,
there is an invisible, intelligent Being, acting on and through it, as and
when He will."[4] Having established this as his grounding metaphor, Newman goes on to list the diverse areas of human accomplishment (pagan,
Jewish and Christian) where the invisible God has been rendered visible.

He begins with a vast, sweeping brushstroke that serves as the stage and
backdrop of his Christian-humanist canvas:

> Man, with his motives and works, his languages, his propagation, his diffu-
> sion, is from Him. Agriculture, medicine, and the arts of life, are His gifts.
> Society, laws, governments, He is their sanction. The pageant of earthly roy-
> alty has the semblance and the benediction of the Eternal King. Peace and
> civilization, commerce and adventure, wars when just, conquest when hu-
> mane and necessary, have His co-operation, and His blessing upon them.
> The course of events, the revolution of empires, the rise and fall of states,
> the periods and eras, the progresses and the retrogressions of the world's his-
> tory, not indeed the incidental sin, over-abundant as it is, but the great out-
> lines and results of human affairs, are from His disposition.[5]

The Bible teaches us in great detail how to read and interpret the history
of Israel; it is left to us to read and interpret the histories of the other great
nations. If we make no attempt to assess the glories and brutalities of ancient Egypt, then we have misunderstood, at least in part, both Moses (the
traditional author of Genesis) and the Exodus. Unless we strive to understand the rise and fall of the four great empires of Babylon, Persia, Greece
and Rome (i.e., the four metals of the giant in the dream of Nebuchadnezzar), we fail to grasp how God works through history. To neglect the
study of Rome is to strip Paul's statement that God sent his Son in "the
fullness of time" (Galatians 4:4) of half its meaning. How can we hope to
understand ourselves if we do not know our own history? And if we do not
know where we came from in the historical realm, how can we know where
we came from in the spiritual realm? If our study of the great pagan historians and political scientists (Herodotus, Thucydides, Plato, Polybius, Ci-

---

[4]Cardinal Newman, Discourse III in *The Idea of a University*, ed. Harold Bloom (New York: Confu-
cian, 1981), p. 55.
[5]Ibid., pp. 57-58.

cero, Livy) can point us toward some of the truths that lie behind these questions, that same study can help us gain a clearer perception of the nature of mankind and the divine purposes that undergirded our creation.

But we mustn't stop there. Once our meditations on pagan history, combined with our reading of the Bible, have helped us sketch out the broad historical picture in which God has worked out his plan, our focus must narrow to the works of those great poets, philosophers and statesmen whose dreams and visions lifted them above their time and culture. Here, too, Newman trusted fully that whatever truths lay buried in these works were compatible with and even identical to the truth of Christ:

> To Him must be ascribed the rich endowments of the intellect, the irradiation of genius, the imagination of the poet, the sagacity of the politician, the wisdom (as Scripture calls it), which now rears and decorates the Temple, now manifests itself in proverb or parable. The old saws of nations, the majestic precepts of philosophy, the luminous maxims of law, the oracles of individual wisdom, the traditionary rules of truth, justice, and religion, even though imbedded in the corruption, or alloyed with the pride, of the world, betoken His original agency, and His long-suffering presence. Even when there is habitual rebellion against Him, or profound far-spreading social depravity, still the undercurrent, or the heroic outburst, of natural virtue, as well as the yearnings of the heart after what it has not, and its presentiment of its true remedies, are to be ascribed to the Author of all good.[6]

Despite the fact that our world and our humanity are fallen, God's hand can still be discerned in the laws and the wisdom that keep the former in motion and the latter in check. Each nation has its torah and its book of proverbs, and, though only the biblical manifestations of these essential elements carry complete authority, traces of God's truth and presence are to be found in all of them. All our works and our ideals are blackened over by the stain of sin, and yet now and again throughout history the light of Christ has broken through in the lines of a poem, the maxims of a philosopher, or the decisions of a lawgiver. Those ancient virtues that the humanist seeks to imitate, those classical deeds of heroism that would incite him to noble action, all find their ultimate source

---

[6]Ibid., p. 58.

in the original agency of the author of all good.

But we must not end our search for wisdom here. From the poetry and philosophy of the ancient world we must advance to a deeper study of their theology, prophecy and religion:

> Anticipations or reminiscences of His glory haunt the mind of the self-sufficient sage, and of the pagan devotee; His writing is upon the wall, whether of the Indian fane, or of the porticoes of Greece. He introduces Himself, He all but concurs, according to His good pleasure, and in His selected season, in the issues of unbelief, superstition, and false worship, and He changes the character of acts by His overruling operation. He condescends, though He gives no sanction, to the altars and shrines of imposture, and He makes His own fiat the substitute for its sorceries. He speaks amid the incantations of Balaam, raises Samuel's spirit in the witch's cavern, prophesies of the Messias by the tongue of the Sibyl, forces Python to recognize His ministers, and baptizes by the hand of the misbeliever. He is with the heathen dramatist in his denunciations of injustice and tyranny, and his auguries of divine vengeance upon crime. Even on the unseemly legends of a popular mythology He casts His shadow, and is dimly discerned in the ode or epic, as in troubled water or in fantastic dreams.[7]

Wherever man has sought with his entire being to perceive the truths of his Creator, God is there. He does not always approve, but he is always present. And at times he speaks through the mouth of the pagan: to announce the coming of the Messiah (the Fourth Eclogue of Virgil), to denounce injustice and cycles of vengeance (the *Antigone* of Sophocles and the *Oresteia* of Aeschylus), to attest to the hidden nature of sin and the need for a scapegoat (the *Oedipus* of Sophocles), to prepare the heart for the arrival of a God-Man who will suffer (the legends of Heracles and the myths of Adonis) and who will expose the impotent legalism of the Pharisee (the *Bacchae* of Euripides), and to warn us against wrath and instruct us in what it means to be human (the *Iliad* and *Odyssey* of Homer). Though the fullness of deity is found only in Christ and the fullness of his revelation in the Bible alone, the shadow of the Almighty yet hovers and broods over the yearnings of the pre-Christian world.

---

[7]Ibid., pp. 58-59.

May we have eyes to catch glimpses of God's presence and glory in the forms and rituals of pagan antiquity.

In the chapters that follow, I seek to live up to Newman's high call by exploring how the faith and discernment of Christian readers can be enhanced by vigorous interaction with the central literary masterpieces of the ancient world. Rather than attempt to encompass the full Greco-Roman legacy (as does Newman in his broad overview), I shall confine myself to the epic and dramatic poetry of Homer, Virgil and the Greek tragedians. Thus, although elements of Greco-Roman philosophy, theology, history, politics and ethics will appear occasionally in this work, the focus will remain firmly on the epics and the tragedies. The book will be broken into three sections: part one will examine Homer's two great epics; part two will take up the plays of Aeschylus, Sophocles and Euripides; part three will consider the origin, plan and contents of Virgil's Roman epic, the *Aeneid*. I will not discuss the works of the supreme proto-Christian Plato, not because he is not vital but because he wrote nonfiction prose rather than fictional poetry and because, in any case, he demands an entire book to himself. The modern Christian is as likely to dismiss the epics of Homer or the plays of Sophocles as sources of truth on account of their pagan origin as he is to dismiss them on account of their being fictional and poetic. By keeping my focus firmly on epic and dramatic literature, I hope to explode (or at least shake) these ingrained modernist, post-Reformation, post-Enlightenment prejudices.

In the chapters themselves, the poetry of Homer, Virgil and the tragedians will be considered from two distinct but overlapping perspectives: (1) as literary works possessing their own separate integrity within the context of the cultures and the poets that produced them; (2) as proto-Christian works of almost prophetic power that point the way to Christ and glimmer with a faint but true light. Not all the works considered point specifically to Jesus as the dying and rising God (most point instead to a virtue, ethos or dilemma that finds its full flowering and expression in Christianity), but I will treat each work as a source of inspired wisdom from which Christians can learn and profit as they might from a devotional work like *The Imitation of Christ* or *Pilgrim's Progress*.

Though capsule plot summaries will be included in each chapter, and though this book can be read profitably on its own, it is my hope that readers will study it alongside the actual works of Homer, Virgil and the tragedians. To facilitate this study, I have included a bibliographical essay in which I point out some key resources that the nonspecialist should find helpful. Indeed, it is my further hope that parents and teachers will use this book as a companion and guide as they lead their children and students on a thrilling odyssey through the enduring masterpieces of the ancient world.

I have dedicated this book to my parents, Tom and Angie Markos, both of whom were born to Greek immigrants and both of whom helped to keep alive in me my Greek heritage. While my father taught me my love of mythology and ancient Greek history, my mother taught me to love all aspects of Greek culture—especially dance. Because of their influence, I can claim to carry the legacy of classical Greece not only in my head (as a student and product of Western civilization) but in my heart and blood as well.

I would also like to acknowledge and celebrate the growing number of classical Christian schools and Christian homeschoolers who have been instrumental in reviving the legacy of the Greek and Roman classics. Thomas Cahill has argued that it was the Irish monks who helped to preserve the pagan classics; it is my belief that the classical schools and homeschoolers will play a decisive role in preserving the classics through a potential new dark age. Indeed, the excellent illustrations at the head of each chapter were made by a young woman, Jennifer Barton, who was homeschooled throughout high school. In addition to being one of the best English majors I have taught at Houston Baptist University and one of the finest Christian women I have had the privilege to mentor, Jennifer embodies the full flowering of her parents' efforts to provide her with a full education in body, soul, mind and spirit. If our Judeo-Christian, Greco-Roman culture is to be preserved, it will be students like Jennifer who will do the preserving. I wish her and her peers Godspeed!

PART ONE

Homer

1

HESIOD'S *THEOGONY*

In the Beginning

WE LIVE IN AN AGE THAT HAS ALMOST completely lost its sense of history. Through a process that might best be described as cultural suicide, we have actively, willfully, systematically severed ourselves from our roots, our origins and our past traditions. Live in the now, we are counseled, or, better, keep our eyes fixed forever forward. If it's not cutting-edge, state of the art, or new and improved, then it is probably not worth bothering with: except perhaps as hip nostalgia to indulge in briefly and uncritically. And the same, alas, too often goes for most of our universities and many of our seminaries: the "progressive" agenda, the "enlightened" view, the "critical" reading will trump the traditional one every time.

Evangelicals and other traditional-minded Christians often complain, and rightly so, that many of our modern and postmodern educators, politicians and media people have attempted to cut America loose from her Greco-Roman and (especially) Judeo-Christian roots. And yet those who would fight boldly against this aggressive and irresponsible form of multiculturalism are often just as cut off from our ancient roots as those who have been lulled or beaten into silence by our modern prophets of progressive thinking. If we are to regain our past, we must reconnect to it our-selves: not only because reconnection will provide us with information, but because the act of reconnection is itself one of the strongest critiques that can be leveled against the anti-traditional ethos of our day.

"The historical sense," writes T. S. Eliot in his essay "Tradition and the Individual Talent," "involves a perception, not only of the pastness of the past, but of its presence."[1] It is only when the past presses itself on us as a felt reality that is both relevant and contemporary that we will be empow-ered to embrace it as a source for determining our own purpose, worth and status as citizens of America, cultural heirs of the Mediterranean world, and members of the human race. The truism that says we can't know where we're going if we don't know where we came from is only half true. The one who knows nothing of his origins is more than merely lost; he is, in the most profound sense, cut off from himself. He knows not who he is.

If, then, we are to regain a sense of who we are, we must not only seek out our origins; we must learn as well to perceive those origins both as de-terminers of the past and touchstones of the present. In the Jewish world, this attempt to perceive both the pastness and presence of the past begins with the book of Genesis; in the Greek, it begins with Hesiod's *Theogony*.

HE ON WHOM THE MUSE BREATHES

Hesiod stands side by side with Homer at the head of that flood we call Western civilization. In keeping with most classicists, I would place both poets near the end of the eighth century B.C., with Hesiod composing on the west coast of the Aegean (modern-day Greece) and Homer on the east (modern-day Turkey). Like Homer, Hesiod begins his poem by calling on the Muses, the nine divine daughters of Zeus and Mnemosyne, goddess of memory, for inspiration. However, whereas Homer's invocation of the Muse is brief and borders on the perfunctory, Hesiod goes into great detail as to how the Muses placed on his heart and on his lips the power of poetry. After a brief preamble in which he lays out his dramatis personae, Hesiod boldly yet humbly exclaims:

---

[1]Hazard Adams, ed., *Critical Theory Since Plato*, rev. ed. (New York: Harcourt Brace Jovanovich, 1992), p. 761.

The Muses once taught Hesiod to sing
Sweet songs, while he was shepherding his lambs
On holy Helicon; the goddesses
Olympian, daughters of Zeus who holds
The aegis, first addressed these words to me:
"You rustic shepherds, shame: bellies you are,
Not men! We know enough to make up lies
Which are convincing, but we also have
The skill, when we've a mind, to speak the truth."

So spoke the fresh-voiced daughters of great Zeus
And plucked and gave a staff to me, a shoot
Of blooming laurel, wonderful to see,
And breathed a sacred voice into my mouth
With which to celebrate the things to come
And things which were before. They ordered me
To sing the race of blessed ones who live
Forever, and to hymn the Muses first
And at the end. No more delays; begin.[2]

Hesiod presents himself here as far more than a frustrated artist in need of an Olympian cure for writer's block. The divine breath of the Muse carries with it a calling; he is to be a channel not only of inspiration, but of revelation. He has been chosen, selected out, to perform a task for which he is not wholly adequate. He is, after all, one of many well-fed, self-satisfied rustic shepherds who live near the crest of the holy mountain. That is, until he is breathed upon by the numinous spirits who make their dwelling on Helicon and given a poetic staff of laurel to take the place of his shepherd's crook.

Jews and Christians who know their Bibles well will immediately see in the quoted passage many parallels to the prophetic books of the Old and New Testament, especially to the Psalms of David, Israel's great poet-shepherd. But the scene, for all its links to David, actually comes closer in detail and spirit to the event recorded in Exodus 3: a well-fed and perhaps self-satisfied rustic shepherd named Moses is tending his flock on Mount

---

[2]My text for Hesiod's *Theogony* is taken from *Hesiod and Theognis,* trans. Dorothea Wender (New York: Penguin, 1973), pp. 23-24.

Horeb when he is chosen, selected out, by a numinous God who speaks to him from a burning bush and gives him a magical rod. In pointing out this parallel, I do not suggest that Hesiod is somehow the Greek equivalent of Moses or that his *Theogony* is to be granted the same status as Genesis. I do suggest, however, that these parallel accounts of the meeting between a poet-prophet and his Muse can teach us something about the nature of origins that our age has forgotten.

Origins, as we are reminded in Genesis, Exodus 3 and the opening of the *Theogony,* are not to be discovered through empirical observation or scientific experimentation, but to be received as a gift of revelation. I expect that this statement will raise the eyebrows of many readers, but I do not retract it. If we are to have any understanding of our own individual birth, we must consult those who gave birth to us, or at least those close to our parents who witnessed the event. In the case of the birth of our species, our planet and our universe, it is only our Creator who can supply us, through inspiration and revelation, the information we desire. True, as rational beings we are able to determine something of our origins by reasoning backward from effect to cause; however, if we are to achieve a full, rounded, intimate picture of our human beginnings, we must rely at least in part on the voice that speaks from outside our spatiotemporal world. In court, judge and jury weigh both physical evidence and the testimony of reliable witnesses when determining their verdict; if the physical evidence does not exist or is impossible to interpret, they must rely on the testimony. Such is the case with the origin of ourselves and our world, but it is also to a lesser extent the case with our ancient human past.

The modern world tends to think that the best way to understand our past is to dig up physical artifacts and analyze the geographical, climatic and sociopolitical-economic factors of the age under study. But it is not so. The best way—perhaps the only way—to understand our great forebears is to lose ourselves in their highest poetry, to absorb Hesiod, Homer and the five books of Moses into our collective veins. If Moses and Hesiod tapped something of the divine mind, then we must seek to tap their minds. If we can't attach our metal ring directly to the magnet, then let us attach it to a larger and older ring that is already attached to the magnet.

In "Tradition and the Individual Talent," T. S. Eliot exhorts the would-be poet to allow his own private mind to be overlaid by "the mind of Europe," to "develop or procure the consciousness of the past and . . . continue to develop this consciousness throughout his career."[3] It is good advice, not only for poets, but for all of us who would reconnect with the past, who would know where we have come from, why we are here, and where we are going.

Of course, we do not and should not read Hesiod the same way we read Moses. The revelation given to Moses was far clearer than that given to Hesiod. Unlike Moses, who spoke with God face to face, Hesiod saw the divine face dimly through a dirty mirror. Hesiod, lacking the direct revelation vouchsafed to Moses and the prophets, knows nothing of creation ex nihilo. He does not know, cannot even conceive, that in the beginning there was not "stuff" but spirit, not matter but God (an inability, ironically, that he shares with our modern, post-Enlightenment world). But then again, Genesis 1 itself tells us very little about creation ex nihilo; only the first verse, in fact, directly addresses this vital biblical doctrine—which Hebrews 11:3 tells us can only be perceived and understood by faith. After the first verse, the remainder of Genesis 1 is concerned with describing how God shaped the primal chaos that he caused to appear out of nothing. And in this sense, the *Theogony* comes close to Genesis. For both Moses and Hesiod, the prime concern of God (the gods) is to bring order and shape to what was originally formless and void.

SHAPING THE CHAOS

Out of chaos, writes Hesiod, were born the primal forces of earth, night and love, and out of the former two came, with the help of Love, heaven and day. As in Genesis 1, order is established through a process of separation: earth from heaven, night from day. But here too there is a difference. Just as Hesiod is ignorant of creation ex nihilo, so does he lack the vision of a higher, self-existent, purely good God who has neither beginning nor end. Forced to conceive of the origins of the divine and the human, the spiritual and the physical apart from the biblical Yahweh, Hesiod must of necessity offer us a far messier and bloodier drama. The divine and perfect

---

[3]Ibid., p. 762.

justice that existed in the mind of Yahweh before the creation of matter must, perforce, come at the end of Hesiod's drama rather than at the beginning. Hesiod is writing, as it were, in the dark: called, yes, inspired, yes, but lacking direct access. Still, he gives it his best shot. He will struggle, poetically and prophetically, toward order and justice.

As Hesiod tells it, earth (Gaia) and heaven (Ouranos) become lovers and give birth to a race of Titans: Prometheus, Atlas, Ocean and so on. Unfortunately, these serene immortals are not all of the offspring of earth and heaven. Gaia bears as well to her sky god husband a brood of proud and insolent monsters. Afraid that one of his monstrous offspring will supplant him, Ouranos takes them and presses them back into the earth—which is to say, back into the womb of his wife. Gaia groans in agony, her belly stretched and bloated by the fierce sons hidden within her. In desperation, she fashions a "mighty sickle" and gives it to her strongest Titan son, Kronos. Sickle in hand, Kronos hides behind a rock, and the next time Ouranos swoops down from the sky to lie with Gaia, he "stretche[s] forth his left hand . . . [and harvests] his father's genitals." Kronos flings his father's testicles behind him and, as they soar over the land, blood drips down and mingles with the earth: out of the blood-soaked earth leap the Furies, hideous goddesses with snakes for hair and venomous teeth who relentlessly pursue those guilty of taboo crimes. In the end, the testicles fall into the ocean, producing a foam out of which rises Aphrodite, goddess of love.

Kronos then rules as king of the Titans and takes his sister Rhea as his wife. But Kronos, like his father before him, grows fearful of his sons and determines that he will not himself be supplanted. Accordingly, each time Rhea gives birth to a new child, Kronos seizes it and swallows it whole. Enlisting the aid of her mother, who perhaps now resents the son who carried out her bloody wishes, Rhea takes her next son, Zeus, and hides him away on the island of Crete. In place of the child, Rhea gives Kronos a large stone wrapped in swaddling clothes, which the ogre-father promptly swallows. When Zeus has grown to manhood, he returns and, with the help of the Titans, overthrows Kronos and releases his brothers and sisters from the belly of his father.

Zeus becomes lord of the Olympian gods along with his two brothers,

Poseidon, lord of the sea, and Hades, lord of the dead, and his sister Hera, whom he takes as his wife. Ares, god of War, is born to Zeus and Hera, but Athena, goddess of war and wisdom, is born out of the head of Zeus. In jealousy, Hera bears Hephaestus, the blacksmith of the gods, without the aid of Zeus. The other gods who dwell on Mount Olympus—Apollo, god of music and the bow; his sister Artemis, goddess of nature and the hunt; and Hermes, messenger of the gods—are born to Zeus and a lesser goddess. Zeus's two sisters, Hestia, goddess of the hearth, and Demeter, goddess of the grain, round out the Olympian gods, though Demeter tends to dwell on the earth.

At first, Zeus, who receives his own prophecy that one of his sons will overthrow him, rules with the same bloodthirstiness and paranoia as his father and grandfather, even showing particular cruelty to one of the Titans, Prometheus, who had helped him overthrow Kronos. When he learns that Prometheus, whose name in Greek means "forethought," knows the name of the goddess who will bear the son that will overthrow him, Zeus tortures Prometheus until he divulges the name. Having secured the name of the goddess, Zeus then forces that goddess, Thetis, to marry a mortal man, Peleus, so that her son, Achilles, will be a mortal and pose no threat to Zeus's rule. These machinations are as unpleasant as they are heartless, and they expose the new monarch of Olympus as cold and Machiavellian. However, once Zeus believes he has neutralized the threat to his rule, a wonderful change comes over him and he becomes a god of justice, order and civilization. Instead of Thetis, he takes as wives both Metis (wisdom) and Themis (justice) and defeats once and for all the more bestial of the primal gods. In a titanic battle, he even defeats with his thunderbolts a hundred-headed, chaos-causing, storm-producing dragon whom he imprisons in a volcano.

If we focus here only on the Oedipal violence of Ouranos's castration or the domestic violence that manifests as lust, betrayal and even cannibalism, we will not move beyond a Freudian reading that would interpret the *Theogony* as a repository of primal urges and repressed sexuality. But if we look to the end and view the cycles of violence and vengeance as culminating in the "civilizing" of Zeus, we will discover something very different, something that finds an echo in Genesis. Like Hesiod, Moses not only presents creation as a kind of ordering, but he structures his narrative around a group of weak and stumbling patriarchs whose story nevertheless culminates in order, justice and promise. What Moses' patriarchs come slowly to learn about Yahweh, Hesiod's gods come to learn even more slowly about themselves.

Viewed from this perspective, the disturbing sexual violence that marks both the *Theogony* and Genesis—not to mention Joshua, Judges, 1 and 2 Samuel, and 1 and 2 Kings—takes on a deeper meaning. Both books begin essentially with a fertility mandate, a cosmic call to be fruitful and multiply, to populate and exert dominion over the natural world. In carrying out this mandate, however, the gods of Hesiod, like the men of Genesis, pervert fertility into a series of intergenerational struggles that either sow strife between half-siblings (Jacob and Esau, Joseph and his brothers) or ultimately prevent fertility rather than encourage it. Thus, as Kronos castrates Ouranos to prevent him from fathering more children, Onan "castrates" himself by spilling his seed on the ground rather than impregnating Tamar (Genesis 38:8-10). Onan is instructed to do this by his father, Judah, who seems as intent on preventing Tamar from bearing a child to his son as Zeus is on preventing his own offspring from being born. And yet, in the end, these despicable, repulsive schemes are used to further a higher divine plan. In Hesiod, we end up with a civilized Zeus and a mortal child, Achilles, who becomes the prototype of all tragic heroes to come. In Genesis, Tamar is impregnated by Judah and becomes the mother of a child whose descendant will be the greatest tragic hero of all: Jesus Christ.

But the biblical parallel does not stop here; physical as well as sexual violence has a role to play in the greater cosmic drama. As part of the long process by which Zeus brings order and balance to the heavens, he imprisons the rebellious Titans in Tartarus, a dark pit which is as far below the earth as the earth is below the heavens. Remarkably, in the New Testament, where hell is generally referred to by the Greek word *Hades*, there is only one instance in which the biblical writer uses the word *Tartarus* for hell: "For if God spared not the angels that sinned, but cast them down to hell [Tartarus], and delivered them into chains of darkness, to be reserved unto judgment" (2 Peter 2:4). Though the Bible offers scanty details, it is clear that before the creation of our world a war in heaven resulted in the expulsion of Satan and his fallen angels. Through that war God restored justice and balance to the heavens, a justice that rested in part on imprisoning those who rebelled against his authority. Again, Hesiod knows nothing of Yahweh (he fails to conceive even of Zeus as a divinity of pure goodness, love and truth), but he knows that if the high God is truly to be the high God, he must have the power and will to control rebellion and disobedience.

And Hesiod knows something else. He knows that the search for origins must involve a study of language. Just as throughout the book of Genesis we are told the meaning of key figures' names—Abraham, Sarah, Isaac, Jacob and so on—so Hesiod shows a near obsession with tracing the meaning behind the names of his key divine players. The word Cyclopes, he informs us, comes from *kuklos* ("circle") because the Cyclopes have a single large eye in the center of their head; *Aphrodite* comes from *aphro* ("foam") because she rose up out of the sea. To be honest, many of Hesiod's etymological attempts are doubtful at best, but the passion he shows to find meaning in names shows a passion for meaning itself.

It is no coincidence that the more our postmodern society loses its grounding in tradition, the more it loses its faith in language. To immerse ourselves in the works of Hesiod, Homer, Virgil and the Greek tragedians, all of whom felt a passion to explore origins, is to renew our love both for the past and for the words our great ancestors used to enshrine and interpret that past.

2

HOMER'S *ILIAD* I

A History of Conflict

WHEN I WAS A BOY, MY MOTHER BOUGHT me a toy airplane powered by a simple but wonderful device. The plane's large plastic propeller was attached to its body by a thick red rubber band. To make the plane work, I would grasp the body of the plane in my left hand and place my right index finger on the propeller. Then I would slowly twirl the propeller in a clockwise motion. Each time I twirled it, the rubber band would form a knot; after twenty or so twirls, the rubber band was transformed into a mass of angry little knots that threatened to explode in my face if I dared to twirl the propeller even one more time. That, of course, was my signal to remove my finger, open my left hand, and let the airplane soar.

WINDING THE PROPELLER

Iliad, in Greek, means "the story of Ilium (another name for Troy)." That is to say, the *Iliad* purports to tell the tale of Troy and of the Trojan War. And yet, as first-time readers of the epic immediately notice, the *Iliad* recounts neither the beginning nor the end of the war. The action of the epic limits itself to a roughly two-week period in the final year of a ten-year war.

Homer, like those who first listened to and then later read his poem, knew full well of Troy's tragic fall, just as he was fully versed in the myths and legends that surrounded the war's divine origins and human heroes. Yet he consciously chose to leave most of this colorful and dramatic material out. Homer was neither an editor nor a historian; his purpose in composing his poem was not to give a blow-by-blow chronicle of the war but to birth a work of art that would endure not for an age but for all time.

What, then, did Homer leave out? In a nutshell, the Trojan War began, according to the myths, when the gods were on Mount Olympus celebrating the wedding of Thetis and Peleus. (I use "celebrating" somewhat facetiously, since the wedding was forced on Thetis by the paranoid Zeus.) In making up the guest list for the wedding, the gods neglected to invite Eris, the goddess of discord. To get her revenge, Eris showed up anyway and tossed into the midst of the divine revelers a golden apple on which she had inscribed the words, "to the fairest." This peevish stunt quickly put an end to the festivities, as each goddess claimed the apple for herself. In the end, the contenders who were still left standing—Hera, Athena and Aphrodite—approached Zeus and asked him to decide. As neither he nor any of the other gods would make the choice, the goddesses were forced to resort to a human judge: a shepherd named Paris who lived in the Trojan countryside. To ensure that the mortal would select her, each goddess proceeded to offer him a bribe. Paris, being young (and foolish?), rejected Hera's offer to make him a great ruler and Athena's to make him a mighty warrior, and he chose instead the gift of Aphrodite: the love of the most beautiful girl in the world.

As it so happened—as it so often happens—the most beautiful girl in the world was already married. Her name was Helen and she was Greek, the daughter of Zeus and a mortal woman. (In Greek mythology, one is not a god unless both parents are divine.) Because of her great beauty, all the kings of Greece, which was broken into a series of independent tribal states, each ruled by a chieftain, competed for her hand. To avoid bloodshed, Helen's mortal father held a great contest, offering his daughter's hand to the winner. In addition, to avoid future bloodshed, he made the kings swear that they would honor the winner of the contest and defend his claim as her lawful husband if anyone attempted to steal her away.

Fast-forward several years, when a suave, ingratiating Paris comes to visit Helen and her husband, Menelaus, at their palace. Though Menelaus showers Paris with hospitality, the Trojan shepherd repays his kindness by seducing his wife and taking her back with him to Troy. This creates something of a problem, for Paris is not in fact a simple shepherd but the son of Priam, the king of Troy. When Paris was born, his father had been warned by an oracle that his son would bring about the destruction of Troy, so he had sent the infant out of the city to be raised as a shepherd. Alas, despite Priam's feeble attempt to avoid the prophecy, his son proved to be the doom of his family and his city.

When he learns of Paris's treachery, Menelaus calls on the kings of Greece to uphold their vow to protect his rights as husband. In response, the Greeks mount a great expedition and sail to Troy, which is on the northwest coast of modern-day Turkey. Though Menelaus is the injured party, his brother Agamemnon, who rules the rich and powerful state of Mycenae, is chosen commander in chief. Still, despite his status as supreme monarch and captain of the expedition, Agamemnon is not the strongest of the Greek general-kings. Surpassing him are Aias, a towering hulk of a man with the strength and endurance of an ox, and Diomedes, slightly less strong than Aias but far more prudent, as well as a third soldier known to be the bravest and strongest, if also the most stubborn and hotheaded, warrior of their day—indeed, of any day. I speak of course of Achilles. On account of his divine mother Thetis, Achilles is as strong as Helen is beautiful, but on account of his human father Peleus, he is a mortal man whose life will someday be taken from him. On the expedition as well come Odysseus, the wisest and craftiest of the kings, and the aged Nestor, who is too old to fight and win glory but who offers experience-based counsel to Agamemnon and lengthy stories and proverbial maxims to his fellow soldiers.

Given the vast number of ships and men the Greeks send against Troy (Homer catalogues them for us in Book II), it might seem that the war would be swift and decisive. But Troy has an unscaleable wall to protect her, and the brave and noble prince Hektor, Paris's brother, to lead her armies. As a result, the war lasts ten long years, with the Greeks and Trojans engaging in sorties and single combats on the grassy plain between the wall of Troy and the Aegean shore. As each bloody and exhausting year drags on, tension in the Greek camp mounts. To relieve the strain and re-plenish their ever-diminishing supplies, the Greeks periodically raid the cities that lie along the coast. If the city is rich and the plunder good, the Greek general-kings divide the best of the loot among themselves: gold, armor, horses—and women. Agamemnon, though neither the bravest nor strongest soldier in these raids, validates his position as commander in chief by always securing the best prize. During one particular assault on the city of Thebe, Agamemnon conspicuously claims the beautiful Chry-seis while tossing to Achilles, the real hero of the raid, Briseis. She is lovely, to be sure, but clearly not the best.

It is in the wake of this raid on Thebe, undertaken in the final year of the war, that Homer chooses to begin his epic poem—not with the golden apple, the judgment of Paris, the abduction of Helen, or the sailing of the Greeks. Aristotle dubbed this technique in medias res ("in the middle of things"), a literary device that poets since Homer have used both to unify an otherwise loose and episodic tale and to add a sense of tension leading to inevitable conflict to a situation that might otherwise seem static. When Homer plunges into the story of Troy, the tensions between god and god, god and mortal, Greek and Trojan, and Greek and Greek have almost reached their breaking point; a multitude of external and internal conflicts have all come to a head. The rubber band is tightly knotted; it is ready to burst.

LETTING IT GO

In the days that precede the opening of Book I of the *Iliad*, Chryseis's fa-ther, a priest of Apollo named Chryses, enters the Greek camp and begs Agamemnon to return his daughter to him. Though Chryses offers great ransom for the return of his only child, Agamemnon rudely and inhospi-tably refuses his request. In retaliation, the grieved father begs Apollo to avenge him. Apollo, who favors the Trojans, answers Chryses's prayer by shooting an arrow of plague into the Greek camp. For nine days soldiers throughout the camp fall sick and die, yet Agamemnon does nothing. Fi-nally, Achilles takes the prerogative to call a meeting of the generals and brings with him a soothsayer, Calchas, to reveal the cause of the plague. It is at this meeting that the action of the *Iliad* begins.

Assured by Achilles that he will be protected, Calchas proclaims boldly what everyone already knows but is afraid to say: that the plague will not end until Agamemnon returns Chryseis to her father. Agamemnon reluctantly agrees to surrender his prize, but on one condition:

> Find me then some prize that shall be my own, lest I only
> among the Argives [Greeks] go without, since that were unfitting;
> you are all witnesses to this thing, that my prize goes elsewhere. (I.118-20)[1]

At this point, if Achilles were wise, he would keep his mouth shut and walk away. In calling the assembly and bringing Calchas, he has done what was necessary. The truth is out, and Agamemnon has promised to return Chryseis. Agamemnon, for his part, has done what a commander must do: save face before his army by demanding another prize. Were the meeting to break up now with no one challenging his demand, Agamemnon would most likely not have gone through with it. He would not have had to. But Achilles refuses to keep silent:

> Most lordly, greediest for gain of all men,
> how shall the great hearted Achaians [Greeks] give you a prize now?
> There is no great store of things lying about I know of. (I.121-23)

For Achilles, this is no mere matter of how Agamemnon chooses to order his affairs or control his troops. For Achilles, it is personal. In response, Agamemnon ratchets up his condition from a demand to a threat. He will not be intimidated, even by Achilles himself:

> Not that way, good fighter though you be, godlike Achilleus,
> strive to cheat, for you will not deceive, you will not persuade me.
> What do you want? To keep your own prize and have me sit here
> lacking one? Are you ordering me to give this girl back?
> Either the great-hearted Achaians shall give me a new prize
> chosen according to my desire to atone for the girl lost,
> or else if they will not give me one I myself shall take her,

---

[1]All passages from the *Iliad* are taken from *The Iliad of Homer*, trans. Richmond Lattimore (Chicago: University of Chicago Press, 1951). Citations are identified by book number in Roman numerals followed by line numbers. In general I have adopted Lattimore's spelling for Homer's characters, though I have chosen in some cases (Achilles, Patroclus) to use more recognizable spellings.

your own prize, or that of Aias, or that of Odysseus,
going myself in person; and he whom I visit will be bitter.
Still, these are things we shall deliberate again hereafter.
Come now, we must haul a black ship down to the bright sea,
and assemble rowers enough for it. (I.131-42)

Everyone, including Agamemnon, knows Achilles is the greater warrior and could easily slay Agamemnon in one-on-one combat. If Agamemnon shows himself weak in the face of Achilles's threats, he risks losing the allegiance and respect of the army. By threatening to steal the prize not only of the muscular Aias and the crafty Odysseus, but of the great Achilles himself, Agamemnon shows himself to be undaunted.

The anger is rising in the chests of both men, but at this point Agamemnon is still in control. It is significant that once he finishes making his threat, he swiftly and smoothly shifts the topic away from his personal dispute with Achilles and tries to refocus everyone's attention on the less controversial task at hand: preparing the ship that will carry Chryseis back to her father. As before, were the meeting to break up now, Agamemnon would most likely not have followed through with his threat. He has preserved his authority by threatening to take Achilles' prize, and he would not need to do anything more—hence his diplomatic attempt to end the meeting quickly. Achilles, unfortunately, does not seem to hear the latter part of the speech. Indeed he most likely hears nothing past the words, "I myself shall take her, / your own prize." Agamemnon's diplomatic attempt to defuse the situation is lost on Achilles; instead, he attacks again:

O wrapped in shamelessness, with your mind forever on profit,
how shall any one of the Achaians readily obey you
either to go on a journey or to fight men strongly in battle? (I.149-51)

Achilles continues to rage in this vein, insulting Agamemnon and questioning why he, Achilles, has come to Troy in the first place. And then the real cause of his anger surfaces:

Never, when the Achaians sack some well-founded citadel
of the Trojans, do I have a prize that is equal to your prize.
Always the greater part of the painful fighting is the work of
my hands; but when the time comes to distribute the booty

yours is far the greater reward, and I with some small thing
yet dear to me go back to my ships when I am weary with fighting.
Now I am returning to Phthia, since it is much better
to go home again with my curved ships. (I.163-70)

This, it becomes clear, is not the first time Achilles and Agamemnon have argued. Clearly the tension has been mounting for years; the knots in the rubber band have been strained to the breaking point, and it is time to let the propeller go. In response to Achilles' threat to abandon the war and return home, Agamemnon replies:

Run away by all means if your heart drives you. I will not
entreat you to stay here for my sake. There are others with me
who will do me honour, and above all Zeus of the counsels.
To me you are the most hateful of all the kings whom the gods love.
Forever quarrelling is dear to your heart, and wars and battles;
Go home then with your own ships and your own companions,
be king over the Myrmidons. I care nothing about you.
I take no account of your anger. But here is my threat to you. . . .
　　　　　　　　　　I shall take the fair-cheeked Briseis,
Your prize, I myself going to your shelter, that you may learn well
How much greater I am than you, and another man may shrink back
From likening himself to me and contending against me. (I.173-87)

For years now Agamemnon has envied Achilles' great strength and courage, and Achilles has resented the lack of respect paid him by Agamemnon. By beginning his epic in medias res, Homer allows us to see nine years of envy and resentment that have built up in his two protagonists. When his epic begins, he presents us with a dual portrait in motion.

Despite the disparity that exists in time and culture between Homer's age and our own, this portrait is remarkably familiar. Between Achilles, the great but impulsive warrior, and Agamemnon, the able but ultimately weak commander in chief, we encounter the age-old struggle between energetic soldier and armchair general, gifted employee and insecure administrator, sanguine professor and choleric dean, dynamic actor and imperious director, popular, easygoing youth pastor and autocratic head minister. The former tend to have a confidence in their own abilities and a charisma that draws people toward them, but with that confidence and charisma comes often a desperate need for applause and attention and a generous dose of bravado. The latter are diplomatic and politically savvy and know how to control people and situations, yet they suffer from low self-esteem and a mild paranoia that others will threaten their authority or steal the allegiance of those under them.

When Agamemnon claims that Achilles' strength is merely a gift of the gods, his envy is apparent. As is often the case with administrators, nothing comes easily or naturally for Agamemnon as it does for the soldier, the professor, the actor: every day and every decision is a struggle. Like the intelligent but overanxious coach, he lies awake at night while his linebackers sleep as deeply and contentedly as bears. Achilles, on the other hand, though he is hailed and loved by the troops in a way Agamemnon will never be, allows his battlefield successes to be spoiled by Agamemnon's lack of appreciation. The impulsive Achilles sees only the insult—and not the diplomatic necessity—in Agamemnon's threat to take Briseis; in response, he throws a public tantrum that forces the paranoid Agamemnon to follow through with his threat.

His pride wounded, Achilles expands his tantrum to epic proportions. Not only does he pull out of the battle; he instructs his divine mother to go to Zeus and ask him to empower the Trojans so that they will start defeating the Greeks. "Then," the spiteful Achilles reasons to himself, "Agamemnon will be forced to come to my tent and beg me to return to the battle." Thetis, an overly anxious mother who has passed her anxieties on to her son, does as he asks, and Zeus with a nod of his head agrees to answer Achilles' prayer. Hera sees Zeus nod his head, and, fearing that her husband is plotting behind her back, accuses him of deceit and treachery.

Zeus shoots back that she should mind her own business and let him run his own affairs, whereupon she says she does not want his job, only his respect. Many attentive readers will note that this second war of words closely parallels the earlier one between Agamemnon and Achilles; however, they often make the wrong connection. Achilles is not to be compared to Zeus but to Hera. Like Hera, Achilles, for all his bravado, does not want Agamemnon's job, only his respect. And Agamemnon, like Zeus, wishes only to rule his realm in peace and quiet, without having to deal with the tantrums of impulsive and overeager upstarts.

I mentioned earlier that Hesiod knows nothing of the biblical concept of creation ex nihilo laid forth in Genesis 1; just so, Homer knows nothing of the biblical teaching laid forth in Genesis 2 and 3 that man was created in God's image but is now fallen. And yet Homer, like Hesiod, nevertheless manages to pierce down to some vital truths about ourselves and our world. He sees with great poetic and psychological insight how Achilles' and Agamemnon's nobility is marred by the lust of the eye, the lust of the flesh, and the pride of life. Homer sees further how human lust and pride can pervert us from within and prevent us from maturing into the creatures we are capable of being. The virtues and vices of Agamemnon and Achilles, and of the other warriors Homer so powerfully brings to life, are not separate things but inextricably linked. As with the great heroes of the Bible, from Abraham to Moses, Samson to David, Homer's warriors are brought down by flaws that stem as much from their virtues as from their vices. Good and evil, darkness and light are knotted together in them just as they were in that fatal fruit our first parents so foolishly devoured.

However, whereas the biblical heroes can measure their failings against a holy and righteous God, those of Homer lack a divine model. Homer's gods are as flawed and deceptive as his mortals, susceptible to the same petty rivalries and ambitions, the same envy and resentment, the same lust and pride. As such, Homer and his world lack a clear sense of sin as that which violates the nature of a holy God. Rather than heaven and earth being distinguished by a perfect state of righteousness above and a fallen state of rebelliousness below, the distinction between Homer's Olympus and his earth is that between frivolous comedy, in which there are no ultimate consequences, and high tragedy, in which bad choices lead always to bad consequences. Thus, although Book I is structured around parallel disputes between Agamemnon and Achilles and Zeus and Hera, only the first produces tragedy. The latter resolves itself in comic frivolity as Zeus and Hera's domestic quarrel gives way to drink, laughter and conjugal love. The former ushers in pain, horror and destruction.

That Homer's warriors are forced to play out their tragic struggles over against a series of divine struggles that are finally comic is a dichotomy that imbues Homer's epic world with an almost existential despair, making it as disturbingly modern (even postmodern) as it is hauntingly remote. It is a

world where the voice of Job cries out for answers, for a mediator, for a re-
deemer, but there is no voice from the whirlwind—only the laughter of the
gods.

THE WRATH OF ACHILLES

Thus far, I have interpreted the characters and events of the *Iliad* in a way
conducive to the experiences and assumptions of the modern reader. However, it is quite probable that Homer and his original audience interpreted
these same characters and events quite differently. Though Homer never
mentions the story, he and his audience would have known that Achilles
had been destined to be the son of Zeus and therefore an immortal god.
Indeed, Homer seems to allude subtly to Achilles' almost-godhood when
he has Thetis address Zeus in these words:

> Father Zeus, if ever before in word or action
> I did you favour among the immortals, now grant what I ask for.
> Now give honour to my son short-lived beyond all other
>   mortals. . . .
> Bend your head and promise me to accomplish this thing,
> or else refuse it, you have nothing to fear, that I may know
> by how much I am the most dishonoured of all gods. (I.503-6, 514-16)

Though she does not state it directly, Thetis speaks as if Zeus owes her a
favor, and as if the favor is tied somehow to the short-lived status of her
son. Her phrase, "You have nothing to fear" may even be a bitter reminder
that because Zeus has forced her to marry Peleus, Achilles can pose no ultimate threat to Zeus's rule. In any case, the scene suggests that Thetis does
have some political clout, for Zeus grants her request immediately, despite
the fact that he knows it will cause him considerable trouble with Hera.

However, the strongest proof that Homer means us to read his epic in
light of Achilles' semidivine status is to be found in Achilles' own reaction
to his mortality. Just as Thetis reminds Zeus of Achilles' short-lived status,
so she reminds Achilles of it every time she speaks with him. This constant
reminder of his impending, inescapable death has clearly affected the great
warrior. Though he fears neither pain nor injury, Achilles is morbidly obsessed with his own mortality. According to legend, early in life Achilles

was given the choice between a long, boring life and a short, glorious one (Homer incorporates this into the action at IX.410-16). He chose the short, glorious life, for he desperately wished to gain through his deeds on the battlefield the glory and immortality stolen from him when his mother was forced to marry Peleus.

According to the opening line of the poem, the *Iliad* is first and foremost about the anger of Achilles. The first word of the poem in Greek is *menin* ("wrath"), a word normally used by Homer and his fellow Greeks to denote the wrath of the gods. Ultimately, the wrath of Achilles is his wrath against Zeus and the fates who have robbed him of the immortality that should have been his birthright. Within the poem, this wrath is sublimated and then rechanneled against Agamemnon, who, by taking Briseis from him, robs Achilles of the martial glory which he has long used as a substitute for his lost divinity.

When seen from this perspective, Achilles' epic tantrum is transformed, if not apotheosized, into something far grander and more tragic. Achilles is more than a soldier enraged by the ill treatment of his commanding officer. He differs not only in degree from Agamemnon but in kind as well. When the elders of Troy, who are watching the war from the top of one of the parapets, look on the face of Helen, they exclaim:

> Surely there is no blame on Trojans and strong-greaved Achaians
> if for long time they suffer hardship for a woman like this one.
> Terrible is the likeness of her face to immortal goddesses. (III.156-58).

In the same way, we are not to blame Achilles for his wrath but to understand that in the person of Achilles we are in the presence of something semidivine. That the gods themselves acknowledge the rightness (if not the righteousness) of Achilles' wrath is demonstrated in Book I, when Athena appears to Achilles in the midst of his war of words with Agamemnon:

> And the anger came upon Peleus' son, and within
> his shaggy breast the heart was divided two ways, pondering
> whether to draw from beside his thigh the sharp sword, driving
> away all those who stood between and kill the son of Atreus,
> or else to check the spleen within and keep down his anger.

> Now as he weighed in mind and spirit these two courses
> and was drawing from its scabbard the great sword, Athene descended
> from the sky. For Hera the goddess of the white arms sent her,
> who loved both men equally in her heart and cared for them.
> The goddess standing behind Peleus' son caught him by the fair hair,
> appearing to him only, for no man of the others saw her.
> Achilleus in amazement turned about, and straightaway
> knew Pallas Athene and the terrible eyes shining. (I.188-200)

In this unforgettable scene, we glimpse not only the full nature of Achilles' wrath, the power of which can barely be contained, but the closeness and even intimacy of Achilles' relationship with the divine. As the Spirit of God lifts Ezekiel into the inner court of the new temple (Ezekiel 43:5), so Athena grabs Achilles by the hair and draws him for a moment just outside the realm of mortal concerns. Her eyes shine terribly, and Achilles is both amazed and transfixed by the goddess. But he quickly regains his balance and addresses the goddess directly as though he were on an equal footing. Athena tells Achilles that she has come to stem his anger and prevent him from killing Agamemnon, and Achilles agrees to stay his hand. By so doing, by choosing to utter through Thetis his prayer to Zeus rather than kill Agamemnon, Achilles sets in motion the tragedy of the *Iliad,* a tragedy that is as much about the horrors of war and the death of soldiers as it is about the wrath of a man who should have been a god.

Greek tragedy deals often with heroes of a divine or semidivine status who are forced to struggle, alone and isolated, in a world of mortality that more often than not fails to recognize their status, virtues and mission. In a way, Achilles is the father of all such tragic heroes, and as such he offers us a glimpse—no more—of Jesus Christ, the God-man who empties himself of his full glory and eventually suffers death (Philippians 2:6-8), who comes to his own but is not received by them (John 1:11), and who fights a series of verbal wars with the religious "commanders" of his day who would prevent him from fulfilling his mission and achieving the glory that is his by birthright (Matthew 21:23—23:39; Mark 1:40—3:6; John 8:12—9:41).

At the end of the next chapter, I shall return to the central theme of Achilles' semidivine status. For now, we would do well to remind ourselves

that it is as difficult for the modern reader to "deal with" the wrath of
Achilles as it is for the modern Christian to "deal with" the wrath of God
in the Bible. Just as it is all too easy simply to dismiss the wrath of Achilles
as an epic tantrum, so it is all too easy to ignore Yahweh's wrath against the
Canaanites of Jericho, whom he orders to be destroyed utterly. That divine
wrath does not confine itself to the pagan tribes of Canaan. As the Achilles
of Homer pours out his wrath on Trojan and Greek alike, so does the God
of Abraham, Isaac and Jacob punish with equal severity the idolatry of the
Philistines and of his own people Israel.

In both the *Iliad* and the books of the Old Testament, there is a power
and a force that is not to be trifled with. Homer understood tentatively and
imperfectly what the Old Testament teaches directly and clearly: that
wrath is as much a quality of the divine as love or mercy. Of course Homer,
lacking direct revelation, could not conceive of the sacred holiness of Yahweh's wrath nor of the righteous anger that impelled Christ to drive the
moneychangers from the temple courts, but he did understand that wrath
is part of the fabric that weaves together the intersecting worlds of mortality and immortality.

3

HOMER'S *ILIAD* II

Civilization versus Barbarism

THOUGH BOOK I OF THE *ILIAD* ENDS with Achilles' rash decision to pull out of the war and his terrible prayer to Zeus, the consequences of that prayer do not begin to manifest themselves until several books later. In the meantime, Homer slows down his narrative and fills in some of the details and the gaps. In Book II, we get a catalogue of the Greek ships and warriors and a fuller sense of the dynamics in the Greek camp, including more insight into the troubled leadership of Agamemnon. In Books III and IV, Homer offers an episode that, logic dictates, would more likely have occurred in the first or second year of the war than in the ninth or tenth: a duel between Paris and Menelaus for possession of Helen. Either way the duel goes, it should bring a cessation of the war. But the gods meddle in the combat, with Aphrodite spiriting away the almost defeated Paris to the bed of Helen and Athena persuading one of the Trojans to treacherously shoot an arrow at the bewildered Menelaus, and the war begins anew. Indeed, in the opening section of Book IV, we overhear Zeus and Hera as they coldly barter over the fate of Troy and the city-states of Greece.

With Book V, we get our first full taste of Homeric battle, with the spotlight fixed on Diomedes as he routs the Trojans in a display of Achillean prowess. At some point in the *Iliad*, every major hero, whether Greek or Trojan, gets just such a moment in the spotlight: a moment of almost godlike prowess that allows the warrior to display his *arete* (which can be translated "excellence," "manliness" or "virtue," and which is similar to the Roman word *virtus*). It is to achieve *arete* that the soldiers strive, and no soldier more fiercely than Achilles. Indeed, each time Homer allows one of his soldiers his moment of *arete* (or *aristeia*), the reader is prepared for the ultimate *aristeia* of Achilles that is recounted in all its bloody glory in Books XX to XXII. In a sense, the godlike Achilles will achieve that which the rest of us lesser mortals merely strive for. The *aristeia* of Diomedes is merely the first in a slow buildup that will culminate with the full wrath of Achilles unleashed on Hektor and his fellow Trojans.

And that brings us to the tightly woven and infinitely subtle Book VI, in which Homer offers what amounts to an *Iliad* in miniature: a self-contained narrative that carries the reader from war to peace, division to reconciliation, barbarism to civilization, the breaking of oaths to the affirmation of oaths.

HOMER'S MORAL COMPASS

As discussed earlier, Homer's warriors must live their lives and make their choices in a world that lacks a single divine standard of holiness and righteousness. They must do so as well in a world that lacks a single human concept of law. That is to say, they live and choose in a world that is both premoral (at least in the full Judeo-Christian sense) and pre-legal (at least in the later Athenian-Roman sense). Still, they are not wholly without an internal sense of that which is moral and lawful. Homer's world, like the pre-Mosaic world of Genesis, does possess a system by which the lust and pride of its elite warriors can be regulated and channeled: a method for keeping order in a pre-law society.

As in Hesiod's *Theogony*, Homer's *Iliad* does at times ascribe to Zeus the potential for just and civilized leadership. And this is no more evident than when Homer uses the divine title of Zeus Xenos. *Xenos* in Greek signifies "guest," "stranger" or "foreigner" (our modern word *xenophobia* means "the fear of foreigners"). As Zeus Xenos, the god of guests, the lord of Olympus was believed to defend the rights of all such guests and to ensure that they were treated with the proper respect and hospitality. According to the laws of *xenia,* known commonly as the guest-host relationship, both guests and hosts are duty-bound to treat each other in a certain manner. The host is to provide hospitality—food, shelter, clothing—to any stranger who comes to his door in a state of need without first interrogating him or hiding the bounty of his house. The guest, on the other hand, is not to treat his host with contempt or take advantage of his hospitality. The same relationship goes between any two people in a similar relationship: most notably, a victorious captor and his suppliant captive. If a defeated soldier on the battlefield grabs hold of the knees of the one who defeated him and begs him to spare his life, the one who holds the position of strength is honor-bound to spare his life—though he is entitled to a fit ransom.

This guest-host relationship, of course, also plays a prominent role in the Old Testament, where Abraham is rewarded for the hospitality he shows the three angels in Genesis 18, while Sodom is destroyed in chapter 19 for (among other things) its egregious breach of this same code. It appears as well in the New Testament, most notably in Hebrews 13:2, where we are told that by showing hospitality to strangers we might find that we have entertained an angel unawares, and Matthew 25, where those who have or have not shown hospitality to suffering people in need discover to their joy or horror that in so doing they have or have not shown it to Christ himself. This guest-host dynamic continued to be vital throughout the Middle Ages, not only in the sanctuary offered by Catholic churches (see Hugo's *The Hunchback of Notre Dame*) but in the code of chivalry by which knights were to ransom rather than kill fellow knights whom they had captured in battle. In the *Inferno,* Dante treats the betrayal of a guest or host as the second-worst sin in the universe, second only to the betrayal of one's lord. And the guest-host relationship to this day plays a central role in many Mediterranean cultures.

In the *Iliad,* the guest-host relationship is the key moral counter by which a character's goodness or evil can immediately be assessed. But there is another. Homer's warriors are also guided from within by a strong sense of *aidos* ("shame") and *nemesis* ("blame"). In all that they do on and off the battlefield, they strive to avoid any behavior or action that will cause them dishonor or that will bring down on them some form of divine retribution. Throughout the epic, soldiers on both sides are stirred to action by generals who accuse them of shamefully holding back (see V.787), an accusation that they are just as likely to throw at themselves (VII.93). As for *nemesis*, when the elders of Troy muse on the godlike beauty of Helen, they exclaim that it would not cause blame to anyone who fought a war on her behalf (III.156-58). In a clever reversal of this pronouncement, Helen, when she is ordered by Aphrodite to go to the bed of Paris (whom Aphrodite has just shamefully rescued from the battle with Menelaus), at first refuses because she fears it would bring *nemesis* down on her to sleep with such a coward and fool (III.410).

Generally speaking, as long as the soldiers on both sides of the war honor the guest-host relationship and steer clear of both *aidos* and *nemesis*, the battle remains honorable and the carnage and ferocity are kept to a minimum. When it is violated, chaos and destruction soon follow. Such a breach occurs at the beginning of Book VI, when Menelaus pins down a Trojan and is about to kill him. In desperation, the Trojan grabs Menelaus's knees and supplicates him to ransom rather than kill him. Though Menelaus has reason to hate all Trojans, his strong, internalized sense of *xenia* and *aidos* nudges him in the direction of mercy. That is, until Agamemnon rushes up behind him and urges him to show neither tenderness nor pity for any Trojan who comes in his path (VI.55-60). Swayed by his elder brother, Menelaus shamefully kills the suppliant Trojan. It is an inauspicious beginning to Book VI, one that threatens to destabilize the moral and ethical balance of the epic. Indeed, it takes Homer the rest of Book VI to restore the balance, a process that prepares us for the greater destabilization that Achilles will eventually bring and the even greater reconciliation that will resolve it.

Restoration begins in the next episode when Diomedes and a Trojan named Glaucus step forward into "the space between the two armies" (VI.120) and prepare to do battle. Before doing so, however, Diomedes questions Glaucus as to his name and pedigree, for he wants to be sure that this noble-looking man he is about to fight is not a god in disguise. In response, Glaucus tells a long and fantastical tale about one of his heroic ancestors. When he has finished his tale, Homer tells us,

> Diomedes of the great war cry was gladdened.
> He drove his spear deep into the prospering earth, and in winning
> words of friendliness he spoke to the shepherd of the people:
> "See now, you are my guest friend from far in the time of our fathers. . . .
> Let us avoid each other's spears, even in the close fighting. . . .
> But let us exchange our armour, so that these others may know
> how we claim to be guests and friends from the days of our fathers."
> (VI.212-31)

Though Diomedes and Glaucus have never met, Diomedes realizes when he hears the Trojan's tale that their two grandparents had once entertained each other as guest and host. That bond is so strong that Diomedes considers it to have passed down two generations to include himself and Glaucus. In the patriarchal world of Homer, as in that of the Old Testament, the friend of my father must necessarily be my friend as well. Despite the passions and brutalities of war, Diomedes and Glaucus are able in the name of the guest-host relationship to rise above the hatred between their people and assert a higher bond that transcends both blood and country.

But it is not quite enough to make up for the breach in *xenia* and *aidos* perpetrated by the two sons of Atreus—Agamemnon and Menelaus. To reset the balance, Homer must offer a fuller countervision, and to do this he takes us into the city of Troy to witness one of the most touching and human episodes in all of literature.

BALANCE IN A WORLD GONE MAD

Though the *Iliad* is told from the point of view of the Greeks, and though it is clear that we are on their side, most readers find themselves drawn more toward Troy. To paraphrase the eighteenth-century critic Edmund Burke, though we respect and fear the Greeks, it is the Trojans whom we love. And while Achilles is, technically speaking, the protagonist of the poem, our sympathy tends to lie more with the antagonist: Hektor, prince of Troy and the greatest warrior after Achilles. Anyone who has read a book about war can guess that Achilles and Hektor will have to meet on the battlefield before the epic closes, and it is no secret as to who will have to win that fight. And yet, despite the inevitability of Hektor's death at the hands of Achilles, Homer refuses to do what a lesser writer would have done: demonize Hektor and his city so that when they are destroyed we will feel a sense of victory and exaltation.

Homer won't make it that easy for us. In the latter half of Book VI, he takes us into a city that, far from being the walled camp of a crude, barbarian horde, is a little utopia of peace, beauty and joy, a sea of domestic tranquility in the midst of a raging bloody ocean. Into this city we follow Hektor, who has left the battlefield to accomplish three goals: instruct his mother to beg the aid and mercy of Athena; shame his brother into returning to the battlefield (since the war is, after all, his fault); and say farewell to his wife, Andromache, and child, Astyanax, since he fears his own impending doom. Once inside the walls, Hektor is accosted by Hekabe, his mother, and Helen, his sister-in-law, both of whom try to prevent him from returning to the battlefield. Hektor is able to withstand their pleas and keep his mind focused on the war, but when he meets his wife, his resolve wavers and he is forced to face a terrible dilemma: should he return to his men and thus fulfill his duty as prince and commander, or should he remain inside with the family he loves.

The dilemma is a very real one. Like all of Homer's warriors but more so, Hektor is a man under great pressure. The burdens he bears are weighty indeed. First-time readers of the *Iliad* always note that Homer rarely names one of his warriors without appending to it either the father's name, or patronymic, or a one- or two-word descriptive tag known as an epithet. Thus we have "swift-footed Achilles" or "Achilles, son of Peleus," "Agamemnon, son of Atreus" or "Hektor, breaker of horses." To be known always by a patronymic or an epithet is to take on the burden of both the past and the present. That is to say, warriors and leaders like Hektor and Achilles are expected not only to live up to the reputation of their fathers but also to fulfill and constantly enhance their own reputation. To make it worse, the warriors also live under what might be called the burden of the future, for they are desperately concerned with what people will say about them after they are dead. On top of these three burdens, a character like Hektor must live up to the expectations of his troops and the people of Troy, who look to him as their prince and savior. All this on the one side;

on the other, Hektor's equally strong—and equally noble—desire to stay with his family.

We, like Hektor, often find ourselves caught in just such dilemmas, situations in which the boundaries of right and wrong, success and failure are blurred. We respond to these situations in one of two ways. Either we fall back on the proverbs, principles and virtues we were taught as children, or we reject these proverbs and invent new strategies. In either case, our choice marks a crucial moment of decision that defines our relationship to the world and forces us to consider that most essential of questions: who am I? In a simple melodrama, the character who chooses the former option is labeled the protagonist, while the one who chooses the latter ends up playing the antagonist. But Homer resists setting up such a simple dichotomy, preferring rather to explore the nature of such choices. The act of choosing is a particularly human one, and it is out of the tension between the forces that would circumscribe all within a fixed circle of codes and destinies and the individual strategies that press at the boundaries of that circle that humanity emerges. This humanity is a thing that, to paraphrase St. Paul, is hard pressed on every side but not crushed, perplexed but not despairing, struck down but not destroyed. Great literature (and this includes both Homer and the Bible) reveals both man's greatness and his limitations, his inner divinity and his unregenerate nature, his God-given capacity for virtue and his fallen propensity toward lust and pride.

Into his final meeting with Andromache Hektor brings the full weight of his many burdens and the anxiety that comes with the dilemma he must face. In this brief yet timeless meeting, Homer not only explores the nature of choice but dramatizes the universal human need to find stability in the midst of chaos and meaning in the midst of existential despair. He also manages to balance out the breach of *xenia* and *aidos* perpetrated by the sons of Atreus at the outset of Book VI.

The scene begins with Andromache begging Hektor to stay with her, reminding him that he is everything to her, since her father and brothers have all been killed by Achilles. In response, Hektor the protagonist-antagonist falls back on the proverbs, the strategies he has been taught from birth:

All these
things are in my mind also, lady; yet I would feel deep shame *[aidos]*
before the Trojans, and the Trojan women with trailing garments,
if like a coward I were to shrink aside from the fighting;
and the spirit will not let me, since I have learned to be valiant
and to fight always among the foremost ranks of the Trojans,
winning for my own self great glory, and for my father. (VI.440-46)

Hektor speaks the last three lines as if they were a code he has memorized; as he says himself, it is something he has learned. It is his own spirit
rather than the gods that will accuse him if he does not live up to the glory
of his father (the burden of the past) and of himself (the burden of the
present). The shame and blame that would ensue if he did not return
would well up inside of him and destroy not only his reputation but his
identity.

Drawn to the plight of his wife and child, the mighty warrior reaches
out to take Astyanax in his hand, but the child, frightened by his father's
horse-hair helmet, cries out in fear. Clad in his instruments of war, Hektor
appears as a menacing figure, one his innocent child does not recognize. In
response, Hektor puts down the child, removes the helmet, and then takes
him back in his arms. He throws the child in the air and laughs, laying a
blessing on him that he would surpass even his father in courage and prowess. Hektor is no toy soldier made of brass, but a real man of flesh and
blood. In the midst of war, he takes the time to allay his child's fears. It is
perhaps the most tender and human moment in the *Iliad*.

Hektor returns the child to Andromache and then speaks again. He
must try once more to explain to her—and to himself—why he must return to the battlefield even if it means his death. He must put into words
the strategies he has learned and fashioned for finding balance in a world
gone mad:

Poor Andromache! Why does your heart sorrow so much for me?
No man is going to hurl me to Hades, unless it is fated,
but as for fate, I think that no man yet has escaped it
once it has taken its first form, neither brave man nor coward.
Go therefore back to our house, and take up your own work,
the loom and the distaff, and see to it that your handmaidens

ply their work also; but the men must see to the fighting,
all men who are the people of Ilion, but I beyond others. (VI.486-93)

The first half of the passage expresses a traditional attitude toward fate
that is echoed quite strongly in the Qur'an. Knowing he can do nothing to
escape his "death day," Hektor resolves to fulfill his duty. Whether he plays
the role of brave man or coward, his death will come at its appointed time.
What good is it to risk shame and blame if the risk will not lengthen his
days? In one sense, Hektor speaks here as a fatalist; he may even be seen to
embody a particular form of stoic despair that often seems to hang over the
best of pagan philosophy and literature. And yet, can we not also perceive
in Hektor's speech an intimation of something else? A desire, perhaps, to
rest secure in a fate that is even higher than Zeus? A yearning for a kind of
divine sovereignty that would lend a final purpose and meaning to human
suffering?

In the second half of the passage Hektor shifts from a concept central
to Islam to one that is central to Hinduism: the concept of duty. In Hinduism, particularly in the Bhagavad-Gita, devotees are called on to do
their duty *(dharma)* and to cleave to their assigned task and portion in life
no matter the sacrifice—a concept foreign to modern democracies. For
Hektor, this division of duty includes gender-specific roles that help define
parameters within which Hektor and Andromache can best serve and survive. As long as he does his duty and she does hers, as long as they stay
within the boundaries set for them, all will be well.

When at the end of Book XII Hektor is killed outside the walls of Troy,
Andromache is not with the rest of her family, who witness his tragic death
from the watchtower. She is in her room, working at the loom, in the very
place where he asked her to be.

HEKTOR VERSUS ACHILLES

At the end of chapter two, I confessed that in describing Achilles' wrath in
Book I as an epic tantrum I was perhaps succumbing to a more modernist
reading of the poem. Here again, at the end of chapter three, I must confess that in depicting Hektor as the true protagonist of the *Iliad* I may be
guilty of the same critical sin. For despite the fact that nearly all modern
readers (myself included) prefer Hektor to Achilles, it is clear that Homer

means Achilles to be the central protagonist of the epic. It is Achilles and not Hektor who is the god-man. Hektor is perfect in his way, but his perfection is a human perfection that others, even we who read the *Iliad*, can imitate and perhaps even achieve. Achilles, like Hercules or Prometheus or Oedipus, is beyond us, a larger-than-life hero whom we cannot imitate and whom we can barely understand.

Hektor stays within human boundaries while Achilles aches to surpass all such boundaries. Hektor knows both his capabilities and his limitations, and his angst is therefore less than that of Achilles. The son of Peleus and Thetis, on the other hand, yearns to shatter the limits of his own mortality and achieve something of the divine glory denied him by Zeus. Homer conceived his epic in ignorance of the Old Testament. Had he had access to Genesis and its teaching that man is both physical and spiritual, akin to the animals in his body and to the angels in his spirit, Homer might have recognized more fully that Achilles, as tragic hero, embodies that part of humanity that is troubled by its own inner transcendence.

Of all the characters of the Old Testament, the one most like Achilles is Samson: he of the uncontrollable wrath whose ability to save is surpassed only by his ability to destroy. Neither warrior seems to understand fully the nature of his own strength, yet both burn to fulfill what they see as their mission. Samson is perhaps the most flawed of the Old Testament heroes; he is surely far less "likeable" than Abraham, Moses or Joshua. Nevertheless, this does not prevent Samson from emerging as one of the key Old Testament types of whom Christ will be the fulfillment. Like Samson, Jesus is betrayed by his people and turned over to the enemy (the Philistines, the Romans), who mock him, scorn him, and rob him of his "life" (blindness, crucifixion). But out of the depths of humiliation and defeat, Samson and Christ both rise again, using their very defeat as a weapon by which to destroy the power of the enemy (the pulling down of the Temple of Dagon, the resurrection).

If God can use the uncontrolled lust and anger of Samson to foreshadow and even prefigure the life, death and resurrection of Christ, could he not also have used the semidivine wrath of Achilles to prepare the pagan world for the coming of one who would, by means of a violent defeat and dramatic victory, conquer the power of Satan, sin and death? (Significantly, when Milton decided to compose his own Christian reworking of a Greek tragedy, *Samson Agonistes,* he chose Samson as his biblical embodiment of the tragic hero.) Please do not misunderstand. Achilles is not a type of Christ in the way Joshua or Elisha is a type of Christ. But he does embody in its most extreme form the wrestling that lies at the heart of man: a dual nature that will never allow him to rest fully contented in the earthly sphere. As such he points ahead to the one who would be both true God and true man, the one who would reconcile man and God, the human and the divine.

Yes, I like Hektor more than Achilles. But there are times when I prefer the sensitive Jonathan to the rash David, the peace-loving, reconciling Barnabas to the rigid, intensely focused Paul. And yet God makes it clear in 1 and 2 Samuel and the book of Acts that it is David and Paul who, for all their propensity to wrath, are the ones appointed by God to embody and carry forward the struggle.

4

HOMER'S *ILIAD* III

A New Ethic

THE *ILIAD* IS, ARGUABLY, THE GREATEST book ever written about war. It depicts the battlefield in all its glory and celebrates the virtues of war and of the warriors who fight it. And yet at the same time it exposes the horrors and injustices that accompany it. Both pro-war and anti-war, the *Iliad* refuses to leave us with simple answers. And to complicate further its almost self-contradictory stance, the *Iliad* presents us with a central character who is simultaneously the greatest warrior ever to take the field and the first pacifist in history.

Though Book VII, following as it does the great reconciliation scenes of Book VI, offers us a second hope for a peaceful conclusion to the war in the form of a second duel, this time between Hektor and Aias, that hope proves to be fleeting. In Book VII the war resumes and Achilles' prayer to Zeus begins to take its effect. By the end of Book VIII, the Greeks have been so battered that Agamemnon concedes he must do something to appease Achilles and convince him to return to the battlefield. He does so in Book IX by sending an embassy to Achilles with an offer of great reward if he will take up his spear again and defend his Greek comrades. The ambassadors chosen to carry Agamemnon's very generous offer are carefully handpicked: Odysseus for his rhetorical skills; Aias, who shares both Achilles' brute strength and his love of battle; and Phoinix, Achilles' boyhood tutor and therefore a surrogate father.

All three ambassadors fully expect that Achilles will accept the reward, which includes vast amounts of gold, horses, land, citadels and women, and rejoin the battle. But he refuses. In what follows, we shall explore exactly why Achilles should have accepted the reward and why he does not.

THE HEROIC CODE

Every work of art, I teach my students, presents its reader with a microcosm, a carefully constructed little world—both akin to and unique from the "real" world—that runs according to its own rules. Each of these microcosms is founded on a certain set of values that gives it a distinctive shape, that helps it maintain that shape, and that lets its inhabitants know when it is proper to laugh or cry, to sing or dance, to love or hate. In order to understand these little worlds, we will often as a class draw up a list of the virtues and behavioral codes that each microcosm holds sacred and the methods used for identifying those who possess these virtues. This list in turn generates deeper questions: What qualities must a hero possess if he is to succeed in such a world? What strategies will he use for dealing with the joys and hardships presented to him by a world thus configured? Such simple but incisive questions can draw students into a work that may at first seem inaccessible and even irrelevant. They can help a class thresh out the issues and conflicts that give resonance to the great works of literature.

We have, of course, already done this to a certain extent for the *Iliad*. The rules of *xenia, aidos* and *nemesis* are all key components of this particular microcosm, just as Hektor's understanding of his "death day" and the role and function of duty represent some of the strategies he uses to survive and thrive in his world. But what of the wider society of the *Iliad*? Clearly, we are dealing with a warrior society, one that privileges virtues like strength, courage and physical prowess. But why do these soldiers fight?

To answer that question, we must look at a passage that critics refer to as the "heroic code." The passage is spoken by a Trojan, but it could just as

well have been spoken by a Greek, for Greek and Trojan alike ascribe to
the code. "Glaucus," the speaker asks,

> why is it you and I are honoured before others
> with pride of place, the choice meats and the filled wine cups
> in Lykia, and all men look on us as if we were immortals,
> and we are appointed a great piece of land by the banks of Xanthos,
> good land, orchard and vineyard, and ploughland for the planting of wheat?
> Therefore it is our duty in the forefront of the Lykians
> to take our stand, and bear our part of the blazing of battle,
> so that a man of the close-armoured Lykians may say of us:
> "Indeed, these are no ignoble men who are lords of Lykia,
> these kings of ours, who feed upon the fat sheep appointed
> and drink the exquisite sweet wine, since indeed there is strength
> of valour in them, since they fight in the forefront of the Lykians."
> Man, supposing you and I, escaping this battle,
> would be able to live on forever, ageless, immortal,
> so neither would I myself go on fighting in the foremost
> nor would I urge you into the fighting where men win glory.
> But now, seeing that the spirits of death stand close about us
> in their thousands, no man can turn aside nor escape them,
> let us go on and win glory for ourselves, or yield it to others. (XII.310-28)

The heroic code stated here breaks into two parts. In the first half, the
speaker reminds Glaucus that the reason they and their fellow warriors are
graced with the best land, the best food and the best wine (not to mention
the best women) is that they possess a type of honor that can only be won
on the battlefield. Unlike our modern American society, which privileges
money, the society of the *Iliad,* like the pre-Civil War South, places its
highest premium on honor. The more honor one has, the more he is entitled to the finer things; conversely, the more one enjoys the perks of his status, the greater is his duty to fight bravely in the front ranks.

Honor then is the supreme virtue for these warriors, but how are we to
know which of them possesses the most honor? Like love, honor is not a
thing that can be calculated in numeric terms. Or is it? In our modern military, one can often identify which soldier is the bravest by counting the
number of medals he has. In Homer's world, there is also a concrete way

of determining which warrior has the most honor. One simply needs to count up the number of prizes, or "meeds" of honor, that the warrior possesses. These prizes consist of gold, horses, armor, trophies and women. The more fiercely and bravely one fights, the more meeds of honor he will win; the more meeds he has, the greater will be his honor; the more honor he has, the higher his status will be in society.

But this desire for status, the second half of the passage tells us, is not the only reason the soldiers fight. They fight as well for the glory that honor brings. And they desire that glory for the simple reason that they are mortal, that they will die, and, unless they have done something to bring glory to their name, they will be forgotten. For the Homeric warrior, collecting prizes and thus gaining honor promises a sure if meager form of immortality. We are all going to die, the heroic code advises, so let us win as much glory as we can before that inevitable day arrives.

With this in mind, we may now understand a little better why Achilles pulls out of the war when Agamemnon steals away Briseis in Book I. When Agamemnon does this, he robs Achilles not only of his meed but of the honor linked to it; worse yet, he demonstrates to Achilles and all of the other warriors that he has the power to rob a man of his honor by stripping him of his prize. Achilles' fellow warriors are fully aware of this, and up until this point, they have not blamed him for his decision—though Achilles' men, who are forced to pull out along with Achilles, are mad at him, for his decision has robbed them of the opportunity to win meeds for themselves. Indeed, Phoinix even admits to Achilles that were Agamemnon

> not bringing gifts and naming still more hereafter,
> Atreus' son; were he to remain still swollen with rancour,
> even I would not bid you throw your anger aside, nor
> defend the Argives, though they needed you sorely. (IX.515-18)

Remarkably, Phoinix is here telling Achilles that even though Greeks are dying because of his refusal to fight, he as yet bears him no ill will; in fact, were Agamemnon not offering him such a rich prize, he would even now not urge Achilles to fight. Up until this point, Phoinix goes on to say, "one could not blame your anger" (IX.523). In other words, up until now,

Achilles' actions have provoked no *nemesis*. But now the situation has changed. Agamemnon is offering Achilles a prize that, if accepted, would immediately make him the most honored warrior of all time (hence the excessive nature of Agamemnon's offer). It is not only inconceivable that Achilles would not accept it; if he does not, he would be acting improperly and foolishly.

To prove this point to Achilles, his former tutor establishes the Homeric equivalent of a legal precedent. He tells him a story of another warrior who was as brave and stubborn as Achilles, a warrior named Meleager who also pulled out of a war because of anger and resentment. In the story, things begin to go bad for Meleager's side, and the leaders try to woo him back with an offer as great as that which Agamemnon now offers to Achilles. But Meleager, his heart still sore, refuses. Despite his refusal, when the war rages more hotly and he hears the cries and groans of men, his warrior heart rises within him and he returns to the battlefield. In a blaze of glory, he saves the day and drives back the evil from his people, but because of his earlier refusal, he loses out on the promised meeds. In case Achilles misses the moral of the story, Phoinix explains it clearly:

> Now, with gifts promised
> go forth. The Achaians will honour you as they would an immortal.
> But if without gifts you go into the fighting where men perish,
> your honour will no longer be as great, though you drive back the battle.
>   (IX.602-5)

To our modern sensibilities, Phoinix's conclusion seems illogical and strained. Honor is honor, is it not? Why should it matter whether or not Achilles has the gifts? For Homer's society, it makes all the difference. Again, it is inconceivable that Achilles should refuse the gifts and remain in his tent. Everything in his society and his upbringing tells him he should accept them. Indeed, Achilles of all men is the last person we would expect to refuse the gifts, for he is the one most concerned with winning fame and glory as a compensation for his mortality.

Yet he refuses.

THE FELLOWSHIP OF LIFE

Since the end of Book I, Achilles has remained completely off stage. What has he been doing in the interim? We might begin by asking what he was doing before Book I. The answer, of course, is fighting, always fighting. Achilles is a creature of the battlefield; he knows nothing else. Since he was old enough to wield a sword, he has stood at the very center of the battle. And now, suddenly, for the space of several days, he is forced to step off the field, to watch from the sidelines. Perhaps as he watches from the wings he begins to do something he has never before had the time or the inclination to do: think.

Imagine if you were the star athlete of your high school for four years, and then, in your senior spring, you broke your leg and were forced to spend your days sitting on the bleachers. What thoughts might run through your brain that never occurred to you before? Might you not, for the first time, begin to question the importance of your sport? Might you not begin to wonder if it was worth the investment you put into it? When you were in the center of the action, it seemed to be everything, but now. . . . And might you not move from there to consider other larger questions: Who am I? Why am I here? What is my purpose? How do I know I am of value?

These, I believe, are the very thoughts and questions that run through Achilles' mind as he sits in his tent, cut off from the only thing that has ever given his life meaning. Indeed, I would argue that this must be the case, for when Achilles tries to explain to the embassy why he will not accept Agamemnon's gifts and return to battle, he says things that are radically opposed to the beliefs of his society: radically different, in fact, from his own beliefs and actions up to this point. Achilles, we must understand, is not only a devotee of the meeds of honor system; he is its poster child. There are few men in his society who are more committed to the heroic code or who have benefited more fully from it. For Achilles to question the code would be like Donald Trump questioning the virtues of capitalism. Yet question he does.

When the three ambassadors first lay forth Agamemnon's offer, Achilles insists that he will not be persuaded. We think, at first, that he is merely angry at Agamemnon and will not back down, but then he says something stunning:

Fate is the same for the man who holds back, the same if he fights hard.
We are all held in a single honour, the brave with the weaklings.
A man dies still if he has done nothing, as one who has done much.
    (IX.318-20)

This is not something Achilles believes, or at least it is not something he believed in the past. If taken to its extreme, a statement like this could fracture the very foundation of the meeds of honor system. If honor is the same for the brave man as for the weakling, then why fight? Why accumulate meeds of honor if all possess the same honor regardless of their deeds or of their courage? Does Achilles realize what he is saying?

Yet he does not stop here. Later in the meeting, he boldly—and, from the point of view of his microcosm, nonsensically—exclaims:

For not worth the value of my life are all the possessions they fable
were won for Ilion, that strong-founded citadel, in the old days
when there was peace, before the coming of the sons of the Achaians.
(IX.400-403)

We cannot, Achilles seems to be saying, put a price tag on a human life. Yes, we agree from our modern vantage point, of course this is true—forgetting that it was most certainly not true in Achilles' day. The Judeo-Christian belief in the intrinsic value of all human beings had yet to be "invented" when the Trojan War was fought (about 1200 B.C.) or when Homer composed his epic (about five hundred years later). We have not even reached the teachings of Socrates and Plato, who themselves do not fully reach this understanding.

But there is more. In answer to Phoinix's warning that if he does not take the gifts, his honor will be lessened, Achilles replies:

Phoinix my father, aged, illustrious, such honour is a thing
I need not. I think I am honoured already in Zeus' ordinance
which will hold me here beside my curved ships as long as life's wind
stays in my breast, as long as my knees have their spring beneath me.
    (IX.607-10)

Are we listening here to a first-century Christian or to a mighty warrior who has killed a thousand men and watched his honor grow with the accumulation of each new trophy? Achilles should not be saying these things;

he should not even be thinking them. If it is true that we all have honor and worth merely because we are alive, then the whole heroic code and the meeds of honor system on which it rests is an illusion, a will-o'-the-wisp.

Achilles has no name for the new ethic he is tentatively proposing, but I like to call it the fellowship of life. According to the meeds of honor system, we are all going to die, so let us win as much glory as we can before the end. But according to the "fellowship of life," we are all going to die, so let us live and enjoy the time that is given us. Let us not rush into our deaths more swiftly, but take honor and dignity in the life that is within us. It is quite understandable that Achilles has no name for his new ethic. For all his prowess on the battlefield, he is not a thinker. He lacks the analytical skills and philosophical tools to take his stray thoughts and synthesize them into a system. He is not Socrates; he is not even Nestor or Odysseus. He simply does not know what to do with the earth-shattering thoughts bouncing around in his head.

And yet, even if he did possess some of these skills, he still might have failed in formulating his thoughts into a workable ethos. Most of us test our ideas by bouncing them off of other people. But this Achilles cannot do. He has no support group, no "think tank," to help nurture and shape his fledgling ethos. None of the ambassadors, not even Odysseus, has any concept of what he is saying. This, according to Homer, is their reaction to Achilles' musings: "So he spoke, and all of them stayed stricken to silence / in amazement at his words. He had spoken to them very strongly" (IX.430-31). And when the embassy returns to Agamemnon and relays Achilles' words, they have the same exact reaction (IX.693-94).

Ironically, the right ideas have come to the wrong person at the wrong time. Alas, not just ironically but tragically. Achilles' new ethos, a message his society needs to hear but will not hear again until Paul speaks at the Areopagus in Athens, prevents him from returning to the war. And it is precisely his refusal to reenter the war that leads to the horrors recorded in the remaining books of the *Iliad.* Instead of fighting himself, Achilles agrees to let his best friend, Patroclus, wear his armor and fight in his place. As if possessed by the very spirit of Achilles, Patroclus turns the tide of battle against the terrified Trojans and almost takes the city single-handedly, but despite the armor, he is no Achilles. Before the wall of Troy, he meets and is killed by Hektor.

When the news reaches Achilles, he is filled with rage and returns to the battlefield, no longer a man concerned with the innate dignity of every human being, but a murderous animal intent on wholesale slaughter. As for his new ethic, his fellowship of life, Achilles rejects it completely, blaming it for the death of his beloved friend. And so is lost to the world an idea—that life has intrinsic value apart from one's status or accomplishments—that could have revolutionized the ancient world. Nevertheless, Achilles' shadowy, ill-defined ethic remains one of the greatest "seeds" of the pagan world, one that will be fully articulated by Christ and go on to provide a foundation stone for the edifice of Western civilization.

5

HOMER'S *ILIAD* IV

From Wrath to Reconciliation

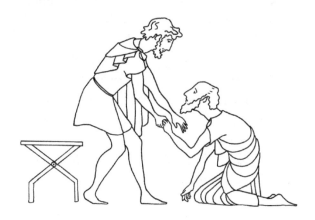

FROM THE MOMENT ACHILLES LEARNS that his friend Patroclus has been killed, an inner metamorphosis begins to take place that slowly transforms him from a noble warrior into a brutal killer. Here is his first reaction to the news of Patroclus's death:

> In both hands he caught up the grimy dust, and poured it
> over his head and face, and fouled his handsome countenance,
> and the black ashes were scattered over his immortal tunic.
> And he himself, mightily in his might, in the dust lay
> at length and took and tore at his hair with his hands, and defiled it.
>   (XVIII.23-27)

On the surface, Achilles is merely engaging in a cultural form of grieving, a method one still might see in parts of the Mediterranean world. On a deeper psychological level, he is defiling his outer countenance as preparation for a greater inner defilement. Like a Native American brave who puts on war paint that he might become something more wild and fierce than he is, Achilles fashions for himself a terrible mask that his face—and soul—will soon come to fit.

The theme of the *Iliad,* as we have seen, is the wrath of Achilles. Until this point, the reader has taken for granted that the wrath referred to in the opening line of the poem is Achilles' wrath against Agamemnon. Now we find that the true and more deadly wrath of Achilles is not against Agamemnon but against Hektor—or, better, his rage against Hektor more fully taps the true source of his wrath: the loss of his immortal birthright. When Achilles in Book XIX reconciles with Agamemnon and declares that he has beaten down his anger, we realize that what Achilles has done is not beaten down his anger but channeled it into a new and more deadly form. From this point until he can kill Hektor with his own hands, Achilles swears that he will neither eat nor sleep. The only food he now desires is "blood . . . and slaughter, and the groaning of men" (XIX.214). Even when Agamemnon graciously announces that he will still give Achilles the prizes he had promised him in Book IX, Achilles shows no interest in the gifts. Only one thing concerns him now: the death of Hektor. Nothing else matters.

THE FELLOWSHIP OF DEATH

Before Achilles encounters Hektor, however, Homer sends his bloodthirsty warrior on an epic killing spree. During this spree, Achilles decimates the Trojan army, cutting through their ranks as a farmer might walk through fields mowing down the ripe grain with his scythe. As he fights his way forward, ever seeking sight of Hektor, Achilles finds himself by the banks of the river Xanthos. There by the shore of the sacred river he encounters the unfortunate Lykaon, one of the many sons of King Priam whom Achilles had earlier captured and sold into slavery. After long years of toil, Lykaon has finally been ransomed and newly restored to his family and city. Now, with terror in his heart and trembling in his knees, Lykaon once again meets the man who caused him such pain. Lykaon throws himself at Achilles' knees and begs the Greek warrior to spare his life in return for a great reward. But the Achilles he meets on this day is a very different man from the one who defeated him several years earlier. The man who stares down at him now with a wild look of hate in his eyes has lost his capacity for pity or *aidos* and cares no longer for the rules of *xenia.* In answer to Lykaon's plea, he speaks out in a "voice without pity":

> Poor fool, no longer speak to me of ransom, nor argue it.
> In the time before Patroklos came to the day of his destiny
> then it was the way of my heart's choice to be sparing
> of the Trojans, and many I took alive and disposed of them.
> Now there is not one who can escape death, if the gods send
> him against my hands in front of Ilion, not one
> of all the Trojans and beyond others the children of Priam.
> So, friend, you die also. Why all this clamour about it?
> Patroklos also is dead, who was better by far than you are.
> Do you not see what a man I am, how huge, how splendid
> and born of a great father, and the mother who bore me immortal?
> Yet even I have also my death and my strong destiny,
> and there shall be a dawn or an afternoon or a noontime
> when some man in the fighting will take the life from me also
> either with a spearcast or an arrow flown from the bowstring. (XXI.99-113)

According to the meeds of honor system and the heroic code, we are all going to die, so let us gain glory. According to the fellowship of life, we are all going to die, so let us live. According to this new ethic of despair—what I call the fellowship of death—we are all going to die, so let's get on with it. In rejecting the ideas he expressed in Book IX, Achilles has not returned to his older, more traditional beliefs, but has gone to the other extreme. Now neither life nor meeds, neither honor nor glory mean anything to him. All has been emptied of its value.

Exacerbated by Patroclus's death, the unresolved conflict between Achilles' human and divine natures engulfs the warrior, plunging him into an early form of existential despair. Achilles must now confront directly what it means to be born of a mortal father and an immortal mother, and he presses that realization upon Lykaon as though he were defying the Trojan to give him an answer to the riddle of his birth. In response to Achilles' agonizing question, neither Lykaon nor Homer has a comforting answer. In the absence of an answer, Achilles concludes his "debate" with Lykaon with these dark words:

> Even so, die all an evil death, till all of you
> pay for the death of Patroklos and the slaughter of the Achaians

whom you killed beside the running ships, when I was not with them.
  (XXI.133-135)

Guilt, it seems, drives Achilles' wrath and despair as much as his obsession with his own brief life. Not only is he powerless to prevent his own death; he cannot even prevent the death of his friend. If this be the case, what is the point of living at all?

Rejecting Lykaon's right as a suppliant and loosing himself from any sense of shame or fear of *nemesis*, Achilles kills the Trojan in cold blood and tosses his body into the river. Then, with renewed fury, he cuts down a dozen more sons of Troy and casts their bodies into the Xanthos as well. So great is the slaughter that the river itself cries out; the blood of the slain is choking it, congesting the flow of its streams. Incensed, Achilles leaps into the water and begins to fight the god of the river. His fury has blinded him even as his wrath has warped and skewed his moral compass.

Fearing that the entire Trojan army will be slaughtered, Apollo deceives Achilles into chasing him while the remaining Trojans run for shelter behind the walls. But Hektor will not run. Even when Achilles realizes he is being fooled and charges back toward the wall of Troy, Hektor remains steadfast and unmoved. Then, in what may be considered to be the first soliloquy in literature, Homer allows us to listen in as Hektor ponders within his breast what he should do (XXII.99-130). For a brief, hopeful moment, Hektor decides that he will strip off his armor and make a promise before Achilles that he will return Helen to the Greeks along with a great ransom. Hypothetically speaking, if Hektor does this the war should end and the killing stop. But Hektor knows in his heart that this will not happen. He and Achilles and all of the key players in the drama have forged too far ahead to turn back now.

Achilles speeds his way toward Hektor and, when Hektor sees the cold, pitiless wrath in his eyes, he turns and flees for his life. Three times Achilles chases Hektor around the walls of Troy.

> It was a great man who fled, but far better he who pursued him
> rapidly, since here was no festal beast, no ox-hide
> they strove for, for these are prizes that are given men for their running.
> No, they ran for the life of Hektor, breaker of horses (XXII.158-61)

Homer's point is subtle but clear: the life of Hektor is now the only prize, the only meed of honor that Achilles cares anything about.

In the end, though he knows Achilles is a force that cannot be beaten, Hektor ceases his flight and bravely faces Achilles for a final combat. But before they close in battle, Hektor calls out to Achilles and asks him to make a pact: whoever is victorious in the battle, he must promise to ransom back the body of the other without desecrating or defiling it. Hektor's request is just and righteous (the proper treatment of corpses is central to the Homeric understanding of ethics and morality), but Achilles, who has forsaken the strategies and virtues of his youth and of his society, refuses to agree:

> Hektor, argue me no agreements. I cannot forgive you.
> As there are no trustworthy oaths between men and lions,
> nor wolves and lambs have spirit that can be brought to agreement
> but forever these hold feelings of hate for each other,
> so there can be no love between you and me, nor shall there be
> oaths between us. (XXII.261-66)

In the face of Achilles' wrath, all that makes human life valuable, all that raises it above the nasty, brutish life of the beast comes crashing down. Living as they do in a pre-law society, Homer's warriors have at best a tenuous hold on the structures and benefits of civilization. Eliminate the laws of *xenia* and *aidos* and the beast in man will eventually tear down all that is good or just or peaceful, all that is worth preserving on this battlefield we call the earth. (Of course, a counterargument could be made that it was the Trojans who broke *xenia* and *aidos* when Paris stole away Helen, and that the wrath of Achilles embodies the judgment of the gods on Troy as the wrath of Samson embodies the judgment of God on the Philistines.)

Hektor's pleas avail him nothing. Once Achilles kills him, he strips his body naked, ties the heels of the corpse to his chariot, and drags it round and round the walls of Troy. It is a terrible act, one that stuns even the gods into silence. It is made even more horrible by the fact that Hektor's family is forced to watch this pitiless display from their vantage point on the watchtower. But Achilles does not care. Just before he begins to drag the body, Achilles addresses his fellow Greeks with words that offer us a window into his warped soul:

> There is a dead man who lies by the ships, unwept, unburied:
> Patroklos: and I will not forget him, never so long as
> I remain among the living and my knees have their spring beneath me.
> And though the dead forget the dead in the house of Hades,
> even there I shall still remember my beloved companion. (XXII.386-90)

The third line of this passage directly echoes one of the phrases Achilles uses to describe the fellowship of life in Book IX:

> I think I am honoured already in Zeus' ordinance
> which will hold me here beside my curved ships as long as life's wind
> stays in my breast, as long as my knees have their spring beneath me.
>   (IX.607-10)

Here, flush with hope in the possibility of his new ethic, Achilles asserts that as long as he has spring in his knees, he will know that he is of value and worth in the eyes of Zeus. But in the passage from Book XXII, the spring in his knees reminds him only of the death of Patroclus. As long as that spring remains, Achilles will live for the dead, will become himself a sort of walking dead.

When Hektor faces Achilles in Book XXII, he is wearing not his own armor, but the armor of Achilles: the armor, that is, which Patroclus had borrowed from Achilles, and which Hektor stripped from Patroclus's corpse after he killed him. In an almost literal sense, when Achilles kills Hektor before the walls of Troy, he kills himself as well. Like Samson, Achilles is finally his own worst enemy, his own executioner.

THE FELLOWSHIP OF SUFFERING

All who seek revenge on those who have done them wrong hope in their heart that if they can see their vengeance through, they will find peace, closure and an end to pain. Alas, those who do follow through with their dreams of vengeance rarely find the peace they seek. "Dearly beloved," counsels Paul, "avenge not yourselves, but rather give place unto wrath: for it is written [in Deuteronomy 32:35], Vengeance is mine; I will repay, saith the Lord" (Romans 12:19). So it is in our day; so it was in the days of Troy.

Achilles' killing of Hektor and defiling of the corpse do not bring him relief. On the contrary, they only fan his grief and pain the more. Thus, as

Homer begins the final book of his poem, we learn that although all the Greek soldiers, who have just celebrated the funeral of Patroclus in an epic manner, are enjoying food and fellowship and sleep, Achilles is unable to partake in their joy. Guilt, despair and an almost unbearable weariness hang on him, crushing out of him his joy, his hope, his life. While the Greeks sleep, Homer tells us, Achilles

> wept still as he remembered his beloved companion, nor did sleep
> who subdues all come over him, but he tossed from one side to the other
> in longing for Patroklos, for all his manhood and his great strength
> and all the actions he had seen to the end with him, and the hardships
> he had suffered; the wars of men; hard crossing of the big waters.
> Remembering all these things he let fall the swelling tears, lying
> sometimes along his side, sometimes on his back, and now again
> prone on his face; then he would stand upright, and pace turning
> in distraction along the beach of the sea, nor did dawn rising
> escape him as she brightened across the sea and the beaches.
> Then, when he had yoked running horses under the chariot
> he would fasten Hektor behind the chariot, so as to drag him. (XXIV.4-15)

Though there is no single proper way to grieve the loss of a loved one, there are surely improper ways for dealing with the pain and sorrow of loss. Restlessly, vainly, Achilles seeks to find a position that will assuage his grief, but all of his efforts seem only to intensify it. Whether he sits or stands or lies on his side, whether he paces the beach or rolls back and forth in his bed, the grief remains. In his madness, Achilles even continues to defile the body of Hektor, but that too only intensifies the pain. If Achilles embodies the pinnacle of glory and honor that a man is capable of, he also embodies the depths of despair to which we all fall prey. Indeed, inasmuch as Achilles is a god-man who foreshadows the God-Man, his depth of grief offers us a possible glimpse of the agonies of Gethsemane.

For eleven days this continues with no one saying a word to Achilles, but finally, on the dawn of the twelfth, Apollo calls on the gods to take pity on the dead Hektor. Apollo realizes, if the other gods do not, that Achilles' actions are a threat to civilization itself. He must be stopped or he will kill all pity and defile all that is sacred and holy. Zeus, as if roused from a slumber, calls Thetis to his side and instructs her to go to Achilles and order him to stop his grieving and return the body for ransom. Then he sends one of his messengers—Iris, an embodiment of the rainbow—to go to Priam and instruct him to enter the Greek camp and offer ransom for his son's corpse.

It is significant, I believe, that when Thetis tells Achilles to stop, he immediately agrees. One feels that Achilles has wanted to stop, has yearned to put an end to his self-destructive grieving, but no one has had the courage—or the love—to risk the wrath that might be unleashed. Still, even though Achilles consents to the orders of Zeus relayed by his mother, the reader waits in quiet fear as Priam makes his way through the Greek camp in search of Achilles' tent. What will happen when Achilles is confronted face to face with the father of the one who killed his friend? Will he truly ransom back the body, or will wrath seize him again and lead him to kill the defenseless Priam?

In a sense, the entire *Iliad* is one long slow buildup to the meeting of Priam and Achilles. On the outcome of this meeting rests not only the continuation, but the very possibility of civilization. If these two enemies can find reconciliation, there is hope for mankind; if not, there is only the jungle.

Helped by the god Hermes, Priam slips unnoticed through the Geek camp, enters Achilles' tent, and throws himself at the knees of the warrior. He begs Achilles to take pity on him and his suffering, and he asks something else. He asks Achilles to look upon him and see not an enemy, but an old, grief-stricken man who might very well be Peleus, the aged father of Achilles. In Book IX, Phoinix acts as a surrogate Peleus and encourages Achilles to return to battle. Here, Priam emerges as more than a surrogate; in a very real sense, he is Peleus. Indeed, as Achilles gazes with wonder on Priam, the old king for a brief moment takes on the visage of a god. Achilles is moved by Priam's plea, and the following scene ensues:

> So [Priam] spoke, and stirred in the other a passion of grieving
> for his own father. He took the old man's hand and pushed him
> gently away, and the two remembered, as Priam sat huddled
> at the feet of Achilleus and wept close for man-slaughtering Hektor
> and Achilleus wept now for his own father, now again
> for Patroklos. The sound of their mourning moved in the house. Then

> when great Achilleus had taken full satisfaction in sorrow
> and the passion for it had gone from his mind and body, thereafter
> he rose from his chair, and took the old man by the hand, and set him
> on his feet again, in pity for the grey head and the grey beard.
> (XXIV.507-16)

Quietly, gently, miraculously, something happens in this scene that we have been waiting for since Book I: the wrath, grief and despair of Achilles ebb away, and he again finds stability. For the first time since the death of Patroclus, Achilles has been released from the weight of his sorrow; he is, at least for now, satisfied and at peace. He has discovered the proper way to grieve, and it has brought him rest. But what has he done? It is certainly not the weeping, for he had been doing that for twelve days. It is not the tears themselves but the fact that he shares them that makes the difference. For the first time he is grieving together with another human being who, like him, has suffered the loss of someone dear. He is even able, in an amazing moment of clarity, to look upon the aged and worn face of Priam and see the face of his father.

Out of this experience arises a fourth ethic: the fellowship of suffering. According to the heroic code, we are all going to die, so let us gain glory. According to the fellowship of life, we are all going to die, so let us live. According to the fellowship of death, we are all going to die, so let's get on with it. But according to the fellowship of suffering, we are all going to die, so let us grieve together. What makes it so difficult to be a human being, so difficult to be a mortal in a world of mortals, is not so much that we will die ourselves but that we will lose the ones we love. In their shared mourning, the two men weep for different people, yet ultimately it is the same grief: the grief of the survivor who must continue to live in a world that has lost much of its light and hope. Even Jesus wept at the tomb of Lazarus, sharing with his good friends Mary and Martha in the fellowship of suffering. "For we have not," the author of Hebrews tells us, "an high priest [Christ] which cannot be touched with the feeling of our infirmities; but was in all points tempted like as we are, yet without sin" (Hebrews 4:15). Achilles, unlike Christ, is neither pure nor sinless, but it is significant that we see in this scene that the great warrior shares our grief in the most humble and intimate way. It is likewise significant that, just as Christ's mercy turns aside God's judgment, so Achilles, the agent of divine wrath in the *Iliad,* is also the one whose mercy stems and exhausts that wrath.

It is here, and not with the death of Achilles or the fall of Troy, that Homer ends his great epic. After Achilles returns the body, he and Priam agree that they will call a truce for twelve days so that both sides may mourn and bury their dead. Yes, when the truce ends the fighting will resume and Troy will be destroyed, but that is a matter that lies outside the scope of the *Iliad:* a poem that neither begins at the beginning nor ends at the ending.

In an essay titled "What I Believe," the British novelist E. M. Forster had this to say: "All the great creative actions, all the decent human relations, occur during the intervals when force has not managed to come to the front. These intervals are what matter. I want them to be as frequent and as lengthy as possible, and I call them 'civilisation.'"[1] It is in the midst of one of these intervals that Homer's *Iliad* comes to a close.

---

[1]Arthur M. Eastman, ed., *The Norton Reader,* 7th ed. (New York: Norton, 1988), p. 1165.

6

HOMER'S *ODYSSEY* I

Coming of Age

IF THE *ILIAD* IS THE FIRST GREAT TRAGEDY in Western literature, the *Odyssey* is the first great comedy. Unlike the former, which ends with a death and a funeral and the sharing of mutual grief, the latter climaxes with a series of recognitions and reunions and a "remarriage" between a husband and wife who have been separated for twenty years. More importantly, whereas Homer's first epic gives us a world where ethical standards are murky and hard to define, where the supposed antagonist, Hektor, identifies himself fully with the mores and codes of his culture while the supposed protagonist, Achilles, breaks and even reinvents them, Homer's second epic gives us a world where ethical categories are clearly defined and adhered to. In the *Odyssey*, which is as much a melodrama as it is a comedy, the line that separates the good guys from the bad is far easier to discern than in the *Iliad*. When the good guys—Odysseus and his son—kill the bad guys—the suitors—in the *Odyssey*, we feel elated and triumphant: which is not the way we feel when Achilles kills Hektor in the *Iliad*. Hektor does not deserve the death visited upon him nor the shameful treatment accorded his corpse; the suitors richly deserve everything they get.

And we know that they do, for the Homer of the *Odyssey* makes it simple for us to distinguish heroes from villains: heroes keep and honor the guest-host relationship; villains break and pervert it. Though we hear little about *aidos* and *nemesis* in the *Odyssey,* the theme of *xenia* is pervasive and all-encompassing. The reason for this is that whereas the *Iliad* defines the nature of the good life and the good man along martial lines, the *Odyssey* defines it along domestic ones. The former upholds honor, courage and prowess on the battlefield as the keys to external and internal success; the latter champions faithfulness, persistence and the preservation of identity. Thus it is that the *Iliad,* like all tragedies, finds its ultimate resolution only in death, while the *Odyssey,* like all comedies, finds its consummation in (re)marriage. The Greek word *oikonomia* (from which we get our word "economy") refers to the management of a family or household; it is a word whose implications are at once social and political, at once economic and domestic. The hero of the *Odyssey* struggles not only to be reunited with his wife but to restore the *oikonomia* of Ithaca. For Achilles, it is enough to achieve personal glory and honor; for Odysseus, the entire sociopolitical-domestic world must be put back in order.

These significant distinctions between the two epics and their heroes have led many critics to assert that the same man ("Homer") could not possibly have written both of them. How, the argument goes, could the same poet conceive of two worlds so vastly different in their ethical outlook and their definition of what constitutes a hero, a villain and a proper resolution. Were I writing this chapter five hundred years ago, I might have acquiesced in this conclusion. But I do not. I live in the wake of one who wrote not only straight histories, comedies and tragedies but who gave us, at the end of his career, a series of genre-defying romances that essentially begin as tragedies but end as comedies—William Shakespeare. If Shakespeare could conceive and inhabit such vastly different worlds, then there is no reason to doubt that Homer could do so as well. After all, the war cannot last forever; sooner or later we must all return home. Homer, as one of the chief architects of Western civilization, helps provide us with strategies for dealing with both stages of life.

NO LONGER A CHILD

Perhaps the best way to begin our analysis of the *Odyssey* is with that very phrase: "stages of life." As a domestic epic, the *Odyssey* is concerned not only with relationships between the sexes (husbands and wives) but with those between generations (parents and children). The *Odyssey* is as concerned with the journey and maturation of the hero's twenty-year-old son, Telemachus, as it is with the development of *Odysseus* himself. Telemachus is, in fact, our central hero for the first four books of the *Odyssey;* his father does not appear until Book V. Homer's critics, both ancient and modern, have noted this peculiar narrative device and have often treated Books I to IV of the *Odyssey* as a sort of self-enclosed mini-epic; they have even given it a name: the *Telemachaia.* Before we even meet the legendary hero of the Trojan War, we watch as his son grows into a man. The *Telemachaia,* like *Huckleberry Finn* or *David Copperfield* or *Catcher in the Rye,* is essentially a coming-of-age story: one that focuses on a young and untested hero who must shape his identity and prove his worth by going through a rite of passage.

In the microcosm of the *Odyssey,* it is not enough for the hero to win glory on the battlefield; it is not even enough for him to return home safely. If he returns only to find that his son has abandoned the ways of *xenia* and dishonored himself and his name, then all is lost. We are all going to die, we might say, but as long as the father passes his legacy down to his son and the son upholds that legacy, then all will be well.

Lest we be too nervous as we follow Telemachus on his coming-of-age journey, Homer kindly provides us with an immediate clue that Telemachus will prove worthy of his father. Just as the *Iliad* ends with Zeus making a decree—that Achilles must return the body of Hektor to Priam—and then setting that decree in motion by sending two messengers, Thetis to Achilles and Iris to Hektor, so the *Odyssey* begins with Zeus making another decree—that Odysseus, after ten years of wandering, will be allowed to return to his island home of Ithaca—and then setting that decree in motion by sending Hermes to help Odysseus and Athena to help Telemachus. Homer holds off Hermes' commission to Odysseus until Book V and begins with Athena alighting on Ithaca and entering the palace disguised as a man.

Our first image of the palace is not hopeful. Odysseus has been away from Ithaca for twenty years and, for the last three, a group of rude and boisterous young men have been ransacking his home. They claim to be there as suitors for the hand of Odysseus's wife, Penelope, but they spend most of their day devouring her stores of food and wine and insulting or seducing her servants. Thus far Penelope, who is as crafty and resourceful as her husband, has successfully held off the suitors by a particularly clever ruse. She tells them that she cannot choose a new husband until she finishes sewing a burial shroud for her father-in-law. Day by day she works diligently at her loom to complete the shroud, but at night while the suitors are sleeping she takes apart what she has completed. Significantly, Penelope protects the *oikonomia* of Ithaca by making use of her domestic (feminine) skill at the loom, just as Odysseus will later make use of his martial (masculine) skill to put the suitors to death. Alas, shortly before the tale begins, one of Penelope's disloyal maids betrays her ruse, and the suitors again press her to marry one of them.

When Athena first enters the palace, the suitors do not offer her/him anything to eat or drink. Since neither the food nor the wine is theirs in the first place, one might expect them to be generous with it and to extend hospitality *(xenia)* to the stranger, but they take no notice and continue carousing. Telemachus, on the other hand, notices Athena's presence immediately and, "ashamed that a stranger should be kept standing at the gate," goes up to her and extends hospitality (I.120).[1] This is our signal that Telemachus has the heart of a hero and has been well bred by his mother. Still, our young would-be hero has a lot to learn. In the second before he rises to greet Athena, he is "sitting disconsolate among the Suitors, imagining how his noble father might come back out of the blue, drive the Suitors headlong from the house, and so regain his royal honours, and reign over his own once more" (I.115-18). The thought that he himself might rise up and drive the suitors from his home does not seem to have regis-

---

[1]All passages from the *Odyssey* are taken from *The Odyssey of Homer*, trans. E. V. Rieu and rev. D. C. H. Rieu (New York: Penguin, 1991). I have chosen a prose translation not only because of the fluidity and accuracy of the translation, but also to emphasize how the *Odyssey*, in contrast to the *Iliad*, reads like a novel. Though Rieu's translation is prose, he provides approximate line numbers in the margins. These numbers are close enough to allow readers with a different translation to find the quoted passages, as long as the translator provides line numbers keyed to the original Greek.

tered in his young untested heart. He is still a boy, dreaming of the day when his heroic father, whom he has never met but about whom he has heard wonderful stories, will ride in on a white horse and save the day. A modern psychologist might describe him as a young man lacking a father figure and raised by an overindulgent mother.

However we categorize him, Telemachus clearly suffers from something of an identity crisis. When Athena asks him if he is truly the son of the famous Odysseus, Telemachus replies, "My mother certainly says I am Odysseus's son; but for myself I cannot tell. No man can be certain of his parentage" (I.214-16). Telemachus does not mean here to question his mother's fidelity but to give voice to a lack of a clear sense of self. "Who am I?" he seems to be asking himself. "Do I have what it takes to be the son of a hero-king?" Athena does not give him the luxury to brood long on his identity crisis—as perhaps Penelope has. She issues him a wake-up call in words that are kind but firm. It is up to Telemachus to fit out a ship, choose a crew, and sail to Greece proper (the Peloponnese) in search of news about his father; he is to visit both Nestor at Pylos and Menelaus at Sparta. If he learns from his father's war buddies that Odysseus is alive, he is to wait for his return. "But if you learn that he is dead and gone," she instructs him,

> return to your own country, build a mound with all the proper funeral rites, and give your mother in marriage to a new husband. This settled and done, you must think of some way of destroying this mob in your house, either by cunning or in open fight. You are no longer a child: you must put childish thoughts away. (I.290-97)

The time for idle dreams about his father's return is past; Telemachus must take the initiative to be both decisive and responsible. It is time for him to grow up.

To help inspire him in this maturation process, Athena holds up before Telemachus a hero of his own age and generation who is likewise the son of a legendary king and warrior: Orestes, son of Agamemnon. In Homer's (as opposed to Aeschylus's) telling of the tale, when Agamemnon returns to Mycenae after the war, he discovers that his wife, Clytemnestra, has been seduced by the wily Aegisthus and is having an affair. No sooner do his people celebrate his return than Agamemnon is treacherously mur-

dered by his wife's lover. Many years go by, and Aegisthus and Clytemnestra rule Mycenae with an iron fist. But Agamemnon's son, Orestes, has
been growing up in a distant city, safe from the treachery of Aegisthus.
Eventually the young prince grows to manhood and, with a courage worthy of his father's generation, returns home and kills Aegisthus. The similarities between Orestes' situation and that of Telemachus (Agamemnon
= Odysseus; Clytemnestra = Penelope; Aegisthus = Suitors; Orestes =
Telemachus) is so threateningly close that Athena hopes it will rouse
Telemachus to emulation and to action. Thus, she concludes her wake-up
call by saying, "Have you not heard what a name Orestes made for himself
in the world when he killed the cunning Aegisthus for murdering his noble
father? You, my friend—and what a tall and splendid young man you have
grown!—must be as brave as Orestes. Then future generations will sing
your praises" (I.297-303). A lesser youth who was the son of a less noble
father might have been crushed by the pressure put on him by Athena, but
Telemachus is inspired by it, and his spirit is uplifted by the challenge to
be the next Orestes.

Athena, seeing that her work—at least for now—is completed, departs
for Mount Olympus. Here is how Homer describes the scene:

> The goddess spoke and the next moment she was gone, vanishing like a bird
> through a hole in the roof. In Telemachus' heart she had implanted spirit
> and daring, and had brought the image of his father to his mind even more
> strongly than before. He felt the change and was overcome with awe, for he
> realized a god had been with him. Then, godlike himself, he rejoined the
> Suitors. (I.319-24)

Like Abraham, like Jacob, like Moses, our hero in training has experienced
a theophany, a divine manifestation that changes the course of his life and
sets him on a new road. In a sense he is reborn. He will fulfill the task for
which he has been appointed and, in his obedience to that task, he will become not a lesser but a fuller person, more true to what he really is.

As he strides out into the room, a bard begins to sing of the return of
the Greeks from Troy. The music draws Penelope out from her upstairs
quarters, and she stands weeping at the top of the stairs. When Telemachus sees her, he looks up at her and says boldly:

You must be brave and nerve yourself to listen, for Odysseus is not the only one who has never returned from Troy. Troy was the end of many another man. So go to your quarters now and attend to your own work, the loom and the spindle, and tell the servants to get on with theirs. Making decisions must be men's concern, and mine in particular; for I am master in this house. (I.352-59)

Penelope is taken aback by Telemachus's words, but she obeys him and returns to her room. It is clear that this speech marks the first time that Telemachus has spoken thus to his mother. One can only imagine her mixed emotions: sad that her son should speak to her so firmly and yet happy that he is becoming self-sufficient and decisive, becoming a man. Every good mother will experience moments like this and feel happy and proud even as she struggles to let her son go. If the words Telemachus speaks to her sound familiar, that is because they are almost identical to the words Hektor speaks to his wife in Book VI of the *Iliad*. Just as Hektor instructs his wife to return to the domestic, feminine sphere of the loom while he returns to the martial, masculine sphere of battle, so Telemachus lays down a similar strategy for ordering society and fulfilling one's duty. Here, however, divorced from an actual battlefield, the role of the male becomes that of protecting the home and serving as its head: both male and female are equally vested in the preservation of the domestic sphere, though they perform different functions within that sphere.

Indeed, when Athena—or, better, Homer—sends Telemachus on his journey to Pylos and Sparta, he does not do so only to enable Telemachus to learn information about his father; as it turns out, he doesn't learn much. In addition to the practical, fact-finding purpose of his voyage, Telemachus needs to be given the opportunity to see what a home looks like when it is well run. In contrast to the heroic code of the *Iliad*, with its focus on martial glory and the collecting of meeds of honor, the overarching ethos that controls the *Odyssey* is focused squarely on preserving domestic bliss and sociopolitical stability. Odysseus himself describes it this way in a flattering speech that he directs to a young unmarried girl:

And may the gods grant you your heart's desire; may they give you a husband and a home, and the blessing of harmony so much to be desired, since there is nothing better or finer than when two people of one heart and mind keep house as man and wife, a grief to their enemies and a joy to their friends, and their reputation spreads far and wide. (VI.180-86)

Telemachus, growing up without a father and with a kingdom in disarray (not once since Odysseus left have the elders of Ithaca been called to an assembly), has never seen this sociodomestic ideal lived out in the real world. At Pylos (Book III), he will see this ideal in action—and he will learn that it is worth fighting for. It is not enough for Odysseus to restore the *oikonomia* of Ithaca; if he does not pass on his patriarchal duties to his son, if Telemachus does not learn and embody the importance of faithfulness and stability in home and assembly, then the community of Ithaca will fall apart.

ENGRAVED IN THE HEART

Of course, there is a third reason Telemachus must go on his journey. At Ithaca, there is no one against whom he can shape his burgeoning identity. Telemachus desperately needs to know if he is worthy, if he is truly the son of his father. What better way to prove that inner worth than to be brought face to face with men who knew his father and were his equals in courage and honor? Just as Shakespeare's Prince Hal must leave behind his drinking buddies (Falstaff and company) and take on new, more noble friends if he is to evolve from a jaded frat boy into the brave and heroic King Henry V, so must Homer's Telemachus remove himself from the company of the suitors and mingle with the legendary warriors who battled against Troy.

Needless to say, the young Telemachus is a bundle of nerves as he approaches Nestor. He is afraid that he won't know what to say, or, worse, that he will speak up and make a fool of himself. In the social-domestic microcosm of Homer's *Odyssey* (as in eighteenth-century Paris or the antebellum South), a man is judged as much by his deeds as by his words: eloquence of speech is as vital as strength of body. In the *Iliad, xenia* manifests itself primarily in how one treats suppliants and captives; in the *Odyssey,* it is part of a much wider sphere of social decorum. At Pylos, Telemachus learns that a good host who encounters strangers on his shore will welcome and feed them before asking their names or their business. Without such courtesy, travel would be both difficult and dangerous. As the battlefield of Troy lacks a Geneva Convention to dictate the proper treatment of prisoners, so the cities that dot the shores of the Mediterranean world lack anything resembling passports or visas or maritime laws. The dividing line between civilization and barbarism is thin. Telemachus must learn to tread that line without allowing himself or his island home to slip into chaos.

To assist him in his education, Telemachus is given two companions on his journey. First, Athena accompanies him on board the ship to Pylos and gently guides, advises and encourages him as he interacts with the heroes of Troy. Throughout this training period, Athena assumes the form of a man named Mentor; as a result, English speakers still refer to an older, wiser person who plays the role of a trusted counselor or teacher to a younger, less experienced person as a mentor. Second, while on Pylos, Telemachus makes a new best friend of his own age: Peisistratus, son of Nestor. Unlike the suitors, Peisistratus is both noble and courteous.

Telemachus is also afforded a more subtle opportunity to grow in wisdom and strength. After visiting Pylos, he proceeds to Sparta in Book IV. Here he meets Menelaus and Helen, whose troubled home exists midway between the "good" home of Nestor and the "bad" home of Agamemnon. Although Menelaus and Helen are reunited in what seems to be marital bliss, we cannot forget that Helen abandoned her husband for Paris. A strange air of uneasiness and tension hovers over most of Book IV, and as Helen and Menelaus in turn recount stories from the Trojan War, it is difficult for the reader to determine the tone of their voice or the look in their eyes. Even more disturbing, at one point in the conversation Helen mixes into the drinks "a drug that [has] the power of robbing grief and anger of their sting and banishing all painful memories" (IV.220-21). Are things so uneasy at Sparta that Helen and her husband need drugs to dull their senses? However we read this strange scene, it is clear that the ideal Telemachus seeks is not to be found at Sparta. If the *oikonomia* of Ithaca is to be restored, it will not be done through drugs that banish grief and pain but by boldly embracing the virtues of the past and even more boldly overcoming the errors of those who violated those virtues.

Much debate has been raised in our country about whether America is primarily the product of secular Enlightenment thought or Judeo-Christian values and beliefs. Perhaps the best solution to this impasse is to acknowledge the secular roots of much of our democratic system while remembering that the only reason that system works is that it is built on a body of citizens who are mostly Christian and therefore morally self-regulating. That is to say, if America were ever to lose her grounding in Christian morality, her governmental systems would eventually collapse from within.

In a very real way, the preservation of civilization in the *Odyssey* rests on the decisions that Telemachus makes. Will he live up to the ideals and the vision of those who are the "founding fathers" of his society, including and especially his own literal father? As we all do, Telemachus must struggle to obey and embody both the letter and the spirit of the law. God gave the Mosaic Law to a group of former slaves in hopes that they would learn to be free, but his ultimate desire was that the Law would be engraved not in stone but on their hearts. If Telemachus finishes his journey merely having memorized the laws of *xenia*, he will have failed. He must learn as well to absorb them into his being.

While in the court of Nestor, Telemachus asks innumerable questions about Orestes and how it was that he avenged his father's murder. He asks why Agamemnon's brother, Menelaus, did not kill Aegisthus and learns that Menelaus arrived at Mycenae several hours after Orestes had done the deed. The message is clear: even if Odysseus is alive and on his way home, Telemachus may still have to be the one to deal with the suitors. Civilization is not a given: it rests on the choices that each of us makes. Telemachus, like the Jews who follow Joshua into the Promised Land, must "choose . . . this day whom [he] will serve" (Joshua 24:15). So must we all choose this day whom we will serve.

7

HOMER'S *ODYSSEY* II

Coming Home

IN CONTRAST TO THE MODERN MYTH that marriage in the ancient world was nothing more than a social arrangement, the marriage of Odysseus and Penelope stands as proof that the husbands and wives of Homer's day were capable not only of deep love but of a kind of intimacy and unity that fully embodies the biblical definition of marriage as two people becoming one flesh.

NEVERTHELESS

At the very moment that Athena enters the palace of Ithaca, Hermes lands on the island of Ogygia. Odysseus has been held prisoner on this remote desert island for seven years by a lovely and amorous nymph named Calypso. Enthralled by his manly beauty and legendary eloquence, Calypso has taken Odysseus as her lover and refused to allow him to return home. As soon as Hermes arrives on Ogygia, he goes to the cave of Calypso, where he finds her singing in a beautiful voice as she goes "to and fro at her loom, weaving with a golden shuttle" (V.63). The detail is an important one, for it presents Calypso to us as both a goddess of ageless beauty and a traditional Hellenic housewife. That is to say, she offers Odysseus both the fulfillment of a "male fantasy" and a surrogate home to take the place of Ithaca and Penelope. If, as our somewhat self-satisfied age likes to think, the men of the ancient world looked on their wives as chattel meant only for sexual pleasure or domestic drudgery, then Odysseus would be foolish to leave Ogygia. With Calypso, he's "got it made."

And yet his only desire is to return to Ithaca. When Hermes arrives at Calypso's cave, he does not find Odysseus there; rather, he finds him "sitting disconsolate on the shore in his accustomed place, tormenting himself with tears and sighs and heartache, and looking out across the barren sea with streaming eyes" (V.82-84). Significantly, our first glimpse of Telemachus in Book I puts him in a similar stance and mood. Father and son are united in their yearnings as they are united in their griefs and their passions. At two separate points in the epic, the two men nearly give away their identities to their hosts because they begin to weep when they hear stories told of the Trojan War. Penelope too weeps when she hears such stories sung, and the nostalgic tears of the three bind them together as a family.

Odysseus desires but one thing: to go home and be reunited with the wife of his youth and the son he does not know. Despite the fact that Calypso has promised to make him immortal, he still wishes to return. Calypso cannot fathom why, and she presses him for an explanation. Surely his wife, a mere mortal, cannot possess a beauty comparable to her own. Why then should he abandon her and her promise of immortality in favor of Penelope? Odysseus's answer offers one of the highest visions of marriage outside the Bible to come out of the ancient world:

> My lady goddess, do not be angry at what I am about to say. I too know well enough that my wise Penelope's looks and stature are insignificant compared with yours. For she is mortal, while you have immortality and unfading youth. Nevertheless I long to reach my home and see the day of my return. It is my never failing wish. And what if one of the gods does wreck me out on the wine-dark sea? I have a heart that is inured to suffering and I shall steel it to endure that too. For in my day I have had many bitter and painful experiences in war and on the stormy seas. So let this new disaster come. It only makes one more. (V.215-24)

Penelope is, to Odysseus, far more than a pretty face. She is a part of who he is as a human being. Odysseus defines himself in great part as the husband of Penelope. Apart from her, he is not fully himself. Apart from her, he is not really Odysseus.

Mostly because of the influence of Alfred Lord Tennyson's stirring poem "Ulysses," we tend to think of Odysseus as the great wanderer, a Greek Sinbad with a desire to sail the seven seas. But Tennyson's Victorian explorer has little in common with the Odysseus of Homer. The hero of the *Odyssey* has one goal: returning home to Penelope, to Telemachus and to Ithaca, to his proper *oikonomia*. For me, the very essence of what it means to be human is contained in the single word *nevertheless*. What Odysseus is trying so hard to convey to the confused and crestfallen Calypso is that his desire to return home is, in fact, not a logical one. Everything the goddess says is correct; her beauty far exceeds that of Penelope and any man in his right mind would choose her for a mate. In any case, Odysseus's chances of reaching Ithaca alive are exceedingly small; he is throwing away an immortal life of bliss on the slim chance that he will make it back to his aging wife and spend perhaps another few decades of declining health by her side. *Nevertheless,* he will go home. If he did not go home, he might be "happier," but he would cease to be himself.

With the help of Calypso, Odysseus builds a raft and sets sail for home, but his journeys are not yet over. As he had earlier been washed ashore on the island of Ogygia, he is washed ashore again on the island of Phaeacia. Here he meets another surrogate Penelope in the form not of an immortal goddess but of a charming young princess named Nausicaa who must surely, one imagines, remind Odysseus of what Penelope was like at that age. Nausicaa falls instantly in love with the handsome, weather-beaten stranger, and her father the king concurs as to the suitability of a royal marriage between Odysseus and his nubile daughter. The incentives for Odysseus to do so are strong. Phaeacia is a great deal like Ithaca, but much, much better. Nausicaa's island is a magical, edenic place where the "fruit never fails nor runs short, winter and summer alike" (VII.117) and where the gods walk undisguised among the people. The citizens of the island live in peace and are well-versed not only in shipbuilding and sailing but in music, dance and athletics. They represent the pinnacle of the guest-host relationship, and they treat Odysseus with honor and courtesy. How easy it would be for him to stay on Phaeacia and begin his life anew.

Nevertheless, he must leave. Phaeacia is not Ithaca, nor is Nausicaa Penelope. Phaeacia is, arguably, not a real place at all: it is more like a waking dream or a realm of the imagination than a real island where one can build something that will last. (In fact, in one of the strangest and most disturbing moments of the *Odyssey*, we learn that after the Phaeacians help Odysseus return home, Poseidon punishes them by surrounding their island with high mountains, preventing them from receiving any more visitors. That Poseidon punishes them precisely *because* of their excessive hospitality to strangers (see XIII.171-79) makes the incident all the stranger. It is perhaps the unreality of the island that makes it the ideal place for Odysseus to tell the tale of his earlier journeys. I shall discuss those journeys in the next chapter; for now, let it suffice to say that the heavily mythic nature of Odysseus's journeys, which contrast sharply with the realistic tone of the rest of the narrative, befit the fairy tale nature of Phaeacia and its inhabitants.

After recounting his journeys, Odysseus is carried back to Ithaca on board a magic Phaeacian ship that boasts neither helmsman nor rudder, for it is guided by its own instinct. During the passage, Odysseus falls into a deep slumber and is still asleep when the ship touches softly on the shore of Ithaca. Not wanting to disturb him, the Phaeacians lift Odysseus off the ship and lay him gently in a cave by the shore. When he wakes, the Phaeacians are gone and he is back in his own country. It is as if all of his journeys have been nothing more than a dream.

KENOSIS

The Odysseus who wakes up on Ithaca in Book XIII is a somewhat more cautious Odysseus than the one we meet in the first half of the *Odyssey*. His yearning for home has not made him into a naïve idealist. He knows that home is often something that must be fought for, and he is prepared to wait, to suffer, to do battle: whatever it takes to win back his home, family and full identity. Almost immediately, he is met by Athena who comes to him disguised as a young shepherd. She asks Odysseus who he is, but he, instead of telling the truth, makes up for himself an alter ego, something he will do several more times in the second half of the epic. In response, Athena resumes her true form, caresses him, and speaks out with a smile:

> Anyone who met you, even a god, would have to be a consummate trickster to surpass you in subterfuge. You were always an obstinate, cunning and ir-repressible intriguer. So you don't propose, even in your own country to drop the tricks and lying tales you love so much! But no more of this. We both know how to get our own way: in the world of men you have no rival in judgement and argument, while I am pre-eminent among the gods for in-genuity and ability to get what I want. (VIII.291-99)

These two, it is clear, will make a good team. Athena loves Odysseus for his roguish character and tricky ways; it is precisely because he is so re-sourceful and cunning that Athena is so quick to help him. Unlike biblical characters, whom God often exalts because they are weak (true also of the entire nation of Israel), the heroes of Greek myth and legend are generally strong before the gods take their side. The notion of God as someone who exalts the humble and humbles the proud—not to mention someone who calls us to forgive and love our enemies—will have to await the fuller rev-elation of Christ. In many ways Odysseus resembles Jacob, the great trick-ster of Genesis, but with this vital difference: Jacob pays for his trickery when he is tricked in turn by his uncle Laban. Odysseus is like a Joseph whose resourcefulness and cunning help him to win the day but who in the end does not forgive his treacherous "brothers."

Still, despite these differences, Homer is quick to show that Odysseus is able to survive and take back Ithaca from the suitors only because he is willing to suffer indignity and humiliation and to take the cautionary ad-vice of Athena. The goddess warns him that a frontal assault on his palace would not be a wise move. Instead, she (with Odysseus's permission) transforms him into an old, distinctly unattractive beggar. In this form Odysseus suffers in silence the abuse of the suitors, taking on the role of a stranger and outcast in his own kingdom. Before he can blaze forth as the messianic savior of his home, he must endure a literal *kenosis* ("emptying"; see Philippians 2:7) and appear in the form of a servant. Though neither the good nor the bad Ithacans know it, the true king is in their midst.

Whereas Books I to XII of the *Odyssey* move swiftly, Books XIII to XXIV are often gruelingly slow in their pacing. Not until the time is ripe will Odysseus shed his humiliating disguise and take vengeance on the suitors. In the interim, he spends most of his time receiving the humble charity of a poor but loyal swineherd named Eumaeus. Homer clearly loves this swineherd, presenting him with a dignity and integrity that far surpass the aristocratic pride of the suitors. He is a character who would have little if any place in the *Iliad,* yet here in the domestic microcosm of the *Odyssey,* his loyalty and steadfastness make him a true hero. Indeed, he embodies one of the essential elements of *oikonomia:* namely, that every person must play his proper role. He is like the good servant who appears in many of Jesus' parables, the one who remains faithful to his master and is honored with the words, "Well done!"

With the help of the cautious Eumaeus, Odysseus makes several forays to the palace to observe the behavior of the suitors. As the good and righteous king, he will sift and test each in turn so that when the day of reckoning comes, he will be able to distinguish the wheat from the tares. Indeed, the second half of the *Odyssey* resembles in many ways the parables of Jesus, not only in the way the master tests his servants but in the way the suitors are judged by whether they welcome the king disguised as a beggar. Just as Jesus tells both the righteous and the sinners that their treatment of "the least of these" shows forth their treatment of him (Matthew 25:31-46), so here the suitors learn to their horror that their ill treatment of the beggar has sealed their doom: for the beggar is also their king. At its fullest, Homer's understanding of the guest-host relationship comes surprisingly close to the biblical understanding of justice. In fact, it is possible that the parable of the sheep and the goats—in which, according to Matthew 25:32, God is judging the nations—gives us insight into how God will judge pagan nations like the Greeks whose citizens are without God's law but who possess an internal sense of *xenia* that they know they should obey.

JUDGMENT DAY

As the epic moves toward its inexorable climax, Odysseus is reunited with Telemachus, and the two plot together to destroy the evil suitors. In brief, their plot consists of calling all the suitors together into the great hall with the promise that a husband for Penelope will be chosen that very night. The method of choosing will be a contest to determine which suitor possesses a strength equal to that of Odysseus. To win the hand of the queen, the suitors must take up the great bow of Odysseus, bend and string it, and shoot an arrow through a difficult target. This mighty bow, Homer tells us, did not come to Odysseus as a meed of honor won in battle, but as part of a guest-host gift exchange. Furthermore, "This bow Odysseus never took on to his black ship with him when he sailed to war, but laid it up at home in memory of a treasured friend, though he used it on his own estate" (XXI.38-40). This is an important detail, and a beautiful one. The instrument that will help Odysseus carry out his plot and win back his home is linked inextricably to his estate, to the domestic sphere. Though Odysseus will use his skills as a veteran of the Trojan War to enact judgment on the suitors, the vehicle through which he will do so will have little to do with the martial ethos of the *Iliad*.

As we expect, none of the cowardly suitors possesses the strength to string the bow, much less shoot the arrow through the target, though Homer makes it clear that Telemachus would have strung the bow had Odysseus not motioned to him to desist. After all have had a chance, Odysseus, still disguised as a beggar, asks if he may try his hand at the bow. The suitors, of course, mock him for his pretensions, though inwardly they are terrified that he might be able to string it. At this point, Telemachus makes sure that all the doors to the great hall are closed and locked and that only the suitors are left inside; he has already ensured that they have no weapons in their possession. When this is done, the bow is put in the hands of Odysseus and all hold their breath. The first thing Odysseus does with it is to twist and bend the bow to ensure that no worms have eaten into the wood during his long absence. It is another lovely Homeric detail to remind us that beneath the revenge tale about to be enacted is a simpler tale of a man returning to the home and wife he loves. Homer then continues with a third detail linked to an apt simile:

> As a minstrel skilled at the lyre and in song easily stretches a string round a new leather strap, fixing the twisted sheepgut at both ends, so he strung the great bow without effort or haste. Then with his right hand he tested the string, and it sang as he plucked it with a sound like a swallow's note. (XXI.405-11)

Though Odysseus will, in the minutes that follow, use his bow to slaughter several dozen suitors, Homer here shows Odysseus as a musician, one whose skill brings beauty and harmony into the world rather than death and destruction. Odysseus is no mere thug: he is a craftsman who understands both the arts of war and those of peace. Having strung and tuned his instrument, he plucks the string, sending out a note like that of a swallow: one of many birds whose instincts drive them over long weary miles to the place of their birth. His bow strung, Odysseus shoots the arrow through the appointed targets. The arrow flies straight and true; Odysseus has passed the test. The rightful lord has returned to Ithaca.

With the help of Telemachus, Odysseus makes quick work of the suitors, slaughtering them as a lion might who finds himself in the midst of a flock of sheep. When all have been killed, the loyal maid Eurycleia (a female version of Eumaeus) enters the hall and finds "Odysseus among the corpses of the dead, spattered with blood and gore" (XXII.400-401). Filled with elation, Eurycleia prepares to let out a cry of triumph, but she is prevented from doing so by Odysseus:

> Restrain yourself old woman, and gloat in silence. I'll have no cries of triumph here. It is an impious thing to exult over the slain. These men fell victims to the will of the gods and their own infamy. They paid respect to no one on earth who came near them—good or bad. And now their own transgressions have brought them to this ignominious death. (XXII.411-19)

For Odysseus, this is more a ritual sacrifice than an act of revenge. These men have soiled and corrupted the domestic sphere and have violated the sacred laws of Zeus Xenos. He takes little joy in the slaughter but rather in the knowledge that his house is now clean of that which had defiled it. In fact, after the bodies have been dragged out of the great hall, Odysseus orders that fire and sulfur be brought to him that he may clean and purify the palace.

Of all the works of pagan literature, Book XXII of the *Odyssey* comes closest to embodying what the Bible refers to as the Day of the Lord. We are warned both by the Old Testament prophets and by Jesus that that dreadful day may fall on us at any moment, that it will come swiftly and unexpectedly, like a thief in the night. May we not be caught sleeping or in sin when that terrible day arrives; may we be prepared to greet the return of the king. As I read *Odyssey* XXII, I can hear the voice of Joel: "Alas for the day! for the day of the LORD is at hand, and as a destruction from the Almighty shall it come. Is not the meat cut off before our eyes, yea, joy and gladness from the house of our God?" (Joel 1:15-16). Of Amos: "And it shall come to pass in that day, saith the Lord GOD, that I will cause the sun to go down at noon, and I will darken the earth in the clear day: And I will turn your feasts into mourning, and all your songs into lamentation" (Amos 8:9-10). Of John the Baptist: "[His] fan is in his hand, and he will thoroughly purge his floor, and gather his wheat into the garner; but he will burn up the chaff with unquenchable fire" (Matthew 3:12).

But most of all, I hear Jesus' parable of the wise and foolish servants, a parable that reads as if it were a gloss on the second half of the *Odyssey:*

Watch therefore: for ye know not what hour your Lord doth come.

But know this, that if the goodman of the house had known in what watch the thief would come, he would have watched, and would not have suffered his house to be broken up.

Therefore be ye also ready: for in such an hour as ye think not the Son of man cometh.

Who then is a faithful and wise servant, whom his lord hath made ruler over his household, to give them meat in due season?

Blessed is that servant, whom his lord when he cometh shall find so doing.

Verily I say unto you, That he shall make him ruler over all his goods.

But and if that evil servant shall say in his heart, My lord delayeth his coming;

And shall begin to smite his fellow servants, and to eat and drink with the drunken;

The lord of that servant shall come in a day when he looketh not for him, and in an hour that he is not aware of,

And shall cut him asunder, and appoint him his portion with the hypocrites: there shall be weeping and gnashing of teeth. (Matthew 24:42-51)

Jesus' description of the evil servant captures perfectly the perfidy of the suitors and their utter disregard for the judgment that awaits them. Their debauchery is not only sinful in itself but is an expression of the arrogant sloth that consumes their souls. Eumaeus and Eurycleia are the good ser-vants who have waited for their master's return and refused to join the de-bauchery of the wicked. The *Odyssey* is more than a simple revenge story. The return of Odysseus is nothing less than apocalyptic; it uncovers that which has been hidden and reveals the righteous and the sinners for who they are.

Ithaca's messiah-king has returned to her and restored peace and justice, and now he will dwell once more in her midst. But still we have not reached the end. Like the book of Revelation, the *Odyssey* ends not with the battle of Armageddon but with the marriage of the faithful bride and the bridegroom-redeemer. As much as it builds up to the battle in the hall, the *Odyssey* finds its true resolution in the reunion of Odysseus and his be-loved Penelope (though Homer, ever concerned with the full *oikonomia*, will follow this reunion with an epilogue in which Odysseus is reunited with his father and restores the social and political stability of the city-state). While the battle rages below, Penelope is lying safe in her upstairs room. She does not have to wait long, however, for the good news. Loyal Eurycleia runs up the stairs to tell her, her enthusiasm so great that she trips over her feet as she ascends. "Your husband," she tells Penelope, "has returned and has killed the suitors in the hall."

We expect Penelope to immediately cry out with joy and fling herself into Odysseus's arms, but she is too cautious and prudent—too much the wife of the wise Odysseus—to do this. She will ensure that this man whom she thought to be a beggar is really her husband before she gives herself over to him and her own anxious desires. So she gives him a secret test, one that only the true Odysseus would recognize. "Come," she instructs Eury-cleia, "pull the bed out of my room and place it here in the hall that the stranger may sleep upon it." At once, Odysseus leaps to his feet and ex-claims:

> Lady . . . your words are a knife in my heart! Who has moved my bed? That
> would be hard even for a skilled workman, though for a god who took it into
> his head to come and move it somewhere else it would be quite easy. No man
> alive, not even one in his prime, would find it easy to shift. A great secret
> went into the making of that complicated bed; and it was my work and mine
> alone. Inside the court there was a long-leaved olive-tree, which had grown

to full height with a trunk as thick as a pillar. Round this I built my room of compact stonework, and when that was finished, I roofed it over carefully, and put in a solid, neatly fitted, double door. Next I lopped all the branches off the olive, trimmed the trunk from the root up, rounded it smoothly and carefully with my adze and trued it to the line, to be my bedpost. I drilled holes in it, and using it as the first bedpost I constructed the rest of the bed. Then I finished it off with an inlay of gold, silver and ivory, and fixed a set of gleaming purple straps across the frame. So I have shown you the secret. What I don't know, lady, is whether my bedstead stands where it did, or whether someone has cut the tree-trunk through and moved it. (XXIII.183-204)

Of all the details in the *Odyssey,* this one is the most lovely, the most moving. Despite the high drama of the scene, Homer pauses to cast his eyes over every line and surface of the bed, as though he were savoring—and wanted us to savor—the exactness of the description. Nothing speaks more powerfully of the true intimacy of the domestic bond between Odysseus and Penelope than this: that the test of both their loyalty and their true identity should be their marriage bed. For that bed is more than just an object: it stands at the very heart of their home. As the bed itself cannot be moved, so the love of Odysseus and Penelope cannot be shaken. The bed, like their love, is a thing of stability in a world gone mad.

No sooner does Odysseus speak these words than Penelope bursts into tears and throws herself into his waiting arms. They spend all night together in the wooden nest Odysseus made for them, sharing not only in the intimacy of physical love but of shared sorrow and longing. All night they are together—indeed longer, for Athena, wishing to give the reunited couple more time to feast on love, uses her divine powers to hold back the dawn. It is an appropriate ending to an epic poem that is, at its heart, a simple fable of a tired and lonely pilgrim who comes home.

8

HOMER'S *ODYSSEY* III

The Journeys of Odysseus

LIKE THE *ILIAD*, THE *ODYSSEY* BEGINS not at the beginning, but in the middle of things: in medias res. Whereas the former begins in the final year of a ten-year war, the latter begins in the final year of a ten-year struggle on the part of Odysseus to return to his home. But the Homer of the *Odyssey* is too seasoned a craftsman simply to repeat a narrative device from his previous epic. He will do himself one better by weaving a richer narrative structure that seems almost modern in its playful handling of time and place. With an almost effortless skill, Homer so constructs his second epic that Books I to IV (the *Telemachaia*) and Books V to VIII (which carry Odysseus from the isle of Calypso to the isle of Nausicaa) occur simultaneously with one another. Even better, while Odysseus is on Phaeacia, he is asked by Nausicaa's father to share with his dinner guests the story of his travels. Accordingly, Odysseus begins his tale and relates to the Phaeacians all that has happened to him from the Fall of Troy to when he washed up on the shore of Ogygia. That is to say, Odysseus's tale, which stretches in a long arc from Book IX to Book XII, occurs before Books I and V. Once he is done, the Phaeacians agree to return him to Ithaca, and the remaining twelve books pick up where we left off at the end of Books IV and VIII.

It is a wonderful narrative scheme that lends the *Odyssey* a type of sophistication and refinement absent from the *Iliad,* whose power is, in the positive sense of these words, both rude and primitive. It also allows Homer to do something he could not do in his former work. Because Books IX to XII are told as a flashback, Homer can use first person for these adventures; they are conveyed from Odysseus's point of view. By so doing, he takes us into the mind and soul of his hero in a way not possible in the *Iliad.* In these books we not only travel alongside Odysseus; we travel through and in him. Further, the fact that the adventures take place in the suspended time of a flashback increases their mythic and timeless quality. In a sense they take place outside of time in a realm of magic and imagination that contrasts sharply with the more realistic treatment of the rest of the epic. Odysseus, we might say, is in Wonderland.

TWIN DANGERS

Odysseus begins his wanderings with two brief adventures that set forth the pattern for the rest of his journeys. Shortly after leaving Troy, he and his crew land on the island of Ismarus, where, as they had done so many times during the Trojan War, they sack the main city and take the spoils for themselves. Their raid successful and the pickings good, Odysseus advises his men to return immediately to their ships and sail off. But the men insist on remaining on the beach to partake in a feast. It is a decision they regret, for while they eat, the men of the island regroup and attack them. They barely escape with their lives, leaving many of their fellow sailors dead on the beach.

In the next brief episode, Odysseus's men, having put a sufficient distance between themselves and Ismarus, land on the sleepy isle of the lotus-eaters. There, the gentle natives treat them with kindness and hospitality. "Now these natives," Odysseus explains,

> had no intention of killing my comrades; what they did was to give them
> some lotus to taste. Those who ate the honeyed fruit of the plant lost any

wish to come back and bring us news. All they now wanted was to stay where they were with the Lotus-eaters, to browse on the lotus, and to forget all thoughts of return. I had to use force to bring them back to the hollow ships, and they wept on the way, but once on board I tied them up and dragged them under the benches. (IX.92-99)

In contrast to their adventure on the island of Ismarus, which threatens their physical survival, their adventure with the lotus-eaters seems almost harmless. And yet the danger it poses is just as great. For any sailor who desires to return home, there are two distinct dangers he must face. The first is the danger of death; the second is the danger of the false homecoming. Though the lotus-eaters have no intention of killing or even injuring Odysseus's crew, they threaten to make them forget their home and lose their desire to return. I think of those GIs in World War II who survived the perils of war only to remain behind in Italy or France or Japan and marry foreign wives. They survived the battles unscathed, but they never returned to their native land. Odysseus, of course, faces just such a test of his loyalty to home and wife on the isles of Calypso and Nausicaa.

In "The Lotos-Eaters," a poetic treatment of this strange, languid episode, Tennyson depicts Odysseus's lotus-drugged men as giving in to a kind of social sloth that forswears all duty to rebuild or further civilization. The true temptation of the lotus, of the false homecoming, is to abdicate all responsibility to one's father, one's patrimony, one's country. "Let what is broken so remain," sing Tennyson's mariners, "The Gods are hard to reconcile; / 'Tis hard to settle order once again." Were Homer's Odysseus to give in to this temptation, it would mark the end not only of marital joy for him and Penelope, but of the very existence of Ithaca as a civilized land where men live by justice and order, not to mention *aidos*, *nemesis* and *xenia*.

Significantly, Odysseus's next adventure—surely his best-known—takes him to an island inhabited by uncivilized and therefore barbaric creatures who know and care nothing for the laws of Zeus Xenos or civil society. They are fierce giants with a single eye in the center of their head, and they are known as the Cyclopes. Rather than build cities or meet in assemblies, each Cyclops lives alone in his cave, an isolated nation of one. Quite by accident, Odysseus and a small band of men find their way into the cave of the shepherd Polyphemus. The cave is alive with the sound of bleating lambs and goats and filled with baskets brimming with cheese. Instead of waiting for the owner of the cave to return and offer them a meal, the men greedily devour the cheese. Then, having made this first breach in the guest-host relationship (for guests, like hosts, are expected to behave in a civilized manner), Odysseus adds insult to injury by waiting for the owner to return, not so he may apologize for their theft but so he may extract from him a guest-gift.

Soon enough, the owner does arrive, and the men realize to their horror that he is a giant. While they huddle in fear in the back of the cave, Polyphemus drives the sheep he has been pasturing into the cave and covers the entrance behind him with a huge stone that fifty men could not hope to move. Were he a good host like Nestor, the Cyclops would first feed his timid guests and then ask their names. Instead, he first asks their names and then eats two of them raw. Having finished his ghastly meal and washed it down with goat's milk, the Cyclops lies down on the cave floor and goes to sleep. Odysseus's first thought is to stab the beast through his heart, but he stops himself just in time. Were he to do so, he and his men, unable to move the massive stone, would be trapped forever in the cave. Having allowed his own greed and folly to get his men into this predicament, Odysseus will now have to rely on his wit and resourcefulness to rescue them.

When morning comes, Polyphemus wakes, devours two more men for breakfast, and then drives his sheep out to pasture, making sure to seal the remaining men in the cave. While he is gone, Odysseus leaps to action. In the back of the cave, he finds a huge staff which he and his crew whittle into a spear and hide under the dung. He then removes from his pack a flask of wine from a vintage far stronger than anything the Cyclopes have ever tasted. When Polyphemus returns and devours yet another two men, Odysseus is ready for him. "Cyclops," he says sweetly, "wouldn't you like a drink to wash down all that man flesh?" Polyphemus agrees, and Odysseus hands him a bowl filled with the sweet and potent wine. The cannibal gulps it down and asks for more, begging Odysseus to tell him his name and promising him a special gift. Three times Odysseus fills the bowl, and three times the foolish beast drinks it down. When Odysseus can see that the wine is taking its effect, he tells Polyphemus that his name is "no man," and then asks for his promised gift. "This is my gift," says the monster, "I shall eat no man last." Then he collapses on the floor and slips into unconsciousness. Immediately Odysseus takes up the spear, heats the point in the fire, and, with the help of his men, drives it into the single eye of the Cyclops. Enraged, Polyphemus leaps to his feet and thrashes around the cave, calling out to his fellow Cyclopes that his eye has been put out by "no man." As Odysseus had hoped, the other Cyclopes think he is crazy and go on their way.

After several hours dawn breaks, and the goats, their udders full, cry to be let out. The Cyclops, taking pity on his beloved animals, removes the stone, but then stands poised in front of the opening with his arms stretched out to catch any man who tries to escape. But Odysseus is too crafty for him. He straps his men under the sheep where the hands of the blinded Cyclops will not feel them. By this method, Odysseus and his men escape from the cave and return to their ships. The fleet pulls out of the cove and moves toward the sea, and it seems that all will be well. The crafty, civilized Odysseus has beaten the fierce, barbaric giant.

Alas, his great success goes to his head. In an act of foolish bravado, Odysseus cries out from the prow of his ship to the blinded Cyclops: "Polyphemus, if anyone asks you who put out your eye, tell him it was Odysseus, King of Ithaca." The Cyclops, enraged by Odysseus's taunt, takes up in his hand a huge boulder and casts it in the direction of the voice. The boulder lands on the far side of the ship and produces a wave that almost pushes the ship back onto the beach. With great effort, the men are able to row themselves back to safety, but the damage has been done. Now that Polyphemus knows the name of his enemy, he is empowered to place a curse on him. With a booming voice, he calls on his father (who, unfortunately for Odysseus, turns out to be Poseidon), and prays that he will punish the Greek sailor for his crime:

> May he never reach his home in Ithaca. But if he is destined to see his friends again, to come once more to his own house and reach his native land, let him come late, in wretched plight, having lost all his comrades, in a foreign ship, and let him find trouble in his home. (IX.530-35)

It is this prayer (like Achilles' equally terrible prayer to Zeus in Book I of the *Iliad*) that sets the rest of the action in motion. Odysseus will indeed arrive home late and alone to find his palace overrun by the insolent suitors. The barbaric land of the Cyclopes will spread its "anti-civilization" to Ithaca, creating a form of social-political-domestic chaos that Odysseus will have to struggle hard to rectify.

Earlier I compared Odysseus to a Jacob who does not receive the comeuppance he deserves for his tricks and deceit. Now we see that this is not totally true. Odysseus does pay in spades for his breach of the guest-host relationship. Just as he played the role of a bad guest in the home of Polyphemus, so will the suitors play the role of bad guests in his home. But it is not only his breach of *xenia* that leads to Odysseus's troubles. When he arrogantly cries out his true name to the Cyclops, Odysseus violates another cardinal rule of the microcosm of the *Odyssey:* he misuses his own identity. For Homer, as for the writers of the Bible, a person's name is inextricably tied to his character, his identity and his status. It is not a thing to be used lightly. The world of the *Odyssey* is rife with disguise, deceit and treachery: Athena herself appears in a dozen different guises by the end of the epic. To survive in such a world, the hero must know when to speak his name and when to conceal it—as Odysseus will learn to do in the second half of the epic. More than that, he must come to know and understand his own true nature and that of the world around him. Above all, he must not allow himself to be fooled by appearances. He must learn to forsake that which is merely bodily and bestial and ascend to a higher understanding of his own soul.

He must move up the rising path.

The Initiate

If I seem to be shifting from the language of concrete reality to a more obscure, even mystical language, it is because when I read the *Odyssey*, I do it partly through the mediation of a group of medieval Christians who read Homer's epics, as well as other classical pagan texts, in just such an allegorical fashion. Inspired equally by Neoplatonic philosophers like Plotinus, who tended to look for deeper spiritual meanings behind everyday realities, and the New Testament, where Paul interprets incidents from the Old Testament as foreshadowings of greater spiritual truths revealed by Christ, many medieval Christians believed that behind the fantastical voyages of Odysseus was a second, allegorical meaning that could inspire Christians in their spiritual pilgrimage. Read this way, the adventures Odysseus recounts in Books IX to XII—adventures that are already somewhat mystical in their timelessness and otherworldliness—become a map for the initiate who wishes to rise above the temptations of the world, the flesh and the devil. If he is to reach a higher spiritual level, if he is to escape the narrow boundaries of time and space to glimpse the eternal, then the initiate must overcome the deadly sin of sloth (the lotus-eaters) and move out of the cave of ignorance and bestiality.

Such an allegorical reading proves especially fruitful for those who continue past Book IX to the major adventure that Odysseus recounts in Book X. Odysseus, having first been robbed of a chance to reach Ithaca by the greed and folly of his men, and then having lost all but one of his ships to another group of giant cannibals, lands his remaining crewmen on the island of Circe. More cautious now since his run-in with Polyphemus, Odysseus splits his crew into two parties and draws lots to see which group will begin exploring the island. The group that is not led by Odysseus wins the first lot and sets off. Not long after, they come upon the shining house of Circe, whom they hear singing in a beautiful voice as she works at her loom. Prowling about the grounds of her home, they encounter a frightening array of lions and wolves, but as they come closer, they find that the beasts are tame. Like domesticated house pets, the wolves and lions fawn on the men and wag their tail. When Circe spies the men, she opens her doors and invites them in. As Odysseus describes it:

> Circe ushered the [men] into her hall, gave them seats and chairs to sit on, and then prepared them a mixture of cheese, barley-meal, and yellow honey flavoured with Pramnian wine. But into this dish she introduced a noxious drug, to make them lose all memory of their native land. And when they had emptied the bowls which she had handed them, she drove them with blows of a stick into the pigsties. Now they had pigs' heads and bristles, and they grunted like pigs; but their minds were as human as they had been before. So, weeping, they were penned in their sties. Then Circe flung them some forest nuts, acorns and cornel berries—the usual food of pigs that wallow in the mud. (X.232-43)

Luckily, one of the men was suspicious of Circe's invitation and has not followed the men into the house but has remained outside. When a long time has passed and the men still have not returned, he sets off to find Odysseus and warn him.

Odysseus tells the rest of his crew to wait and heads out alone to meet the witch. On his way, he is met by Hermes who warns him of Circe's powers and gives him a magic herb that he can use to counteract her noxious drugs. Armed with the herb, Odysseus approaches the shining house and is greeted warmly by its mistress. As she had done with his men, Circe invites Odysseus to dinner and offers him a drink laced with her magic drugs. After Odysseus has drained the brew, Circe touches him with her wand, beckoning him to join his men in the pigsty. To her surprise, Odysseus does not become a pig but instead grabs her by the throat and draws his blade as if to kill her. Circe begs him to spare her life and to join her in her bed, but before releasing her he makes her swear (in accordance with Hermes' instructions) not to make any attempt to rob him of his manhood. Circe swears the oath and the two repair to her bed, after which she treats Odysseus as if he were the lord of the house, instructing her maids to bathe and feed him in royal style. At Odysseus's urging, she restores his men to their human form, and the entire crew spends a happy year on Circe's island.

Taken by itself, the adventure is a grand one, and Odysseus tells it with gusto. But does it conceal a deeper, more spiritual meaning? For both the pagan Neoplatonists and the medieval scholars, the answer was a definite yes. To them, Circe symbolized the physical world. When we give in to our base, carnal appetites and look only to the world and to our flesh, we end up turning into swine, like the bad boys in *Pinocchio* who turn into donkeys. But if we are armed with true spiritual knowledge (the divine Word) as Odysseus is with the magic herb,[1] then we can extract spiritual knowledge and power even from the world. When the body rules us, we become weak and enslaved like the fawning wolves and lions; when we learn to rule it, we become the master in the house. When we overindulge the flesh, we

---

[1] Given him by Hermes ("hermeneutics" is derived from *Hermes,* whom the neo-Platonists considered to be the bearer of the divine word).

are robbed of our virility; when we rise above it, we are protected from the wiles of the witch. Jesus counsels his followers not to cast their pearls before swine. In *Odyssey* X, Odysseus's men partake of a brew that is, in a sense, too precious for them, and it converts them into swine. But Odysseus the initiate, because he is discerning and properly armed, is strengthened by that which weakens his men.

And now that he is strengthened, Odysseus must face what every initiate must face if he is to ascend the rungs of the spiritual ladder: the fear of death. When the year comes to an end and Odysseus tells the heartbroken Circe that he must leave and return to his true home, she tells him that before he can return, he must lead his crew to the very door of Hades. Time and space do not permit me to describe all the details of Odysseus's descent into the underworld (nor his later adventures with the sirens, Scylla and Charybdis, and the cattle of the sun); suffice it to say that after the *Odyssey,* almost all subsequent heroes of literature must face the psychological and spiritual dread of peering into the abyss as one of their trials. Indeed, the church fathers interpreted the Bible to say that before Jesus was resurrected and ascended into heaven, he first descended into the pit: an episode known as the harrowing of hell. In keeping with this belief, Dante, in his Christian epic of an initiate who ascends the ladder from hell to purgatory to paradise, has his pilgrim follow, both allegorically and literally, in the footsteps of Jesus. In the *Divine Comedy,* Dante the pilgrim enters into hell on Good Friday and departs from the pit on Easter morning.

But let us end our journey through Homer's *Odyssey* not on the plane of the allegorical but on the more familiar domestic plane that has been our focus for most of the last three chapters. I mentioned earlier that Odysseus asserts the fullness of his identity when he tells Calypso that, despite her indisputable superiority in form and grace to Penelope, he nevertheless longs to return to his true home and true wife. In making this decision, Odysseus necessarily forsakes Calypso's offer to make him immortal. Part of the power of the narrative structure of the *Odyssey* is that although Odysseus has seen Hades before rejecting Calypso's offer, we do not know this as readers until much later. Only when we actually accompany Odysseus in Book XI on his descent into the underworld—and learn what a dreary and awful place it is—do we realize the extent of the sacrifice he makes when he leaves Calypso's island. Odysseus has looked into the face of death and seen its horrors (Homer holds out little hope for a blissful afterlife), and yet still, nevertheless, he chooses Penelope and home.

THE GODS

Before moving on, I would like to consider one element of Homer that tends to confuse readers in general and Christians in particular: his treatment of the gods. At first glance, Homer's gods seem to be nothing more than humans who live forever. They are just as likely, if not more so, to indulge in lust, greed, pride and wrath as Homer's warriors. At times, Homer seems to depict them as cold, uncaring and arbitrary. At others he seems to use them as comic relief: Hera seducing Zeus in *Iliad* XIV or Hephaestus ensnaring his adulterous wife, Aphrodite, and her lover in a net in *Odyssey* VIII. Plato, though he loved the *Iliad* and the *Odyssey*, was scandalized by this depiction of the gods as imperfect and given to inordinate appetites. Part of the reason Plato banished the poets from his ideal republic was to prevent the spreading of such impious stories. Though he lived four centuries before Christ, Plato understood that a god cannot truly be a god if he is not perfect, unchanging, and removed from our world of sin and illusion. Both the pagan and Christian philosophers and theologians who followed in Plato's wake felt more or less the same about Homer's gods; indeed, the Neoplatonic and medieval allegorizing of Homer was partly a way to "clean up" the unacceptable actions of Homer's gods and goddesses.

My own reading of Homer's gods has been strongly influenced by Plato and the allegorizers, and I think that there is much truth to this approach. Nevertheless, it must be noted that Homer most likely viewed his gods more seriously and reverently than do we today. First of all, the anthropomorphic gods of Homer are far less beastly and horrific than the animal-headed gods of Egypt, Canaan, Assyria and Babylon. In Zeus, Apollo and Athena—who would come to embody most fully the high civilization of Greece—we glimpse a divine beauty whose counterpart is found in the well-toned and well-oiled physique of the young Olympic athlete in his prime. Second, the gods display a wisdom in keeping with their beauty.

Their knowledge transcends that of the shortsighted mortals, and their vision soars above even that of Nestor and Priam. Theirs is a lordly view from above, tranquil and undisturbed. Third, their power and wrath inspire awe and trembling in the mortals with whom they interact. They may seem petty in their squabbles with one another, but they are by no means to be trifled with.

In these three areas, at least, the gods of Homer afford a glimpse of the divine that comes much closer to the God of the Bible than do the pagan deities with whom the Jews had to contend. There is, however, one further way in which Homer's gods may have prepared the hearts of the Greeks for Christ, a way that would have confounded Plato and many of his heirs. Far from the impassive god of Plato and the Stoics (not to mention a number of church fathers), who is blissfully unmoved by the strivings of mortals, Zeus's Olympians are passionately involved in the affairs of men. Each god and goddess has at least one favorite among the mortals whom they try to save from earthly consequences. In the case of the comic *Odyssey*, Athena several times helps her beloved Odysseus escape death, but in the tragic *Iliad*, the gods are generally unsuccessful in their rescue attempts.

As he watches the death match of Achilles and Hektor from above, Zeus ponders whether he should save Hektor, despite the fact that he himself has prophesied that Hektor would be killed by Achilles in retaliation for the death of Patroclus:

> Ah me, this is a man beloved whom now my eyes watch
> being chased around the wall; my heart is mourning for Hektor
> who has burned in my honour many thigh pieces of oxen . . .
> Come then, you immortals, take thought and take counsel, whether
> to rescue this man or whether to make him, for all his valour,
> go down under the hands of Achilleus, the son of Peleus. (XXII.168-76)

Such a heartfelt cry from an immortal deity who has nothing to fear from god or man cannot help but remind the Christian reader of the pain Yahweh expresses when his people commit spiritual adultery and run after pagan idols. "How often," cries the Lord of Hosts again and again throughout the sacred history of Israel, "did I reach out to you, did I rescue you, did I hide you under the shadow of my wings? And yet you rejected my help and scorned my presence." If there is one thing the God of the Bible is not, it is uninvolved; neither unmoved nor dispassionate, he suffers with his people. And he often suffers most when it is he himself who meted out the punishment.

In the same divine utterance in which he prophesies that Achilles will kill Hektor, Zeus also prophesies that his own son, Sarpedon, will be killed by the spear of Patroclus. When the time comes, however, for his son to go down to Hades, the Lord of Olympus has second thoughts and wishes to pull him out from the fighting. Zeus shares his desire with Athena, but she warns him that if he does so, all of the other gods will want to save their sons and favorites as well. Zeus knows she is right, knows that he must allow Sarpedon to die, but that knowledge does not lessen the pain of his grief: if anything, it increases it. When he realizes he cannot hold back the death of Sarpedon, Homer tells us, in what is perhaps the single most moving line in the epic, "the father of gods and men . . . wept tears of blood that fell to the ground, for the sake / of his beloved son" (XVI.458-60).

The God and Father of our Lord Jesus Christ is absolutely sovereign; nothing lies outside his knowledge or his will. And yet he too is moved with sorrow at the death and destruction of his people. In the gods of Homer, we catch a very real glimpse of an all-powerful God who is neither a passive onlooker nor an armchair general. A God, in short, who knows our sorrows and is acquainted with our grief.

PART TWO

The
Greek Tragedians

9

AESCHYLUS'S *PROMETHEUS BOUND*

The Birth of Tragedy

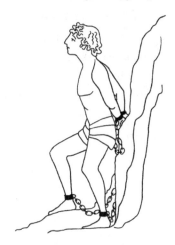

TRAGEDY IN GREEK MEANS, LITERALLY, "goat song." On the one hand, this etymological oddity is easy to account for. The Greek tragedies written by Aeschylus, Sophocles and Euripides during the golden age of Athens, the fifth century B.C., were first performed at an Athenian festival known as the Greater Dionysia. During the festival, held annually in the early spring, three different dramatists would present a tetralogy of plays composed of three (usually linked) tragedies followed by a satyr play that parodied the tragic form and offered comic relief. A group of judges would select a winner among the three tetralogies, and the winning playwright, so Horace tells us in his "Art of Poetry," would be awarded a goat. Such is the simple explanation. (Another simple explanation is that the actors in the satyr play were dressed in goatskins.)

But I would suggest a deeper origin for the word *tragedy:* not "goat song," but "song of the scapegoat." The distinction here holds profound implications for the way we read and absorb Greek tragedy. It is a distinction that when properly understood can empower the discerning Christian to perceive in the pagan dramas of Aeschylus, Sophocles and Euripides seeds of truth that only reach their full flowering in the person of Christ.

SONG OF THE SCAPEGOAT

In Leviticus we are given a detailed description of the rituals and sacrifices God commanded his people to perform on the Day of Atonement, or Yom Kippur. On this one sacred day, the high priest would enter into the most holy place, where the Ark of the Covenant was kept and where God's presence hovered, and make atonement for the people's sins, both revealed and hidden. Just to approach the most holy place the high priest had to sacrifice a bull on his own behalf. After completing the proper purification rituals, he would choose two goats through which to effect the reconciliation of God and his people. The first goat was sacrificed and its blood sprinkled on the altar, but the second was reserved for a different purpose:

> And when he [Aaron, the high priest] hath made an end of reconciling the holy place, and the tabernacle of the congregation, and the altar, he shall bring the live goat [known as the scapegoat]:
>
> And Aaron shall lay both his hands upon the head of the live goat, and confess over him all the iniquities of the children of Israel, and all their transgressions in all their sins, putting them upon the head of the goat, and shall send him away by the hand of a fit man into the wilderness:
>
> And the goat shall bear upon him all their iniquities unto a land not inhabited: and he shall let go the goat in the wilderness. (Leviticus 16:20-22)

In first placing his hands upon and then ejecting from the community the scapegoat—that is to say, the "escape-goat" or "goat of removal"—the high priest ritually transferred and then expelled the guilt and sins of the people. Though the scapegoat may be said to have carried the specific sins of each member of Israel, the ritual itself was essentially communal: its focus was on ridding the community of all sins committed during the previous year. The ultimate end of the ritual was to reconcile Yahweh and Israel, the divine God and the human community.

Though the exact origins of Greek tragedy are somewhat obscure, it is clear that the tragic performances were tied closely to the cult of Dionysus, or Bacchus, in whose honor the Dionysia was celebrated. Indeed, drama itself seems to have arisen out of choral songs sung or chanted in honor of the god; these were later interspersed with dramatized events taken from his life. These events were performed by an actor who would step out from the chorus and speak his lines alone, rather than chant them in unison with the rest of the chorus. Eventually, chorus and actor took up other mythic themes and heroes and the dramatic element increased, with Aeschylus adding a second actor and Sophocles a third (see Aristotle's *Poetics* IV.13-14). Still, even when tragedy turned for its material to the heroic age—that is, the legendary generations living before, during and just after the Trojan War—it maintained its traditional link to Bacchus. The Greater Dionysia was ushered in by the sacrifice of a bull and other animals sacred to Dionysus, especially goats. Throughout the four-day festival, a cult statue of Bacchus would adorn the center of the circular orchestra on which the chorus chanted and danced.

Unlike the Day of Atonement, the Dionysia was a secular festival, and yet it was also profoundly religious and spiritual in a way that is foreign to the post-Enlightenment West. Athenians who were drawn to the theater—and there were thousands of them from every walk of life—came to experience something as communal and ritually cleansing as the Hebrew Yom Kippur or the Catholic Mass. This was something more than entertainment; it was something to be endured, suffered, lived through. As the Athenians watched those twelve plays over three long days, they witnessed—and participated in—titanic struggles between men and gods, order and chaos, justice and revenge, guilt and expiation. The political (having to do with the *polis,* or city-state) and the ethical, the philosophical and the theological: all were wrestled out before them on the stage. Imagine a combination of a night at the opera, a July Fourth celebration and a solemn Good Friday service, and you will get a sense of how the Greater Dionysia touched every aspect of the lives of the Athenians.

In nearly all the extant plays, the action pivoted around the uncovering of some hidden taboo sin, a stain or curse with the power to drag down a hero, a heroine or an entire house. Like the children of Israel, the citizens of Athens were keenly aware that the breaking of taboos would bring down retribution on both the individual and the *polis,* and that to avert such a disaster, the divine wrath had to be diverted onto a surrogate. The Athenians, being ignorant of God's revelation to Moses on Mount Sinai, understood neither that God was One nor that he was holy, and as such they did not recognize sin as that which violates the nature of a holy God. But they certainly did have an inchoate (and, I would add, essential) sense that even if Zeus and his fellow Olympians were imperfect, a divine order of right and wrong existed and could not be trampled upon with impunity.

I discussed in the introduction how the secret rites performed at Eleusis near Athens centered around the seasons of nature as embodied in the myth of Demeter and Persephone. It seems clear from ancient references to the Eleusinian mysteries that the rites also involved the worship of Bacchus, a dying and rising vegetation god linked to the cycle of the grape as Demeter was to that of the grain. Though the ceremony held at Eleusis was primarily sacred while the performance at Athens was primarily secular, both were at their essence communal rituals that celebrated order, balance and reconciliation. Indeed, as the bread and wine of Demeter and Dionysus are a pagan seed that finds its ultimate consummation in the Eucharist (or Lord's Supper), so the tragic song of the scapegoat is an additional seed that finds its consummation in the crucified Savior whose death brought atonement to the world.

Throughout the golden age of Athens, which stretched from its defeat of Persia in 479 B.C. to its own defeat by Sparta in 404 B.C., the citizens of Athens gathered annually to witness—not in a temple but in a theater—the struggles of mortal men and women as they suffered the consequences of their sins (often committed in ignorance) and the strife of the world into which they were thrust (often unwillingly). Though the Greeks did not possess a biblical understanding of original sin, they were convinced that the present race of men had fallen away from an earlier ideal and grown both violent and disobedient in their hearts: the classic statement of this can be found in Hesiod's epic poem *Works and Days*. During the heroic age, which lasted from 1500 to 1200 B.C., tentatively, the tide of decay was temporarily halted; however, by the time we reach the children of the Trojan warriors, moral entropy has set in and the downward slide cannot be averted. With the exception of Aeschylus's *The Persians*, which is set in 480 B.C. (the eve of the golden age), all of the thirty-three extant Greek tragedies are set in the heroic age and focus on tragic heroes in whom we glimpse both the glory of that age and the decline soon to set in.

Let me qualify that last statement. One of the seven extant plays of

Aeschylus takes place on the threshold of the heroic age; it is, in fact, prophetic of that coming age. The play is *Prometheus Bound*, and it offers us
the only tragic hero who is not mortal, although Prometheus, rather in the
manner of Norse mythology, is a god who must endure a degree of pain
and isolation usually reserved for mortals. Though depicted in some ver-
sions of the myth as a man, Prometheus is considered by most mythogra-
phers and poets to be a Titan, one of that intermediary race of giants born
between the primal deities of earth and sky and the later, more sophisticated gods who dwelt on Mount Olympus. This is how Aeschylus depicts
him in his timeless tragedy *Prometheus Bound*.

THE SCAPEGOAT IN CHAINS

As Aeschylus tells the myth, Prometheus was not only the god who stole
the gift of fire from Zeus and gave it to man, he was also the one who en-
dowed mankind with all the gifts that allowed him to rise above the beast
and aspire for higher things. In fact, the fire Prometheus stole was as much
a fire of protection as it was the crucible out of which human creativity was
born. "For men at first," Prometheus explains to the chorus,

> had eyes but saw to no purpose; they had ears but did not hear. . . . All their
> doings were indeed without intelligent calculation until I showed them the
> rising of the stars, and the settings, hard to observe. And further I discov-
> ered to them numbering, pre-eminent among subtle devices, and the com-
> bining of letters as a means of remembering all things, the Muses' mother,
> skilled in craft. It was I who first yoked beasts for them. . . . Through lack
> of drugs men wasted away, until I showed them the blending of mild simples
> wherewith they drive out all manner of diseases. . . . Beneath the earth,
> man's hidden blessing, copper, iron, silver, and gold—will anyone claim to
> have discovered them before I did? . . . One brief word will tell the whole
> story: all arts that mortals have come from Prometheus. (444-505)[1]

The Prometheus of Aeschylus is no mere fly-by-night benefactor who
signs a large humanitarian aid check and then returns to his guarded man-

---

[1] All references for *Prometheus Bound* are from *Aeschylus II*, vol. 2 of *The Complete Greek Tragedies*, ed.
David Grene and Richmond Lattimore (Chicago: University of Chicago Press, 1956). In this and all
other plays in this excellent series, line numbers are keyed closely (but not exactly) to the Greek original; as such the line numbers I provide in the text will also be very close approximations.

sion. Prometheus is fully invested in man's growth and development and is willing to pay any price to protect the fledgling human race from the envy and malice of Zeus.

Like Hesiod, Aeschylus makes it clear that Zeus and his fellow Olympians would never have been able to seize power from the Titans had not Prometheus aided Zeus in his struggles. Now, however, Prometheus has come to regret his decision to help Zeus; the son of Kronos has become, like his father before him, a tyrant and an oppressor. As part of his rebellion, Prometheus steals the sacred fire from Olympus and gives it to man. But this act is not the only reason for which Zeus punishes Prometheus. Prometheus, as we saw in chapter one, knows the name of the goddess who will bear Zeus the child destined to overthrow him. To force Prometheus to stop aiding mankind, to submit to his authority, and to divulge the name of the goddess, Zeus chains the Titan to a high rock in the Caucasus and sends a ferocious eagle to devour his liver. Each night the liver regenerates, and when each new dawn arrives, the eagle returns to feast again. In the play we meet Prometheus at the beginning of his punishment, though we are told he will continue to suffer in torment for many generations to come. But the Titan remains undaunted. He will neither divulge the name nor bend his knee to Zeus. He will remain a foe of tyranny and a friend of man no matter the pain.

And yet, Aeschylus makes clear, a time will come when Zeus and Prometheus are reconciled. *Prometheus Bound*, like all the extant plays except the *Oresteia*, represents a single work that was originally part of a trilogy. Plays two and three of Aeschylus's *Prometheus* cycle are lost, but clues in the play we do have suggest that by the end of the trilogy, Zeus will have unconditionally released the chained Titan, who will respond by acknowledging Zeus's authority and revealing the name of the goddess. Zeus's decision to unilaterally free the Titan will prove that he has changed into a just ruler, and Prometheus, recognizing this, will extend to him the right hand of fellowship.

Twenty-three hundred years after Aeschylus, the Romantic poet Percy Bysshe Shelley (child and heir of the French Revolution) would balk at this reconciliation and compose his own sequel to the play. In Shelley's *Prometheus Unbound*, Zeus is pulled down from his throne, a utopia of perfect freedom and equality is established, and the freed Titan ushers in the new age. For Shelley, as for his fellow Romantic Lord Byron, Prometheus represented the ideal revolutionary hero: a strange blend of the Christ of the Gospels, who is purified and perfected by unmerited suffering, and the Satan of Milton's *Paradise Lost,* whom they saw as an appealing and charismatic hero who bravely resisted the "tyranny" of Milton's Jehovah.

Shelley's play is rich in ideas and imagery, and it is almost unsurpassed in its lyrical beauty and power, but it embodies a profound misunderstanding of Aeschylus and his play. *Prometheus Bound* is not a drama about the downfall of the divine-human hierarchy but about the transformation of divine rule into something just and even merciful. Aeschylus's cycle stands at the transition point between barbarism and civilization, brutality and compassion; indeed, Prometheus himself is that crux point, that nexus between unjust law and merciful law. In that sense, Aeschylus's pre-Christian play is more profoundly Christian than Shelley's post-Christian play. Though bereft of the Scriptures, Aeschylus saw that reconciliation would come not through the abandonment of law, order and force, but through something very much like the atonement: Zeus's wrath is turned aside by the sufferings of a divine (and yet somehow also human) scapegoat. And Zeus's wrath, Aeschylus makes clear, is just; Prometheus, for all of his heroism, is a rebel against the divine monarch, and the Greek playwright, unlike the English one, presents him as prideful and even self-righteous. From the Christian point of view, of course, Prometheus—and this I think Shelley understood—can be interpreted in a different way: like the serpent in the Garden, he tempted mankind with a type of knowledge (the fire of creativity) that Zeus had withheld and declared forbidden. Still, the central focus of the play is not Prometheus's crime but his role as scapegoat.

Indeed, Aeschylus increases the force of his scapegoat theme by weaving into his play an unexpected subplot that complicates what is perhaps the simplest and most austere of all Greek tragedies. Throughout the play, the scene is that of a bare crag in the Caucusus; the time, equal in duration to the actual playing time, remains delicately poised between a past crime and a coming future of pain; the action, straightforward and uncomplicated, focuses exclusively on Prometheus's stubborn refusal to submit to the will of Zeus. After a prologue in which we see Might and Hephaestus chain the Titan to the rock, the drama moves forcefully through three extended dialogues between Prometheus and three visitors to his isolated prison. Between the dialogues are lyrical meditations on Prometheus's sufferings by a chorus of ocean nymphs, along with dialogues between Prometheus and the leader of the chorus. The play is a masterpiece of dramatic unity: an integrated, self-enclosed whole, complete and perfect in conception and execution.

Well, almost. Prometheus's first visitor, Oceanus, who pompously advises him to give in to Zeus, and his third, Hermes, who delivers Zeus's ultimatum and ushers in the cataclysmic ending in which the icy crag splits and Prometheus is catapulted into the abyss, are tightly woven into the unity of the play. But his second visitor, Io, a mortal woman first beloved and then victimized by Zeus and the jealous Hera, seems at first to intrude on the main action and temporarily shifts our attention away from Prometheus. And yet as she shares her tale of woe and Prometheus prophesies what more she will suffer, we come to realize that here on display are two lonely figures—one male, the other female—who are both victims of Zeus's transition from usurping tyrant to just king, and who both must suffer that transition in their flesh, whether immortal or mortal. Furthermore, whereas Prometheus is chained and motionless, Io suffers because she is ever on the move, unable to find rest or refuge. Together they are like the two goats sacrificed for Yom Kippur: Prometheus on the altar, Io cast out of her community to wander in the wastelands outside the *polis*. And they are further linked together, Prometheus prophesies, for in the thirteenth generation to come, one of Io's descendants will kill the eagle and break Prometheus's chains. That descendant will be none other than Heracles (Hercules), a mortal son of Zeus who will eventually be lifted up to Olympus, even as Prometheus has been lowered to the realm of human pain and suffering.

However, it is not Prometheus's prophecy to Io that lingers in the mind after the play ends, but a prophecy spoken by Hermes to Prometheus. After detailing the pain the eagle will bring him as it devours daily his liver, Hermes offers a faint ray of hope for the suffering scapegoat:

And of this pain do not expect an end
until some God shall show himself successor
to take your tortures for himself and willing
go down to lightless Hades and the shadows
of Tartarus' depths. (1026-30)

Hermes' prophecy seems to refer to Heracles (who will as one of his twelve labors go down to Hades and kidnap Cerberus, the three-headed dog of hell), but for the Christian reader who lives on this side of the cross, it suggests something quite different. Could the One God, who instructed Moses to perform the day of atonement annually until his Son would come, be speaking here through the mouth of a pagan poet—as he spoke through the mouths of the pagan prophet Balaam, the pagan kings Neb-uchadnezzar and Cyrus, and the pagan Magi of the Nativity story? Does the prophecy not point uncannily in the direction of Calvary?

According to Christian tradition and a few riddling passages of Scrip-ture, between his death and resurrection Christ descended into hell and re-leased from bondage the righteous souls of the Old Testament. Among those rescued were David, who sang the song of the coming scapegoat-Messiah in Psalm 22, and Isaiah, who sang his own version in Isaiah 53. The sufferings of Prometheus as dramatized in Aeschylus read almost like a pagan gloss on those two prophetic songs of the Old Testament. When I meditate on these strange, shadowy parallels, what remains in my mind is an image that is fictional in the literal sense but that embodies both a mythical and mystical truth: an image of the risen Christ freeing the suf-fering Titan from bondage. Or, to put it in allegorical terms, of a greater Christian truth fulfilling—and thus setting free—a pagan glimpse of that greater truth to come.

10

AESCHYLUS'S *ORESTEIA*

Pagan Poets and Hebrew Prophets

ACCORDING TO ARISTOTLE'S *POETICS*, the tragedians were the true successors to the epic poets. This comment, accurate as it is when applied to Athenian tragedy in general, takes on even greater truth when applied specifically to the *Oresteia* of Aeschylus. Here, in the only complete trilogy to survive intact (the *Oresteia* is the collective name given to the three plays that make it up: *Agamemnon, Libation Bearers* and *Eumenides*), Aeschylus paints with a poetic brush that is as vast and sweeping as Homer's. Like the *Iliad*, the *Oresteia* chronicles the movement from war to peace, division to reconciliation, barbarism to civilization. As we saw in the previous chapter, *Prometheus Bound* (and the lost trilogy of which it was once a part) also captures some of that movement from chaos to order; however, in the *Oresteia* the magnitude of that movement is so much greater that it is Homeric in proportion.

As in the Prometheus trilogy, the *Oresteia* concerns itself with the transition from the violent overthrow of Ouranos by Kronos and Kronos by Zeus to the wisdom and mercy that ensue once Zeus has learned to rule with justice and compassion. But this time the divine conflict recedes into the background and is represented instead in the tragic House of Atreus, whose successive generations echo the transition from bad Titans to good Olympians. In the first half of this chapter we will trace that conflict-transition as it is told by Aeschylus: a conflict even more rich in taboos, bloodguilt, and festering crime than the story of Oedipus. In the second half we will consider how in the *Oresteia* Aeschylus embodies that conflict-transition in a unique way that rivals the prophetic books of the Old and New Testaments.

Suffering into Wisdom

The tragic tale of the House of Atreus begins with its dynastic founder, Tantalus, a mortal son of Zeus. Of all the men who ever lived, Tantalus is surely the most blessed, for the immortal gods so love and honor him that they often invite him up to Mount Olympus to dine with them. Even more wonderful, they visit Tantalus in his home and deign to share meals with him. Yet despite his many blessings, Tantalus decides to do a terrible thing. No reason is given for his dreadful act; perhaps he envies the gods' immortality, though even that is not certain. Whatever his motivation, the next time the gods visit his home, he secretly kills his own son, Pelops, cooks the flesh, and serves it to them. The gods, discovering the treachery, are enraged and punish Tantalus. But they take pity on the innocent Pelops and restore him to his previous state.

Pelops grows to manhood and remains until death a righteous man. The same cannot be said of his two sons, Atreus and Thyestes. In an act of treachery, Thyestes seduces the wife of Atreus. Atreus discovers the act and vows to match Thyestes' betrayal. In good family tradition, he invites his brother to a feast and feeds him the cooked flesh of Thyestes' children. Thyestes, lacking the gods' foresight, eats the food unknowingly. After dinner, Atreus brings a tray out to his brother and opens the cover; on it are the heads and hands of his children. Thyestes vomits up the meal and goes into exile with his one remaining son, Aegisthus, swearing eternal vengeance on the House of Atreus.

Reunited with his wife, Atreus fathers two sons, Menelaus and Agamemnon, who marry two sisters, Helen and Clytemnestra, and become the kings of the city-states of Sparta and Argos. All are happy until one day Paris, the son of the Trojan king Priam, travels to Greece as the guest of Menelaus and Helen. Though Menelaus treats him with the respect due a guest, Paris repays him by kidnapping Helen and carrying her back to Troy. In response, all the kings of Greece rally to Menelaus's cause, and Agamemnon, having the most ships, is chosen commander in chief.

On the way to Troy, tragedy strikes. Because of the anger of the goddess Artemis, the ships are grounded at the port of Aulis. When Agamemnon inquires of the oracle, he is told that he has two choices: abandon the expedition to Troy, or sacrifice his virgin daughter Iphigenia. Unwilling to forsake the glory the war will bring him, Agamemnon chooses the second option and sends a letter home instructing his daughter to come quickly and alone to Aulis, where she will be married to the great hero Achilles. Iphigenia suspects nothing and rushes to Aulis dressed in a bridal gown. But when she reaches the altar, there is no bridegroom waiting—only a sacrificial knife. After the sacrifice is completed, the fleet sails for Troy, leaving the dreadful news to find its way back to Clytemnestra. During the ten long years of war at Troy, Clytemnestra's anger over the sacrifice of Iphigenia festers, and her mind turns toward revenge. Meanwhile Aegisthus, whose father, Thyestes, has long since died but who has taken on his father's hatred of Atreus and his family, sidles up to the despairing queen and, like his father before him, seduces his brother's wife.

Ironically, just as the war began with an act of treachery, so it ends with an equally treacherous act: the Trojan horse. As the walls of Troy have proved for ten years to be impregnable, the Greeks devise an ignoble plan. They construct a large wooden horse with a hollow belly and leave it outside the city; then they pretend to sail off in their ships. The unsuspecting Trojans take the horse into their city and begin to celebrate. During the night, a group of Greeks who have been hiding in the wooden belly pour out of the horse and open the gates. The Greeks are barbaric and savage in their victory. They torch the city, demolish the temples, slaughter the men, and drag the women off into slavery. Each Greek king takes a noble Trojan woman to be his concubine: Agamemnon chooses Cassandra, the prophetess daughter of King Priam. The Greeks' impiety does not go unnoticed. The gods wreak vengeance on the Greeks, each of whom suffers an evil homecoming. Some are killed; others wander many years before reaching home. Agamemnon's fate is the most terrible of all. On the day of his return, he and his war-prize are murdered by Clytemnestra.

Though all the details described above find their way into the *Oresteia,* usually in the form of a choral lyric, the plot of *Agamemnon* focuses on the day of Agamemnon's return and his death at the hands of his wife. During the course of the play, the audience watches in horror as Clytemnestra smoothly deceives the vain and prideful Agamemnon, flattering him coyly, feasting him lavishly, and then stabbing him mercilessly in a bathtub. Though Cassandra appeals to the chorus of Argive elders to help her, they prove impotent (if sympathetic), and Clytemnestra kills her as well. Clytemnestra and Aegisthus then become the new king and queen of Argos.

The tragedy does not stop there. Many years later (as Aeschylus dramatizes it in *Libation Bearers*), Orestes, the exiled son of Agamemnon and Clytemnestra, returns home, and with the help of his sister Electra he kills his mother and stepfather. This act of matricide brings down on Orestes the wrath of the Furies, who pursue him like bloodhounds in a hunt. Orestes (in the *Eumenides*) flees to Athens to expiate his crime; there he is defended by Athena and Apollo and judged innocent by a council of elders. With this judgment peace is restored, and the Furies, who make up the final chorus of the *Oresteia,* are "domesticated." Swayed by Athena, they agree to leave their wrath behind and become protectresses of marriage and childbirth.

As in the divine saga of Ouranos-Kronos-Zeus told by Hesiod in the *Theogony,* Aeschylus's human saga climaxes not with revenge but with a higher vision of law, order and civilization. For the Greeks, the dark *chthonic* ("of the earth") deities like Gaia and the Furies represent an older form of law based on bloodguilt and kinship ties, while the "newer" deities of Olympus (especially Zeus, Athena and Apollo) represent a more abstract, objective form of law based on reason and impartiality. Whereas the former privileges the claims of family and demands blood for blood, the latter privileges the needs of the *polis* and seeks communal decisions based on a law that supersedes individual claims. As Greek tragedy was strongly concerned with the competing claims of family and *polis,* these contrasting visions will surface again in the plays we examine in subsequent chapters.

In his monumental trilogy, Aeschylus encourages his audience to celebrate the shift. (In fact, many readers, myself among them, have interpreted the council of elders that declares Orestes innocent as a progenitor of the Supreme Court.) To achieve this end he draws together all of the most ancient taboos—cannibalism, the sacrifice of a child, the murder of a spouse, the slaying of a guest, matricide—and allows us to witness the consequences of breaking such taboos. Under the old dispensation of the Furies, there is no way to escape the cycles of vengeance initiated by these broken taboos; only with the triumph of a higher abstract law can peace be found. Aeschylus celebrates this triumph in a way that would have spoken strongly to his Athenian audience, but his message also has a deeper meaning for the Christian. Aeschylus's play, in a turn that looks forward to the Christian victory born out of suffering, also marks a movement toward a divine and human reconciliation that allows mercy to win over eye-for-eye justice and that allows characters and audience alike to suffer into wisdom.

A SWIRL OF SYMBOLS

The universe of Aeschylus's trilogy is one in which human and divine actions parallel each other and where vast eschatological patterns of force are worked out over long years of ignorance and pain. Justice does prevail in the end, and harmony and fellowship are restored, but the road to peace is a long one. As in the Bible, this dramatic *via dolorosa* winds among the generations of a chosen family and is replete with riddling prophecies, Jacob-like tricksters, epic struggles and even a messianic figure: Orestes. To survive in such a world, one must learn to read the signs, to see which way destiny is leading. It is therefore not surprising that Aeschylus presents much of his play through a dense weave of images that point simultaneously in a number of different directions. Like the prophetic books of the Old Testament or like Revelation in the New, the *Oresteia,* especially the *Agamemnon,* assaults our eyes and ears with a swirl of symbols that are hard to interpret and even harder to assemble.

To illustrate this, let us look closely at seven lines from the opening chorus of *Agamemnon*, lines that retell the Trojan War in symbolic terms:

> So towering Zeus the god of guests
> drives Atreus' sons at Paris,
> all for a woman manned by many
> the generations wrestle, knees
> grinding the dust, the manhood drains,
> the spear snaps in the first blood rites
> that marry Greece and Troy. (66-72)[1]

The reference to Zeus as the "god of guests" is more than poetic decora-
tion. As discussed earlier, the ancient Greeks believed Zeus to be a protec-
tor of the sacred rights and duties of guests and hosts; a violation of *xenia*
was thought to bring down the wrath of Zeus—as it often does in the *Iliad*
and *Odyssey*. In the passage above, Zeus, working through Agamemnon
and Menelaus, exacts revenge on Paris and his city for his betrayal of Menelaus. (Paris broke the laws that bind guest to host when he abducted
Helen.)

Such is the theme of *xenia* as it is used in the Homeric epics. Here, however, Aeschylus lifts the theme of *xenia* into the symbolic realm. The entire
history of the tragic House of Atreus is predicated on a series of bad guests
and hosts who violate *xenia* and thus bring down wrath on themselves and
their heirs. Tantalus is a bad host who feeds human flesh to his guests;
Atreus likewise when he feeds a similar meal to his brother. Agamemnon
is a bad host to Iphigenia as Clytemnestra is to Agamemnon. The Greek
fleet as a whole is a bad "guest" of the city of Troy as Aegisthus is of Argos.
That Aeschylus means for all these levels of meaning to abide simultaneously in the guest-host symbol is borne out by the fact that phrases and
images containing guests and hosts appear and reappear in a pattern of
repetition throughout the play.

More powerful, though, than the guest-host symbol is a second symbol

---

[1]Citations are taken from *Oresteia*, trans. Robert Fagles, in *The Norton Anthology of World Masterpieces*,
ed. Maynard Mack, 6th ed., vol. 1 (New York: Norton, 1992), pp. 548-652; line numbers are given
in the text.

that rises up in the last two lines of the above passage: "the first blood rites /
that marry Greece and Troy." The image here is of a blood wedding, a marriage that leads not to happiness but destruction. The "marriage" of Greece
and Troy is, of course, metaphorical; however, if we review the greater story
we will find a succession of actual blood weddings: Kronos and Rhea, Paris
and Helen, Agamemnon and Clytemnestra, Achilles and Iphigenia. Each
of these weddings is marked by treachery and betrayal and leads in one way
or another to bloodshed. The marriages themselves are both human and
divine, legitimate and illegitimate, real and feigned; like the guest-host
symbol they exist on multiple levels, mediating and communicating between diverse states and realities. Together the two symbols reveal a fallen
world of treachery, bloodlust and taboo crimes, a chaotic world that, Saint
Paul might say, has been "subjected to futility."

As the chorus continues their song of the war, they focus on a sign that
appeared in the sky on the day Agamemnon and Menelaus were to set out
for Troy, a prophetic sign that is promptly interpreted by the seer of the
Greeks:

The kings of birds to kings of the beaking prows, one black,
    one with a blaze of silver
        skimmed the palace spearhand right
        and swooping lower, all could see,
            plunged their claws in a hare, a mother
    bursting with unborn young—the babies spilling,
quick spurts of blood—cut off the race just dashing into life!
Cry, cry for death, but good win out in glory in the end.
But the loyal seer of the armies studied Atreus' sons,
two sons with warring hearts—he saw two eagle-kings
    devour the hare and spoke the things to come,
"Years pass, and the long hunt nets the city of Priam,
    the flocks beyond the walls,
a kingdom's life and soul—Fate stamped them out.
Just let no curse of the gods lour on us first,
    shatter our giant armor
        forged to strangle Troy. I see
            pure Artemis bristle in pity—
                yes, the flying hounds of the Father

> slaughter for armies . . . their own victim . . . a woman
> trembling young, all born to die—She loathes the eagle's feast!" . . .
>
> I beg you, Healing Apollo, soothe her before
> her crosswinds hold us down and moor the ships too long,
> pressing us on to another victim . . .
>> nothing sacred, no
>>> no feast to be eaten
>>>> the architect of vengeance. (118-38, 145-50)

Though there is no dramatic action in this passage, the symbolic action is intense and overwhelming. The passage begins with a disturbing omen: two eagles pounce on and devour a pregnant rabbit. The scene in itself, though violent and bloody, does not lie outside the normal bounds of nature; however, when the seer of the armies sees it, he reads in these natural objects and events a higher, symbolic meaning. The eagles are not just birds but represent the two eagle-kings: Agamemnon and Menelaus, twin commanders under whom and on behalf of whom the army proceeds to Troy. The hare is not just a hare but Troy herself, whom the two kings will not only kill but devour utterly—as the hare and her unborn children are killed together, so the savage Greeks will not only kill the Trojan men and their sons but drag off their women so as to prevent a new generation from rising out of the ashes.

So far the symbols are fairly straightforward: eagles = kings; hare = Troy. But then Aeschylus, sensing with great insight that symbols are far more slippery than that, complicates the passage. It is not just the seer who has witnessed the murder of the hare. Artemis, too, the divine protectress of nature, has seen and grown fierce with anger at the bloodthirsty eagles and their murder of a pregnant mother. Unfortunately for the sons of Atreus, in a symbolic universe like that of the *Oresteia*, to be enraged at the eagles is to be enraged as well at those whom the eagles represent; to pity the hare is to pity Troy, even though Troy will not be destroyed for another ten years. The killing of a hare now and the destruction of a city ten years hence are, in the world of the *Oresteia*, the same event. Time, place and identity are in flux, similar to what we find in the long prophetic passages of Isaiah, Jeremiah and Revelation. Those whom the eagles symbolize must be punished now for a crime they have not yet committed. There is

a delicate weave in the ordering of the universe and the progression of historical events, and although this order is ultimately linear and forward-
moving (i.e., eschatological), it has a tendency to bend back on itself, form-
ing mini-cycles within the overall march of time.

The punishment Artemis will inflict on Agamemnon—for, as commander in chief, the brunt of the penalty presumably falls on him—is the
sacrifice of his daughter, Iphigenia: "no feast to be eaten." The literal
meaning of this phrase is that Iphigenia, as a human sacrifice, will not have
her flesh eaten, as would have been the case with a sacrificial bull. However, as in the blood wedding symbol, this symbol has a greater resonance
within the overall story. Both Agamemnon's father and great-grandfather
literally served up feasts that should not have been eaten. Likewise Kronos,
in swallowing his newborn children, consumed that which was forbidden.
Returning to the passage, the chorus informs us that this feast not to be
eaten is "the architect of vengeance"; the sacrifice of Iphigenia is to spur on
the murder of Agamemnon. Here again, the deeper, fuller meaning of the
phrase points back to the dreadful act of Tantalus, which was the original
spur for the long cycle of suffering inflicted on the House of Atreus: an act,
we must remember, that, like Adam and Eve's eating of the fruit, was utterly irrational.

Thus far we have analyzed three symbols: guest-host, blood wedding
and forbidden consumption. Though each of these symbols carries its own
individual force and meaning, together they are interwoven with a fourth
symbol that appears in line 129: "The long hunt nets the city of Priam."
This image of a death-bringing net occurs again and again throughout the
trilogy and is, it could be argued, the foundational symbol of the *Oresteia*.
With almost physical force, the net draws into itself nearly all the scattered
symbols of the play. In all its incarnations, the net represents not only destruction, but destruction by treachery; furthermore, it points toward a destruction that slowly pulls its victim in, that in fact tightens its grip the
more the victim struggles. In the passage above, the net is a hunting symbol enriched by Aeschylus's at-first inexplicable reference to the eagles as
"flying hounds." Viewed symbolically, it is neither odd nor inexplicable:
Agamemnon and Menelaus are hounds who smell the blood of Troy, who
hunt their victims the same way Kronos, Atreus and Clytemnestra hunt

theirs. And they are flying hounds because the ultimate hunters in the play are those dread goddesses born of blood and earth: the Furies. It is the Furies, finally, who tighten the net and who embody the hatred, wrath and vengeance that fuel the trilogy. The audience then is not surprised when in the third play of the cycle, the *Eumenides,* the Furies appear on stage and function as the chorus.

With consummate skill, Aeschylus arranges it so that nearly all his symbols find some kind of physical embodiment in the dramatic action of the play. When near the end of *Agamemnon* the doors of the palace are thrown open and a bloody Clytemnestra is revealed standing triumphant over the dead bodies of Agamemnon and Cassandra, we are invited to gaze on the very embodiment of a bad host. When she cries out, unafraid and unapologetic, that her murder was in reality a sacrifice, we witness on the stage a feast not to be eaten. Even more powerfully, when we note that the two bodies are wrapped in a purple cloak, we understand that the symbolic net has flung itself out of the night and strangled its victims. Agamemnon, he who cast a figurative net over Troy, is now caught up, literally, in a net. Finally, and perhaps most disturbingly, when we look on the warrior and his concubine united in blood, the symbol of the blood wedding leaps into physical reality.

It is a strange and disturbing literary device, but it is one Christians should recognize as central to the Bible. The crucifixion of Christ on Good Friday is prefigured not only theologically but symbolically. Throughout the Old Testament a number of images point forward to Calvary: the serpent that bites the heel of the woman's seed (Genesis 3:15), Abraham's near sacrifice of Isaac (Genesis 22), the blood on the lintel that protects the dwellers within from the angel of death (Exodus 12), David's cry of the forsaken man (Psalm 22), Isaiah's song of the man of sorrows (Isaiah 53), Zechariah's stricken shepherd (Zechariah 13). Aeschylus may have been ignorant of Isaiah and Zechariah, of Moses and David, but he understood as well as they that the great, overarching symbols of literature can function as they do only because history and the universe are inherently meaningful and moving toward a purposeful end.

What happened two millennia ago on the first Good Friday and Easter Sunday was neither haphazard nor unexpected. The sacred history of the

Bible that takes us from the beginning of human history (the fall of man) to the end (the new Jerusalem) is also a sacred drama that presents its reader with a unified aesthetic whole, a rich tapestry that like the *Oresteia* is woven of symbolic strands repeated and reworked across the whole sixty-six books of the Bible. When Jesus refers to himself as the good shepherd or the vine or the bread of life, he makes use of images and symbols that run throughout the Old Testament. When New Testament writers refer to Jesus as our Passover or the chief cornerstone or the high priest, we are meant to interpret these symbolic titles in the context of the full and miraculous history of Israel. Though Aeschylus did not have access to the Old Testament, he seems to have understood in a rude, inchoate form that if history is indeed meaningful, if there is a greater destiny being worked out in what seem at first to be random human events, then we should be able to discern in those events patterns that mark the hinge points of that greater cosmic plan. Perhaps he understood as well that such symbols are essentially and profoundly sacramental, that they can bear a freight of meaning that points, simultaneously, downward to the human and upward to the divine.

11

SOPHOCLES' *OEDIPUS*

The Human Scapegoat

OF ALL THE SCAPEGOATS THAT PARADED across the theater of Dionysus during the golden age of Athens, the best known and most fully developed was surely Oedipus. Like the *Oresteia* of Aeschylus, Sophocles' *Oedipus* is a play about ill-fated heroes who have broken taboos and must pay the consequences for doing so: in the case of Oedipus, those taboos are patricide and incest. Just as the modern day Christian who attends a passion play knows in advance the story of Christ, so Sophocles' original audience knew full well the basic outlines of Oedipus's story.

Here is that story in a nutshell: Laius and Jocasta, the king and queen of Thebes, receive a prophecy that their newborn son will kill his father. In order to avoid the prophecy, Laius gives the helpless infant to one of his herdsmen and tells him to take it to the top of Mount Cithaeron, pierce together its feet (*Oedipus* means "swollen foot"), and leave it to die of exposure. But the servant takes pity on the babe and gives it instead to another herdsman from the city of Corinth. At the time, the king and queen of Corinth, Polybus and Merope, are childless, so when the Corinthian herdsman returns to the city with a foundling, they adopt the child as their prince and heir. Oedipus grows up believing he is the natural son of Polybus until one day a man gets drunk and blurts out to Oedipus that he is not his father's son.

Rash and headstrong, the young Oedipus, unable to get a straight answer from his "parents," journeys to the oracle at Delphi and demands to be told the truth about his parentage. Instead the oracle drives him away as though he were cursed, prophesying that he will kill his father and marry his mother. Desperate to escape this fate, Oedipus runs in the opposite direction, away from Corinth. After a time he finds himself at a crossroads where three paths come together. There he runs headlong into a hunting party. The head of the party—who, as it turns out, is Laius minus his courtly robes—rudely orders Oedipus to move aside; instead, the impulsive Oedipus leaps on the party and kills all but one of them, a servant who escapes. Shortly thereafter Oedipus encounters the dreaded Sphinx, who tells her riddle to everyone who would go in or out of the city of Thebes. If they answer incorrectly, she devours them. Her presence has caused a great fear to fall on Thebes and has prevented the Thebans from engaging in trade. Oedipus boldly accepts the Sphinx's challenge and correctly answers her riddle, whereupon the Sphinx kills herself and Thebes is saved.

The Thebans hail Oedipus as their savior. As their former king, Laius, has recently died, Oedipus is made king and marries Laius's widow, Jocasta, with whom he has two sons and two daughters. Fast-forward several years: suddenly and unexpectedly, a plague falls on Thebes and crops, cattle and men begin to die. The people beg Oedipus to save them from this devouring plague, and he accordingly sends Creon, Jocasta's brother, to Delphi for an answer. Creon returns and tells Oedipus that the plague will continue until the murderer of Laius is revealed and expelled, scapegoat-like, from the city. Though he is warned to stop his investigations, Oedipus makes a vigorous search for Laius's killer. In the end he discovers his true identity and that of his wife. Jocasta, unable to bear this revelation, hangs herself; Oedipus, in an agony of remorse, takes two of the brooches from his wife-mother's robe and uses them to gouge out his eyes. He then orders Creon to banish him from the city. With the expulsion of Oedipus, the plague ceases and peace returns to Thebes.

Such is the story of Oedipus, a story that one would hardly pick to be the raw material for one of the greatest and most perfect tragedies ever constructed. Yet this is the story that Sophocles chose to rework into one of the enduring masterpieces of the Western world. By the almost magical power of his art, Sophocles not only transforms a repulsive story about patricide and incest into a triumphant journey of self-discovery, he also transforms a pathetic puppet fated to commit the worst of sins into a courageous hero who risks all to learn the truth and save his people. Even more amazingly, he constructs his plot so that an audience that would normally feel disgust at the events performed on stage instead leaves the theater feeling purged and purified.

STORY VERSUS PLOT

Though we often identify Aristotle with the golden age of Athens (the fifth century B.C.), Aristotle actually lived in the fourth century, when the greatness of Athens had fallen into eclipse. Like many in his day, Aristotle surely yearned to return to the glory days when Aeschylus, Sophocles and Euripides thrilled audiences with their dramaturgy. Indeed, I would argue that one of the main reasons he wrote *Poetics*, his groundbreaking treatise on the nature of epic, lyric and dramatic poetry, was to help inspire a new golden age of theater. Casting his eye back a century, Aristotle sought in his *Poetics* to systematically list and define the elements that made their plays so enduring. To help illustrate his list of criteria, Aristotle quotes frequently from Sophocles and his contemporaries, but the play that he quotes most often and with the most enthusiasm is *Oedipus*. Clearly, the great philosopher-critic considered this play to be the best of them all. Most critics today would agree with his assessment.

But why did Aristotle favor *Oedipus* so highly? The answer surely lies in its amazing plot. According to the *Poetics*, the plot "is the first principle, and, as it were, the soul of a tragedy" (VI.14).[1] Whereas most modern playgoers tend to focus on character, Aristotle firmly believed it was plot that made a tragedy weak or great. By plot, however, he did not mean simply the story behind the action. For Aristotle, tragedy was the result of a

---

[1]References for Aristotle are from *Poetics*, trans. S. H. Butcher, in *Critical Theory Since Plato*, ed. Hazard Adams, rev. ed. (New York: Harcourt Brace Jovanovich, 1992); references are by book and chapter number.

process of imitation (*mimesis* in Greek) by which the playwright transformed a long, haphazard story into a focused, unified plot. Or, to use Aristotle's succinct definition, the imitation of an action (or story) is a plot.

The story of a man, for example, begins with his birth and ends with his death and includes all the various incidents in between. But an Aristotelian plot constructed around that biographical story would confine itself to a single day in the man's life when everything that is most essential to him comes to a head. Whereas the events in a story (like those in real life) follow each other in simple chronological order, the events in a plot should move forward in accordance with necessity, probability and inevitability. The plot, we might say, is life with all of life's contradictions purged out of it. To imitate life is to present life not as it is but as it should be, not as it manifests itself in an imperfect world, but how it would appear in a more perfect world where there is a rational link between cause and effect, where the stable, meaningful laws of probability determine action, and where a sense of inevitability, of a higher controlling fate, is felt.

For Aristotle, the worst kind of plot is an episodic one: that is to say, a plot with no internal cohesion between the scenes. In a well-constructed plot, there is a causal relationship between each scene that propels the reader forward toward the unstoppable conclusion. In the best and most complex plots, that conclusion is brought about either by a sudden reversal of fortune (from good to bad or bad to good), a sudden recognition (in which the hero moves from ignorance to knowledge) or, best, by both at the same time. The reversal or recognition, however, must not appear contrived when it occurs. It should arise, Aristotle explains, "from the internal structure of the plot, so that what follows should be the necessary or probable result of the preceding action" (X.3).

When judged by the standards of Aristotle, *Oedipus* emerges as the embodiment of perfect plot construction. Thus, whereas the story of Oedipus is filled with long, dull stretches during which the tragic pieces of his life slowly coalesce, the plot of *Oedipus* is concentrated into an intense, dramatic period of less than a day during which all the secrets of his life are revealed. Like the *Iliad* and the *Odyssey, Oedipus* begins in medias res. When the play opens, the people of Thebes are crowding around Oedipus and begging him to free their city from the plague. Oedipus assures them that he feels their pain and has taken the proper steps to end the plague. Almost immediately, Creon, whom Oedipus sent to Delphi before the opening of the play, appears on the stage and reveals the words of the oracle. In a moment of great dramatic irony, Oedipus swears that he will seek out the killer of Laius as though Laius were his own father. A choral interlude follows, and then Tiresias, a blind prophet whom Oedipus summoned before the beginning of the play, appears on the stage. He warns Oedipus to stop his search, but when Oedipus forsakes his advice and accuses him of being a traitor, Tiresias blurts out that Oedipus himself is the killer he seeks.

After a second choral interlude, Oedipus has a long dialogue with Jocasta in which he shares his fear that Tiresias's words may be true. Jocasta assures him of the impotence of prophets and prophecies by revealing how she and her husband had been warned falsely that their child would kill Laius. Oedipus in turn tells his own story of how he escaped a terrible fate prophesied by the oracle. Feeling invulnerable, the two shake their fists at fate and the gods and leave the stage. After a third choral interlude, they return to the stage and are met by a messenger from Corinth who has come to inform Oedipus that Polybus is dead and that Oedipus is the new king of Corinth. This makes Oedipus and Jocasta ecstatic, for it seems to prove that Oedipus too has escaped his evil destiny—since his "father" is dead, he cannot kill him. The messenger, overhearing Oedipus's words, tells him that if he feared killing his father and marrying his mother, he need never have left Corinth: Polybus and Merope are not his real parents. The messenger, it turns out, is also the Corinthian herdsman who carried the infant Oedipus to Polybus.

Jocasta, piecing together what has happened, leaves the stage, only to be replaced by the Theban herdsman who gave the infant to the Corinthian. As it turns out, the Theban herdsman is also the servant who survived when Oedipus killed Laius and the rest of his hunting party (he is present because Oedipus had earlier summoned him for questioning about the murder of Laius). The Corinthian herdsman immediately recognizes his Theban counterpart, and Oedipus, to his own destruction, forces the Theban to divulge the identity of the infant he gave to the Corinthian. The truth out, Oedipus rushes off the stage. After the fourth and final choral interlude, he returns, blind and in agony, and forces Creon to expel him from the city.

True to Aristotle's criteria for a complex plot, *Oedipus* not only moves forward, scene by scene, in accordance with necessity, probability and inevitability, but it reaches its climax through a sudden reversal and recognition that occur simultaneously. The reversal occurs when the Corinthian herdsman, thinking to free Oedipus from his anxiety about killing his father and marrying his mother, actually causes Oedipus to discover that he has done both. Along with his Theban counterpart, he also effects the moment of recognition in which Oedipus progresses from ignorance of his parentage to a tragic awareness of his true identity. Though the plot is filled with coincidences that seem on reflection to be contrivances, we do not feel this when reading or watching the play. Within the plot, all moves forward so swiftly and logically that we accept it as real and inevitable.

As an aesthetic work, *Oedipus* is surely a masterpiece, and yet its carefully constructed Aristotelian plot lends it an additional level of greatness that moves it to a higher plane where theology and philosophy meet. As far back as Homer, the Greek mind had struggled to reconcile the twin claims of fate and freedom. The Greeks understood the existence of a greater and older force of destiny that operated through the Olympian will of Zeus but that was not identical with it. The Greeks came to represent this higher destiny as the Moirai or Fates: three goddesses who assign each mortal a lot at birth, who spin the thread of that lot as it unfolds, and who cut the thread when the appointed hour of death arrives. Generally speaking, the Greek view of the Fates was both pessimistic and fatalistic. Alongside this view, however, grew a counter vision that was more optimistic and humanistic: a view that can also be seen in Homer, whose heroes (especially Achilles) struggle valiantly to assert their glory and honor over against what appears to be an uncaring, deterministic universe. As we approach the golden age of Athens, this struggle between the inexorable and inescapable Moirai and the force of human freedom and dignity heightens, spurred on perhaps by Greece's defeat of Persia: an event that seemed to result from both divine providence and human valor.

Needless to say, the Greek struggle between fate and freedom is of particular importance to Christian readers of Sophocles' play. Of all the theological paradoxes that Christians have attempted to resolve, surely the most puzzling (and distressing!) is that which concerns the seemingly opposing forces of predestination and free will. If we fully accept the former, we are trapped in an absurdist universe in which each human being is no more than a puppet on a string. If we celebrate only the second, we are in a world over which God has no control. *Oedipus,* because of its plot, allows for a reconciliation in which both fate and freedom, divine sovereignty and human volition are equally affirmed. Let us consider first how the plot allows for the reality of choice.

The story of Oedipus, we must admit, is a despicable tale about a man categorically fated to commit the double taboo of patricide and incest. Why would anyone be interested in a play about such a character? The answer, of course, is that the plot of *Oedipus* is not about a man who killed his father and married his mother. It is rather about a man who discovers late in life that he has killed his father and married his mother. The distinction here is vital. Whereas the story of Oedipus is about committing a taboo sin, the plot of *Oedipus* is about the triumph of self-discovery. In terms of his overall story, Oedipus is one of the most pathetic men imaginable, trapped by a cruel and evil fate he cannot escape. In the confines of the plot, however, he is a noble, courageous man who chooses to seek the truth about himself no matter the consequences.

Though generations of readers have tried to pin on Oedipus a "tragic flaw" that leads to his downfall, a careful reading of the play shows that Oedipus's demise is not brought about by his negative qualities—his pride or rashness or paranoia. Rather, it is his good qualities—his love of his people and devotion to the truth—that propel him to uncover secrets about himself that a less brave or dedicated man would have left alone. (We could say the same thing of Achilles: that his wrath rises up more from his noble qualities than his ignoble ones.) Oedipus is, supremely, the riddle solver, and he will not let fear or danger hold him back from a pursuit that will lead him to the truth. Oedipus loves Thebes as much as Hektor loves Troy, and he will not allow her to suffer from a plague—even if in healing that plague he brings about his own destruction.

The riddle of the Sphinx that Oedipus answers runs as follows: What animal walks on four legs in the morning, two legs in the afternoon, and three legs at night? The answer is Man: As a child he crawls on all fours, as an adult he walks on two legs, and as an old man he walks with a cane. Man in the generic sense is the answer to the Sphinx's riddle, but the answer to the riddle of the play is a specific man named Oedipus who is unafraid to risk all for the goal of self-discovery.

The Oedipus of the story is an unwilling victim, thwarted on every side by fate. The Oedipus of the plot is a willing scapegoat who chooses to bear upon himself the weight of a sin for which he is not morally or consciously responsible. In the opening scene of the play, he tells the Thebans who crowd around him:

> Your several sorrows each have single scope
> and touch but one of you. My spirit groans
> for city and myself and you at once. (62-64)[2]

Like the scapegoat of Yom Kippur, Oedipus feels as though the sorrows of every citizen have been transferred onto his head. In the concluding scene, he takes those sorrows (and sins) and carries them with him out of the *polis*.

At the end of the play Oedipus is triumphant, but it is a tragic triumph, the realization that what he now bears can be borne by him alone. Further, he realizes that although the god Apollo, who issued the oracle from Delphi, is responsible for his fate, he alone chose his punishment:

> It was Apollo, friends, Apollo,
> that brought this bitter bitterness, my sorrows to completion.
> But the hand that struck me
> was none but my own. (1329-31).

Oedipus, who has been morally blind all his life to his true identity, finds in physical blindness true insight and understanding. In fact, in his late play *Oedipus at Colonus* (part of a different trilogy), Sophocles allows us a glimpse of the final day of Oedipus's long and tragic life. Old, blind, exiled, Oedipus (like the Orestes of Aeschylus's *Eumenides*) finds rest in the environs of Athens. No longer a moral contagion, he has been trans-

---

[2]Citations are from *Oedipus*, trans. David Grene, in *Sophocles I*, vol. 3 of *The Complete Greek Tragedies*, ed. David Grene and Richmond Lattimore (Chicago: University of Chicago Press, 1954).

formed into a holy figure whose mystical death brings blessing upon the city of Athens. As a proud citizen of the Athenian *polis*, Sophocles, like Aeschylus before him, seems to be assuring his fellow citizens that Athens offers the outcasts and exiles of the world a place of refuge where they can find not only rest for their souls but reconciliation for their spiritual and emotional struggles.

CATHARSIS AS CLARIFICATION

In the face of a cruel and crushing fate, *Oedipus* champions the free will and integrity of its hero. That does not mean, however, that the play simply dismisses divine necessity and the overarching rule of destiny. Like the Bible itself, the play affirms both sides of the apparent paradox. The playgoer who experiences the tragedy—and *Oedipus* is something that must be experienced—leaves the theater not only with a respect and even awe for its central scapegoat but with a renewed sense that there is a higher purpose at work in the universe.

To explain how this is achieved, however, I need to back up and return to the *Poetics*. According to Aristotle, tragedy "is an imitation of an action that . . . through pity and fear effect[s] the proper purgation of these emotions" (VI.2). The Greek word here translated as "purgation" is *catharsis*, a word that has entered our own language unaltered and that has proved to be the single most controversial word in the entire *Poetics*. *Catharsis*, which Aristotle uses but once in the *Poetics*, has been translated by critics in at least three different ways: "purgation," "purification" and "clarification."

According to the purgation theory of catharsis, tragedy is a therapeutic experience that works on us like an enema or an emetic. It cleanses us of our emotions of pity and fear and thus leaves us more fit and able to face the rigors of life. When viewing *Oedipus*, the tragic end of the hero is so pitiful and fearful, so emotionally overwhelming, that we leave the theater feeling drained, as if our emotions have been swept away on a tide. We feel pity, Aristotle tells us, when we watch a good man suffer undeservedly; we feel fear when we realize that the same may happen to us. *Oedipus* rouses both emotions in us, for not only do we know he committed his crimes in ignorance, but we also realize, perhaps unconsciously, that we might someday discover something in our own past that will destroy us. If we are believing Christians, we might even see in Oedipus the reflection of our own inherited sinful nature.

According to the more spiritual purification theory of catharsis, tragedy does not so much purge our emotions as purify them. Just as God uses suffering to strengthen our faith (Job 23:10; 1 Peter 1:7), so the hot furnace of tragedy tests and tries our emotions like gold in the fire. To experience *Oedipus*, to see that a man can rise above himself and put self-discovery ahead of all else, is to have our emotions raised to a higher level. In the end, we are left with a strange sense of calm. We feel, along with Julian of Norwich, that "all will be well, and all will be well, and all manner of thing will be well."

According to the clarification theory of catharsis, tragedy sparks in us an intellectual response, a searing moment of perfect clarity. In this almost mystical moment of enlightenment, our ill-defined emotions are carried up into a higher realm of balanced, harmonious rationality, a realm where the higher patterns and forces of the cosmos are suddenly made visible. This is how we feel at the end of *Oedipus*, when we realize that Oedipus must suffer; if he does not, the prophecy will prove untrue and fate will be exposed as arbitrary and chaotic. The sudden illumination or epiphany that we experience at the end of the play is that order and purpose do exist in the universe, even if we cannot fathom the exact nature of that order and purpose. Of course, such a cosmological scheme places limits around mankind; in fact, the plot of *Oedipus* reminds us that the divine will is ultimately impenetrable and irresistible and that to attempt either to understand or resist it is futile. However, as noted earlier, within this limited, restricted world-order we are still able to act freely and boldly. As human beings we may be limited, but we are not powerless; like Oedipus, we are capable of greatness. A verse from the Proverbs comes to mind: "It is the glory of God to conceal a thing: but the honour of kings is to search out a matter" (Proverbs 25:2).

In reading the Gospels or viewing a passion play, we experience a similar catharsis but on a much larger, grander scale. In the Gospels (especially John), Christ is portrayed as the Lamb of God, the sinless scapegoat who takes on the sins of the world and, by so doing, cleanses away original sin and restores balance to the divine scales of justice. Whereas in *Oedipus* the only people directly purged are the Thebans, in the tragedy where the hero is Christ, the entire world is purged. We discover, to our great joy, that though the cosmic order is limited and restricted and though the divine will is ultimately inscrutable, behind that will is a personal, merciful God whose great love drove him to be both Prometheus and Oedipus: both the divine scapegoat who ends the cycle of vengeance and the human scapegoat who rescues us from the plague.

12

SOPHOCLES' *ANTIGONE* AND *ELECTRA*

Questions of Duty

SOPHOCLES WAS CLEARLY DRAWN TO the tragic tale of Oedipus and his descendants. In addition to the two separate trilogies that include *Oedipus* and *Oedipus at Colonus*, he wrote at least one more trilogy on the family of Oedipus that includes the tragedy *Antigone*. Along with *Oedipus*, it is the most enduring and often staged of Sophocles' seven extant plays. It is also arguably the play from ancient Athens with the most direct parallels to our own day. (In 1942, the French playwright Jean Anouilh presented an updated version of *Antigone* as a means of protesting the hypocrisy and suppression of the Vichy government; tellingly, Anouilh's version does not stray far from the original.) In *Antigone*, Sophocles—in a manner that has lost none of its relevance—pits the needs of the state against the needs of the individual, duty to the *polis* against duty to one's family. As I shall show, the decisions Antigone makes in the play not only challenged the ethics and mores of Sophocles' contemporaries, but continue to challenge us today.

THE UNWRITTEN LAW

According to a legend that would have been well known to Sophocles' audience, after Oedipus is sent into exile, the kingship is turned over to his two sons, Eteocles and Polyneices, with Creon, their uncle, acting as regent. When the two boys come of age, they agree to share their rule by alternating back and forth between them. Eteocles takes the first "shift" and rules Thebes well; however, when his year is up and the time comes to release control to his brother, he refuses. Sibling rivalry quickly escalates into civil strife, and Polyneices, along with six other hand-picked warriors, attacks Thebes (an event immortalized in Aeschylus's *Seven Against Thebes*). In the ensuing battle the two brothers kill each other, and the rule of the city passes to Creon. Hoping to prevent any further strife, Creon issues an edict that while Eteocles is to be given a lavish state burial, the body of the traitor Polyneices—who despite his just grievance did betray Thebes—is to be left unwept and unburied, food for birds and dogs. He further decrees that anyone who violates the edict will be put to death as an enemy of the state.

Unfortunately for Creon, Antigone, the sister of Eteocles and Polyneices, cares little for her uncle's reasons of state and secretly sprinkles the dirt of burial on Polyneices' body. Antigone knows, as did all the Greeks of Sophocles' day, that the spirit of a dead man cannot find rest in the underworld unless he is given the proper burial rites. A modern reader need not stretch too much to understand Antigone's determination to supply her brother with such rites. Even in our own day, which has moved beyond ancient superstitions, most people would be angry and scandalized if a corpse—even that of an enemy—were to be mistreated and left to rot. We may no longer believe that a proper burial is necessary for the soul of the deceased to find rest, but we do maintain our essential, inborn sense that to desecrate a human body is to break a very ancient and very real taboo. Indeed, we need not work too hard to construct a hypothetical modern parallel. Imagine if a pious Roman Catholic woman were to be forbidden by an authoritarian and insensitive priest from saying a rosary in memory of her dead brother, because her brother had committed acts of which the priest did not approve. Like Antigone before her, I'm sure that this woman would say the rosary nonetheless, even if the priest were to threaten her with excommunication.

Antigone's moral dilemma is a universal one, and its dimensions extend not only to the religious sphere but to the social and political as well. In chapter nine I argued that the Athenians who gathered at the theater of Dionysus were participating in an experience that was at once aesthetic, religious and political. In chapter ten I suggested that Aeschylus's *Oresteia* sought not only to celebrate on the religious level the triumph of the gods of civilization over the vengeful Furies, but to contrast on the political level an older law that privileged blood ties with a newer one that hailed more abstract notions of justice as supreme, even over the claims of individual piety. Sophocles takes up a similar dichotomy in his play, but he narrows the scope of the conflict to a single decision between a *polis*-minded ruler and his family-minded niece, and he allows the claims of blood to have a fuller say than they do in Aeschylus's trilogy. Furthermore, at a crucial dramatic moment he boldly reaches out to an older, immortal law that is higher and deeper than either the family or the *polis*. Before considering that immortal law, however, let us step back and consider the political state of Athens at the time of Sophocles' writing.

During the golden age, when the plays of Aeschylus, Sophocles, and Euripides were first seen, Athens was still a fledgling democracy. Though she had survived a foreign invasion by Persia, the most powerful empire of the time, and had gone on to become the premier *polis* of Greece, her experiment in democracy was still very much an experiment. Like modern Americans, the citizens of Athens were required to serve periodically on juries, but their duties did not stop there. The majority of citizens were also expected to serve directly in the inner workings of the government. If you were an Athenian citizen, you could count on at least two things: (1) that significant power would be put into your hands at several points in your life; (2) that once you had exercised that power, it would be taken away from you and passed on to a new individual or group. In most cases, those who wielded power were placed there because they were selected by lot rather than elected by vote. Even Socrates, that most apolitical and impractical of philosophers, found himself once in a situation where the power of life and death was put in his hands (don't worry: he did the right thing!). Oddly, one of the few times citizens actually voted was in the uniquely Athenian practice of ostracism. If the people felt that a certain politician was getting too powerful, they could write his name on a broken potsherd (*ostrica* in Greek) and throw it into a well. If enough *ostrica* were cast, the politician would be exiled from Athens for ten years, during which time his property and possessions were kept safe. This political safety valve was practiced quite often in fifth-century B.C. Athens and often resulted in the ostracism of powerful generals—including several who had been responsible for saving Athens from Persia.

Needless to say, the Athenians who attended the first performance of *Antigone* in 441 B.C. understood intimately the intricacies of power and how easily such power could corrupt those who wielded it. After all, it had been only forty years since they had defeated an Asiatic tyrant and only seventy years since they had expelled the last Athenian tyrant from their *polis*. Neither politics nor religion was a taboo subject in Athens; to the contrary, public discussion of the major ethical-religious and sociopolitical issues of the day was frequent and continuous. That discussion extended into the precinct of the theater. To most modern Americans, the idea that the stage could serve such a function seems strange indeed. Indeed, most tend to view the arts in general as either simple mass entertainment or a source of private controversy indulged in by marginalized elites. Our government may engage in periodic political debates over the status and funding of the arts, but alas, the arts themselves rarely draw together a large body of citizens into any type of serious debate over public standards, decisions or policies. When an Athenian citizen entered the arena of the theater of Dionysus, he went to see, to wrestle, and to be challenged, not to be seen or to be amused or to pass the time.

As though he expects his audience to be geared up for serious wrestling, Sophocles, in a manner typical of his dramaturgy, immediately catapults his audience into the dilemmas that will be showcased in his tragedy. On to the stage rush Antigone and her sister Ismene. Creon has already passed his decree, and Antigone has already vowed that she will violate it. Ismene sympathizes with her but is reluctant to break the law set forth by her uncle. The play is less than five minutes old, and we in the audience are already being forced to take the side of either Antigone or Ismene. This is not an easy task; though Antigone has the greater claim to our respect, the gentle and cautious Ismene is more likeable than her rash, headstrong, somewhat prideful sister. Of course Antigone is morally right, but why must she make such a fuss and make things so difficult for her sister and, by extension, her fellow citizens? Cannot she just let the matter drop? Later in the play, when she has a second encounter with Ismene, we discover that Antigone (like Prometheus, Oedipus and Thomas Becket, the hero of T. S. Eliot's modern Greek tragedy *Murder in the Cathedral*) suffers from something of a martyr complex; she feels that she alone is strong enough and worthy enough to suffer. Sophocles, like Homer (who depicts Hektor in more "likeable" terms than Achilles), refuses to make it easy for us.

After Ismene and Antigone leave the stage, the chorus appears and takes the side of the status quo, as is the case in nearly all Greek tragedies. Creon, who enters as the first choral song ends, is convinced he is doing the right thing, and the chorus does not tell him different. They, like Ismene, are eager to see Thebes return to her former life of peace and security. For his own part, Creon sees himself as objective and selfless; he does what he does for the state and not to satisfy any individual desire. But Creon's smug assurance will not last long; a messenger rushes onto the stage to inform him that the dirt of burial has been found on the body of Polyneices. For a second, the timid members of the chorus risk pricking Creon's conscience, suggesting that this mysterious rite of burial may have been the work of the gods.

Creon turns against them in anger and begins to accuse the soldiers who were supposed to guard the body of accepting bribes. Ironically, Creon here hurls the same paranoid accusations against his guards that Oedipus hurls against him in *Oedipus*. As if to further connect the two plays (with *Antigone*, written about fifteen years before *Oedipus*, being the antecedent play), Sophocles later has Creon fall into a debate with the prophet Tiresias. Just as he warns Oedipus, Tiresias warns Creon to stop what he is doing, but Creon, like Oedipus, responds by accusing him of taking bribes. Clearly the sins of pride and rashness are engraved deeply in the tragic House of Thebes. It is as if the characters of Creon and Antigone represent two sides of Oedipus warring against each other. The family of Oedipus is a family that devours itself, for it cannot reconcile within itself the competing claims of political necessity and filial ties, duty and piety, law and nature, passivity and aggression. These tensions are held in suspension within the tightly woven plot of the play, and the audience that experiences them—whether in ancient Athens or modern America—cannot help but join the wrestling.

Inevitably Creon and Antigone meet face to face, and when Creon accuses her of deliberately breaking the law, Antigone speaks the lines that express the central dilemma of the play:

> For me it was not Zeus who made that order.
> Nor did that Justice who lives with the gods below
> mark out such laws to hold among mankind.
> Nor did I think your orders were so strong
> that you, a mortal man, could over-run
> the gods' unwritten and unfailing laws.
> Not now, nor yesterday's, they always live,
> and no one knows their origin in time. (450-57)[1]

Whether the hearer of these lines is a pagan, Christian or agnostic, Antigone's plea for the existence of a higher law that trumps human laws cannot help but inspire awe and fear. Indeed, the very power of Antigone's words rests on the fact that both she and Creon—and all human beings whose consciences have not been seared—are aware of the existence of this immortal, unwritten law. Paul declares boldly in Romans that "when the Gentiles, which have not the law, do by nature the things contained in the law, these, having not the law, are a law unto themselves: which shew the work of the law written in their hearts, their conscience also bearing witness, and their thoughts the mean while accusing or else excusing one another" (Romans 2:14-15). Anyone who doubts Paul's assertion that the pre-Christian, unregenerate Greeks were capable of grasping the existence of the law need only read this passage from *Antigone*. The pagans of classical Greece, despite their tales of deceitful, violent, and philandering gods, knew that such things as justice and law existed and that these could not be breached with impunity.

---

[1]My text is *Antigone,* trans. Elizabeth Wyckoff, in *Sophocles I,* vol. 3 of *The Complete Greek Tragedies,* ed. David Grene and Richmond Lattimore (Chicago: University of Chicago Press, 1954).

Politics was more than a game for the citizens of Athens; like religion, it rested on the dim but real perception of an unchanging moral law that was not manmade but revealed through the conscience. As Paul suggests, in the absence of the direct revelation of Scripture, it is precisely through the conscience that God speaks the rudiments of his law. In reading *Antigone,* we who live this side of the Enlightenment and the New Testament see that our ethical struggles and debates, both in the political and spiritual realms, are not all that different from those of fifth-century B.C. Athens. In America today, the legal and judicial battle over the nature of choice, whether it relates to homeschooling and school vouchers, abortion and euthanasia, or sodomy laws and gay marriage, ultimately pits the wants and needs of the individual against those of society as a whole. Even issues like states' rights, gun control and social security are framed in a family-versus-*polis* paradigm that bears comparison with the central dilemma of Sophocles' play. Furthermore, and this is where the connection becomes the most trenchant, when Americans debate these issues, they eventually attempt to call on a higher law against which the two sides of the debate can be measured. And it is not just traditional orthodox Christians who do so. In the case of gay marriage, for example, many secular progressives appeal to what they perceive as a higher law of inclusivism and egalitarianism to justify their side of the argument.

As for the more theological dimensions of Antigone's speech, they too are compelling and suggest a strong link between the ancient Greek and the modern Christian. According to orthodox doctrine, human beings, though fallen, were created by God as moral, volitional agents with a sense of right and wrong and an inner impulse to seek the former and shun the latter. If Creon had no sense of the law of which Antigone speaks, he would not be a tragic figure; if the audience did not share this sense, the dilemma of the play would be meaningless and they would experience no catharsis. The very existence of *Antigone*—and of Greek tragedy in general—presupposes our innate status as ethical animals who know we should live and act a certain way but find that we cannot. Is it not ironic (and thrilling) that a pre-Christian play written by a pagan could have the power to convince an audience of a truth that Christian apologists spend their lives trying to prove?

By the end of the play, Creon, with the help of the chorus, comes to see the error of his ways and repents of his actions—but it is too late. In quick succession he learns that not only Antigone but his son, who intended to marry Antigone, and his wife have all committed suicide. Creon has violated the very order of things, has upset both the moral law and the law of the *polis,* and he must live to see the destructive effects of that violation. "Whoever thinks that he alone is wise," his son Haemon warns him, "his eloquence, his mind, above the rest, / come the unfolding, shows his emptiness" (707-9). Though Antigone may be seen as the sacrificial lamb slaughtered on the altar of state, Creon is arguably the real scapegoat—the one who must bear on his head the full weight of the sins of his community and his family. He is not, like Oedipus, exiled, but he is condemned to live the rest of his life in an inner self-exile; he shall be quite literally his own executioner.

THE PIETY OF WOMEN

In addition to dramatizing the eternal struggle between the state and the individual, the *polis* and the family, *Antigone* sets in opposition a more masculine reverence for law and order with a more feminine reverence for piety. Modern feminism has attacked the traditional practice of defining women in terms of their relationships with other people (especially other men) rather than as separate, self-defined beings. Thus, they argue, while we think of a man as an island or a country unto himself, we categorize a woman as the mother or sister or daughter or wife of someone else. Ironically, many of those who would consider themselves traditional orthodox Christians have jumped on this feminist bandwagon. I say ironically because many of these same Christians have rightly critiqued the exalted place our modern, post-Enlightenment world has ascribed to the autonomous individual. Rather than inscribing the individual within a web of mutual duties and responsibilities, the modern world seeks to free the individual from all entangling alliances. In the place of communal man (defined by his role and status in the family or the group), we get existential man (born without purpose or essence and left to make his own way in an alienated world).

Traditionally it has been the females of the species who have reminded

us of our interconnectedness, who have in fact been proud to be thought
of primarily as sisters and daughters, mothers and wives. Indeed, this feminine insistence on the centrality and inviolability of familial and provincial
ties has acted, as it does in *Antigone,* as a counterbalance to the male tendency to surrender himself, like Creon, to abstract causes and principles.
As living apologists for the blood that links us to our family and the social
obligations that tie us to our neighbor, women have always exerted considerable influence in society, even (and especially) when they have been denied the direct reins of political power. The feminine voice is one that remembers and enshrines, grieves and binds together. While male
politicians run after utopian dreams of power, world government or global
peace, women have reminded us of the smaller, dearer things that truly
matter.

Though women held little to no political power in ancient Athens, and
though they did not possess equal rights in our modern sense of the phrase,
their voice was strongly heard in the works of Aeschylus, Sophocles and
Euripides: works that were created for public consumption. In both *Antigone* and *Electra,* the eponymous heroines speak for the rights of the dead
and the bonds of familial piety. Indeed, Electra, who holds true the memory of her father Agamemnon and waits patiently for her brother Orestes
to return and take vengeance against Clytemnestra and Aegisthus, is a subject that clearly interested tragedians and audiences alike. It is, in fact, the
only subject for which we have extant plays from all three dramatists:
Sophocles' *Electra,* Euripides' *Electra* and Aeschylus's *Libation Bearers.*
Significantly, when Eugene O'Neill set himself the task of updating
Aeschylus's *Oresteia,* he chose to name his trilogy not after Orestes but
after his sister. His title, *Mourning Becomes Electra,* is of especial interest,
for although Aeschylus was O'Neill's primary source, the title of his play is
more indicative of Sophocles' treatment of the character.

In the Sophoclean version, Electra is first and foremost one who
mourns. At the outset of the play, she informs the chorus, "I will not / leave
my mourning for my poor father" (133-34).[2] "Suited rather to my heart,"

---

[2]My text is *Electra,* trans. David Grene, in *Sophocles II,* vol. 4 of *The Complete Greek Tragedies,* ed. David
Grene and Richard Lattimore (Chicago: University of Chicago Press, 1957).

she asserts, "[is] the bird of mourning / that 'Itys, Itys' ever does lament, / the bird of crazy sorrow, Zeus' messenger" (146-49). Though all may forget, she will not. She has forsaken all her chances to have a husband and children of her own and lives only for the hope that her brother will return. "But I am waiting for Orestes' coming," she tells the chorus, "waiting forever for the one who will stop / all our wrongs. I wait and wait and die" (302-4). Though the situation is essentially the same in Aeschylus's *Libation Bearers*, Sophocles adds a detail that binds brother and sister more closely together: it was Electra who saved the young Orestes from Clytemnestra and Aegisthus after her father's murder. Sophocles also adds another sibling, Chrysothemis, whom he can set in contrast to Electra in a manner similar to the Ismene-Antigone contrast. Though Chrysothemis honors her father and brother, she considers Electra both foolish and stubborn. She counsels her to give over her grief and be reconciled with her mother, but Electra, like Antigone (and Prometheus and Oedipus and Achilles) scorns such cowardly and ignoble advice.

Oddly, the person in the play who is most like Electra is not Chrysothemis or even Orestes, but the person she most despises: her mother. Sophocles makes it clear that Clytemnestra grieves as strongly and inconsolably for Iphigenia, the daughter her husband killed, as Electra does for Agamemnon, the father her mother killed. Perhaps Electra must grieve for Agamemnon rather than Iphigenia precisely because her mother has done the opposite. They are two sides of the same coin: women who have allowed their grief to consume them. Though Sophocles ultimately celebrates Electra's devotion, he does not do so uncritically. Like Hamlet, the grieving Electra is both moody and unstable; much of her hatred of her mother (like that of Hamlet for Gertrude) is based on an intense, repressed sexual disgust over her mother's relations with the less worthy Aegisthus. And yet the passion Electra expresses throughout the play seems somehow more appropriate than the colder, more methodical approach taken by Orestes. The latter is concerned simply with righting a breach in the laws of justice; the former seeks atonement for a broken taboo, restitution for a father shamed, and healing for a shattered family. Orestes' character in the play rises up from what he does; Electra's character is defined by who she is and how she relates to those around her.

In the extreme form represented by Creon, male rage for abstract order and justice can backfire and leave us empty and alienated; in the equally extreme form represented by Electra, the female rage for undying familial piety no matter the cost can also backfire and leave us bereft of a future and a hope. Only when these two forces are kept in a complementary balance—and aligned with a higher, eternal standard of truth—can family and *polis* alike find peace. The fact that neither Creon nor Electra finds this balance is what makes their stories so tragic. But in presenting these tragedies, Sophocles surely hoped that we in the audience might find that elusive balance for ourselves and our communities. "But now," Paul exhorts the mostly Greek church of Corinth, "hath God set the members every one of them in the body, as it hath pleased him. And if they were all one member, where were the body? But now are they many members, yet but one body" (1 Corinthians 12:18-20).

13

SOPHOCLES' WOMEN OF TRACHIS AND PHILOCTETES

The Tragedy of Character

OF THE THREE GREAT TRAGEDIANS OF the golden age, Sophocles is considered to have most perfected the tragedy of character. Despite the fact that Aristotle privileged plot over character, it is nevertheless the resolute nature of Sophocles' heroes and heroines that drives the plots and resolutions of his plays. Whether solving the riddle of the Sphinx or the riddle of his own birth, Oedipus is supremely the riddle solver; he cannot allow unknown things to remain hidden but must seek out the truth that waits in the dark. Antigone must obey the higher laws of piety even when they clash with the human laws of state; indeed, she is as faithful to these laws as she is ruthless in trampling down those who would prevent her from fulfilling them. Electra, the one who mourns, will not change in her devotion though love, youth, freedom and joy should all desert her.

In cataloguing the intransigent natures of these three Sophoclean protagonists, I do not mean to reduce their characters to a single "tragic flaw." Earlier I argued that if Oedipus does have such a flaw, it is more closely tied to his virtues than his vices: namely, his love of his people and commitment to the truth. Aristotle makes it clear in his *Poetics* that the true tragic hero must be a good man; if he were a simple villain we would feel neither pity nor fear over his fate. The point of Sophocles' plays is not to blame the victim but to understand in that moment of tragic clarification that though we are not beasts, we are also not gods. Our nature lies somewhere in between, and we are just as incapable of achieving human perfection and immortality as we are of completely eradicating the beast within. As we saw in part one, this central Sophoclean struggle also lies at the heart of Achilles and his godlike wrath.

In what is most likely his earliest play, *Ajax*, we already see Sophocles' fascination with characters whose natures are fixed and unswerving. When Ajax's wife counsels him to soften his anger, he replies, "You have a foolish thought / If you think at this late date to school my nature" (595-96).[1] Although the Greeks lacked a clear concept of original sin, Sophocles understood the inner contradictions of human nature and the universal tendency toward self-destruction. He knew as well the paradoxical truth that what destroys us is often that which defines us. For we who have access to the Bible, the answer to the riddle at the core of our nature appears obvious: we are beings who were created in the image of a good God but who have fallen. But like so many simple truths, it is obvious only because it has been revealed. The Greeks, bereft of the Torah, were left to wrestle their way into their own tentative answer. And one of the arenas in which they chose to wrestle was the theater.

THE BEAST WITHIN

Heracles (Hercules in Latin) was, along with Theseus, the hero most responsible for freeing Greece from bestial rule. Before their time monsters like the Hydra, the Minotaur and the Nemean lion, along with monstrous men like Procrustes, who forced travelers to fit his bed by either stretching them on the rack or lopping off their feet, held the ancient Greeks in perpetual fear. That is, until these two legendary strongmen arrived on the

---

[1]My texts for *Ajax*, *Women of Trachis* and *Philoctetes* are taken from *Sophocles II*, vol. 4 of *The Complete Greek Tragedies*, ed. David Grene and Richard Lattimore (Chicago: University of Chicago Press, 1957).

scene to clean up the roads and liberate the forests. Heracles, the son of Zeus and a mortal woman, was most responsible for ridding civilization of the beasts that wanted to destroy it. During the course of his many labors, he not only killed the many-headed Hydra and the Nemean lion (whose pelt he wore as a trophy), but the boar of Eyrmanthus, the Stymphalian birds and the fire-breathing bull of Crete. He even traveled to hell, where he captured Cerberus, the three-headed dog of Hades.

And yet for all his victories over these beasts, Heracles (like Achilles or Samson) could never quite conquer the beast within. His temper was as legendary as his exploits, and his lust for battle and beautiful women (again like Samson) ultimately undid him. Indeed, the events that led to his tragic end, which Sophocles dramatizes in *Women of Trachis*, was set in motion by his defeat of two beasts who threatened the chastity and honor of his most lovely battle prize, Deianira. The first was a fearsome god named Achelous; by besting him in close combat Heracles won the hand of Deianira. On the day of their wedding, the newlyweds came to a river, where the centaur Nessus offered to ferry Deianira across on his back. When they were midway across the river, however, the lewd and brutal centaur attempted to assault the new bride. Hearing her cries for help, Heracles drew an arrow tipped with the Hydra's poison and shot Nessus. As the centaur lay dying, he encouraged the naïve bride to take some of his blood, mingled now with the venom of the Hydra, and keep it as a potion. If ever Heracles were to fall in love with another, he promised her, she had only to dress him in a shirt dipped in the blood and it would act as a strong love charm to turn Heracles' thoughts back to her.

When the play opens in medias res, Heracles and Deianira have been married for many years and are the parents of a grown son, Hyllus. Heracles has been away performing his labors, but word has just reached Deianira that he is on his way home. As she muses on his long-awaited homecoming, Deianira shares with her nurse her memories of her first suitor:

> While I still lived in Pleuron, with Oeneus my father,
> I conceived an agonizing fear of marriage.
> No other Aetolian woman ever felt such fear,
> for my suitor was the river Achelous,

who used to come to ask my father for my hand,
taking three forms—first, clearly a bull, and then
a serpent with shimmering coils, then a man's body
but a bull's face, and from his clump of beard
whole torrents of water splashed like a fountain.
I had to think this suitor would be my husband
and in my unhappiness I constantly prayed for death
before I should ever come to his marriage bed. (6-17)

Sigmund Freud found in Sophocles' *Oedipus* the unconscious dramatization of a repressed libidinous desire he believed all male toddlers felt for their mothers. He found the flip side of this so-called Oedipus complex, a libidinous desire felt by female toddlers for their fathers, in Sophocles' *Electra,* and appropriately dubbed it the Electra complex. Whether we agree or disagree with Freud's psychoanalytical readings of *Oedipus* and *Electra,* it is clear in the passage quoted above that Sophocles did understand the nature of repressed sexuality.

In her powerful use of imagery—the shimmering coils, the man's body with a bull's face, the clump of beard, the torrent of water—and in equating death with the marriage bed, Deianira betrays a deepset, probably unconscious fear of male sexuality. She seems unwilling to move from innocence into experience, partly because she can think of physical union only in terms of brutality and even bestiality. Like many young (and not-so-young) people, she fears intimacy and wants to protect herself from passions she cannot control or understand. I do not say these things to shock the reader but to emphasize how quickly and efficiently Sophocles delves into the inner workings of his heroine's psyche. We not only understand and sympathize with her fears and anxieties, but we feel a strong urge to protect and console her. She has bared her soul to us, and we will not abandon her even when she makes her fatal decision.

As the play progresses, Deianira learns that Heracles has essentially destroyed a kingdom, all because he has developed a lustful passion for the daughter of a king—a passion no less strong or brutal than that of Achelous for Deianira. The unfortunate princess, Iole, has been brought into Deianira's home to await the arrival of Heracles. When the sensitive and high-strung Deianira realizes that she will have to share her bed with this captive whom she both hates and feels drawn to, she becomes desperate to regain her husband's affections. It is then that she remembers the lustful centaur who had given her a vial of his blood. Naively trusting Nessus's words, she dips a shirt in the blood and has it sent as a present to Heracles to wear for his homecoming. Alas, the moment he puts on the shirt, the Hydra-tainted blood clings to Heracles' flesh and begins to consume him. Though we in the audience cannot blame the desperate Deianira for her folly, she finds it impossible to forgive herself and commits suicide. Significantly, she does not hang herself, as do Jocasta and Antigone, but penetrates her body with a sword while lying on the sheets of her marriage bed. It is as if the fears expressed in the opening lines of the play have seized control of her and shaped themselves into a self-fulfilling prophecy.

It is telling that of the seven extant plays of Sophocles, only this one does not bear as its title the name of its protagonist. Rather, like Aeschylus's *Libations Bearers* and *Eumenides,* the title *Women of Trachis* refers to the chorus. By choosing such a title, Sophocles perhaps cautions his readers against placing either Deianira or Heracles at the center of the play. Whereas the former dominates the first half of the play, the latter dominates the second; in fact, they do not interact at all during the course of the action. On the one hand, this split focus weakens the play's plot structure; it is far less "tight" than *Oedipus* or *Antigone.* On the other hand, it deepens the characterization, for it pits husband and wife against each other in a mirror-image structure. Like his wife, Heracles does not understand the full nature of lust or its potentially destructive power. Like her husband, Deianira burns with an inner hatred and fear that would strip all that is bestial from the world. Heracles, like Deianira, also ends the play as a suicide; tormented by the shirt of Nessus, he can find relief only by forcing his unwilling son to immolate his pain-wracked body on a sacrificial pyre. As Deianira's fear of male sexuality ends with her own self-penetration, so Heracles' inability to control the passionate fire raging within ends with his being consumed by fire.

In *Ajax,* Sophocles' invincible warrior commits suicide by stabbing himself with the sword of the dead Hektor; in *Women of Trachis,* Sophocles' equally invincible hero is killed by the blood of the dead Nessus. In both cases, a famous slayer is himself slain by a token from the past, something he thought was powerless to hurt him. Near the end of *Women of Trachis,*

Heracles remembers that his father, Zeus, had prophesied that he "should die by nothing that draws breath / but by something dead, an inhabitant of Hell" (1160-61). Heracles learns too late that the lust for steel has the power to breed its own destruction, that it is hard to put the sword back in its sheath once it has been drawn. Ajax, Heracles and Deianira (like Oedipus, Antigone and Electra) are powerless to escape from their own natures, from what Paul calls the "old man" in Romans 6:6. Their own tragic ends are written deep in their characters.

"Mother!" says Hyllus to Deianira after he learns that his father is being consumed by the shirt of Nessus, "I wish I could have found you not as you are / but no longer alive, or safe but someone else's / mother, or somehow changed and with a better heart / than now" (734-37). But alas, the pre-Christian world of Sophocles knew of no power that could change the inner nature of fallen humanity. That may be the greatest tragedy of all.

OUT OF THE WHIRLWIND

Along with *Ajax* and *Heracles,* Sophocles provides us in his extant plays one final soldier whose unswerving nature makes him both nobly heroic and tragically inflexible. His name is Philoctetes, and he bears the distinction of having in his possession the very bow and arrows used by Heracles to kill Nessus. He travels with the Greeks to fight at Troy, but he accidentally breaks a taboo when he trespasses on a sacred shrine. As a result of this trespass, Philoctetes is bitten in the heel by a poisonous serpent, which leaves a festering wound from which he can find no release. Eventually, the stench of his wound and his incessant cries of pain lead the Greek generals to maroon the wretched soldier on the deserted island of Lemnos. There Philoctetes lives as a miserable castaway throughout the long ten years of the war; only his bow allows him to capture small game and survive.

Philoctetes the play begins in the tenth and final year of the war. Though the uncaring generals have long erased the suffering Philoctetes from their memory, they learn from a prophecy that they will never be able to take Troy without the bow of Heracles. As they have treated Philoctetes so treacherously, they know full well that he will not simply give them the bow, so Odysseus, who was originally responsible for having him marooned, devises a plan to wrest it from him. Although in the *Odyssey*

Homer portrays Odysseus as a crafty but noble hero, in the Greek tragedies Odysseus is a Machiavellian villain who uses his craftiness to deceive
and manipulate. The Odysseus of Sophocles (and of Euripides) is first and
foremost a practitioner of political expediency; like the sons of Atreus
(Menelaus and Agamemnon), he does whatever it takes to achieve his
goals. In our day of increasing corporate greed and white-collar fraud, he
is an all-too-familiar figure.

As he knows Philoctetes will kill him the moment he lays eyes on him,
Odysseus takes with him Neoptolemus, the young and noble son of the
recently deceased Achilles. Like Achilles, Philoctetes is a pure and honorable soldier who despises the wiles of both Odysseus and the sons of
Atreus; Odysseus reasons correctly that Philoctetes will see in Neoptolemus a kindred spirit whom he can trust. In the opening scene of the play,
Odysseus explains the situation to Neoptolemus and instructs him to win
over the confidence of Philoctetes so that he can then steal the bow of
Heracles. Their differing views on the matter show the contrast in their
natures:

> ODYSSEUS: I know, young man, it is not your natural bent
> to say such things nor to contrive such mischief.
> But the prize of victory is pleasant to win.
> Bear up: another time we shall prove honest.
> For one brief shameless portion of a day
> give me yourself, and then for all the rest
> you may be called most scrupulous of men.
>
> NEOPTOLEMUS: Son of Laertes, what I dislike to hear
> I hate to put in execution.
> I have a natural antipathy
> to get my ends by tricks and stratagems.
> So, too, they say, my father was. Philoctetes
> I will gladly fight and capture, bring him with us,
> but not by treachery. (79-92)

As in *Women of Trachis*, Sophocles shows here his ability to quickly and efficiently lay bare the depths of his characters' souls. We know immediately
who these two men are, and we feel confident that though Neoptolemus
will be initially swayed by Odysseus's crafty words, he will in the end return

to his true nature. And that is exactly what happens.

But in working out Neoptolemus's moral dilemma, Sophocles turns what might be a cliché into a dramatic revelation of how character is formed. While Odysseus and Philoctetes are seasoned soldiers, Neoptolemus is a neophyte. Like Homer's Telemachus, he is the young, untested son of a legendary hero who has come to the point where he must choose his path. Over the course of the play, we watch intently as Neoptolemus subtly shifts his allegiance from Odysseus to Philoctetes, from one role model to another. At first, convinced that his primary responsibility is to assist Odysseus (and thus the Greek host), Neoptolemus models his behavior and even his speech patterns on those of the crafty son of Laertes. We see that he is uncomfortable doing so, that the effort runs counter to his unformed ideals, but he nevertheless persists in what he thinks is his duty. To make the whole situation more complicated, and more psychologically acute, Odysseus instructs Neoptolemus to win over Philoctetes' confidence by telling him that he, Neoptolemus, has been the victim of one of Odysseus's many deceits. Of course, as long as Neoptolemus struggles against the goodness that is in him, he is the victim he purports to be. As long as he allows Odysseus to ventriloquize him, he is nothing more than the puppet of a master politician.

Slowly, however, as he gets to know Philoctetes and perceives in him the true nobility that shone so brightly in Achilles but is absent in Odysseus and the sons of Atreus, the young soldier begins to see the situation through different eyes. Philoctetes has a dual effect on Neoptolemus that pulls him in two opposing directions. On the one hand, Philoctetes draws out depths of courage and integrity that Neoptolemus never knew he possessed; at one point, Philoctetes even allows the young man to hold the bow. On the other hand, as Hamlet does for his mother Gertrude, Philoctetes turns the mirror upon this deceiver-in-training that he might see the depth of the villainy into which he has fallen. Neoptolemus is horrified. "All is disgust," he cries, "when one leaves his own nature / and does things that misfit it" (902-3). In the end Neoptolemus does steal the bow from Philoctetes, but then in a fit of remorse he returns it to him. His experiences, however, have matured him, and he prevents Philoctetes from using his bow to kill Odysseus. Instead he begs Philoctetes to come with him to

Troy, where he may not only help the Greeks defeat their enemy but be healed of his wound by the sons of Asclepius. Though Neoptolemus speaks well in an ennobled rhetoric purged of the deceit of Odysseus, Philoctetes stubbornly refuses his request.

And that is when we remember that the title of the play is not *Neoptolemus* but *Philoctetes*. Though the young Neoptolemus has shown that he is capable of shuffling off the corrupting education of Odysseus, Philoctetes has grown too set in his ways to change. He will not—and ultimately cannot—change his inner nature; he prefers to nurse his grudges and pains rather than return home and be healed. The play has come to a deadlock: it will end neither with a suicide, like *Antigone;* a tragic clarification, like *Oedipus;* nor a longed-for resolution to cycles of vengeance, like the *Oresteia*. Suddenly, out of the sky, the spirit of the deified Heracles appears and commands Philoctetes to go to Troy. "Voice that stirs my yearning when I hear," cries the raptured Philoctetes, "form lost so long, / I shall not disobey" (1445-47). And so Philoctetes relents, and the play ends happily.

Though this manner of resolution may seem odd to modern readers, it was actually common among the tragedians of ancient Athens. Aristotle referred to such an ending as a *deus ex machina* ("god from the machine") after a crane-like device by which an actor could be lowered onto the stage in the guise of a god or goddess. The deus ex machina was used by dramatists as a way of resolving "from above" all manner of difficulties and misunderstandings. If the characters found themselves in a situation from which they could not extricate themselves, a god could be brought in to tidy up the loose ends and warn them away from disaster. Euripides used the device often, as we shall see later, and the seventeenth-century French playwright Molière even used it to comic effect in his play *Tartuffe*, in which Louis XIV must resolve, godlike, the troubles of the desperate characters.

Not surprisingly, Aristotle strongly disapproved of the deus ex machina; he considered it an artificial and illogical way to end a tragedy. A well-constructed plot, he felt, should be strong enough to resolve itself in a manner consistent with necessity, probability and inevitability. There should be no need for a divine intervention from above. Of course, in making this aesthetic pronouncement Aristotle betrays his commitment to a balanced, rational cosmos in which everything makes sense: a sort of deistic universe in which God need not intervene. Surely as a literary critic Aristotle was right in critiquing plots that could not resolve themselves. But was he right to do so as a philosopher?

What if a great playwright like Sophocles chose to employ the deus ex machina not as a dramatic crutch but as a way to comment philosophically on the nature of God, man and the universe? Might Sophocles not have used the deus ex machina at the end of *Philoctetes* to suggest that when the stubbornness of our intransigent human nature fails us, the gods can still rescue us from our folly? Despite the good choices made by Neoptolemus, his choices are rendered ineffective until a god appears to override the willfulness of Philoctetes. And not just any god, but the god-man Heracles: a savior who knows what it is to suffer as a human being but who dwells now on Mount Olympus with the deathless gods. Only to such a god will Philoctetes pay heed.

Midway through the play, Philoctetes calls out a challenge to the gods above:

> Nothing evil has yet perished.
> The Gods somehow give them [evil men] most excellent care.
> They find their pleasure in turning back from Death
> the rogues and tricksters, but the just and good
> they are always sending out of the world.
> How can I reckon the score, how can I praise
> when praising Heaven I find the Gods are bad? (446-52)

In his words of challenge, and in the torment that provokes them, Philoctetes sounds strangely like Job. In the language of theology, we would call Philoctetes' challenge a *theodicy* (an attempt, to quote Milton's *Paradise Lost*, to "justify the ways of God to man"). In the Bible, the fullest theodicy is the Book of Job, and indeed Philoctetes' sufferings are not far removed from those of the tormented Job. Like the biblical hero, Philoctetes calls out for an answer, and it comes to him not from nature, nor from his conscience, nor from his fellow "actors" on this great stage we call the world. Nothing, in fact, within his sphere of knowledge can supply him with the wisdom he seeks. The answer must come from above: out of the machine; out of the whirlwind.

14

EURIPIDES' *ELECTRA* AND *MEDEA*

The Naïve and the Sentimental

IN THE SIXTH OF HIS *Letters on the Aesthetic Education of Man* (1795), German poet and theorist Friedrich Schiller looks back with awe on the golden age of Athens. Unlike the Neoclassicists of the eighteenth century, who found in the ancient Greeks a love for harmony and balance that spoke to their own fascination with order and system, Schiller, who looks forward to and greatly influenced the Romantics of the nineteenth century, found something far different. For Schiller, the Greeks of the golden age had a natural humanity and integrity that we have lost. They possessed a fullness and simplicity that allowed them to experience life emphatically; compared with them, we moderns live divided, fragmented lives. One year later, Schiller would develop this distinction between ancient and modern in his *On Naïve and Sentimental Poetry*. Here Schiller links the naïve to the ancient Greeks and defines it as a state of mind or soul that is simply and directly tied to nature, that rejects everything artificial or clever, and that is uncorrupted by society or civilization. Whereas the naive is unreflective and unmediated, the sentimental is complex, artistic and overly self-conscious.

Though Schiller meant his definition of the naïve to encompass the full extent of fifth-century B.C. Athens, I would argue that it is in the midst of that century that we see the first stirrings of the sentimental. For although the three great tragedians of Athens worked with the same raw material and through the same dramatic conventions, the work of Euripides reflects a modern, sentimental spirit that is at odds with that of Aeschylus and Sophocles. The tragedies of Aeschylus and Sophocles come from a removed, distant past populated by titanic men and women who speak in a purified language of abstract ideals and who act in accordance with higher codes and destinies. Euripides' tragedies, on the other hand, take place in a familiar, almost mundane world; they seem at times as if they were written yesterday. Despite the fact that the same characters populate the work of all three dramatists, in Euripides these kings and queens, warriors and saviors are demoted to the ranks of politicians and panders, gossips and schemers. To move from Aeschylus to Euripides is to move from the epic, heroic realm of the *Iliad* to the petty, bourgeois world of *Madame Bovary*, from the days of the Hebrew patriarchs to the days of Johnson and Nixon, from characters who remind us of the Knights of the Round Table to those who remind us of our next-door neighbors.

That is not to say that Euripides is a bad dramatist. On the contrary, what his plays lack in simplicity and grandeur they more than make up for in psychological depth and realism. The "sentimental" Euripides is a self-conscious artist who cannot ignore his own age to sweep his reader off to a mythic neverland. He was keenly aware of the injustices of his day—the brutalities of war, the subjugation of women, the ill treatment of foreigners and illegitimate children—and he projected these contemporary issues and struggles back into the legendary settings of his tragedies, rather as Arthur Miller's *The Crucible* projects the dangers of McCarthyism back into the "legendary" days of Puritan New England. That the plays of Euripides make their points without sinking into polemic or allegory is a tribute to the complex and subtle artistry of their maker. They are a tribute as well to his insight into human nature and his gift for giving dramatic voice to the mental anguish and internal rage of the dispossessed.

If Sophocles is the master of the tragedy of character, then Euripides is the master of a more psychological and sociological type of drama. In the former the protagonists suffer tremendously, but their suffering takes place in an aesthetic vacuum cut off from everyday indignities; in a sense their characters are too grand, too noble to be assimilated into our shrunken world of petty politics, corporate back-stabbing and keeping up with the Joneses. True, we see the specter of *realpolitik,* of an ends-justifies-the-means ethos, rise up in Sophocles' depictions of Odysseus and the sons of Atreus, but the protagonists who are injured by them remain in a realm apart and ultimately fall victim to their own fixed natures. In contrast, Euripides' protagonists are smaller, more anxious, more compromised. They are not the living avatars of grand Freudian complexes, but eccentric, angst-ridden neurotics desperate to save what little dignity they have. Sophocles' protagonists set the stage for the sweeping, larger-than-life Caesars, Hamlets and Othellos of Shakespeare's stage; those of Euripides look forward to the frustrated, middle-class characters we meet in Ibsen's *Doll's House,* Shaw's *Major Barbara* and Miller's *Death of a Salesman.*

Ironically, although Euripides used the deus ex machina more frequently than his slightly elder contemporaries, his dramas seem less controlled by an overarching fate. The gods are present in Euripides—they often speak at the beginning and end of his tragedies—but they seem in the final analysis to be irrelevant, or at least inconsequential, to the characters' struggles. Euripides does not completely "psychologize" the gods (as O'Neill does in *Mourning Becomes Electra*), but he does show that what we call Zeus or Aphrodite is often simply a mask for the laws of reason or a justification for human lust. Euripides is less concerned with necessity (a favorite word of Sophocles) than with the psychological and sociological forces that shape us and limit our freedom of action and thought. He hems in his characters on all sides, allowing them to be almost crushed by forces outside their control. Rather than uplift and ennoble them, he observes and analyzes and dissects their tortured psyches. In this Euripides is one of the progenitors of the naturalistic novels of Honoré de Balzac, Emile Zola, Thomas Hardy, Frank Norris and Theodore Dreiser, all of whom were deeply influenced by a deterministic, Darwinian, ultimately anti-humanistic view of man.

Euripides may seem an unlikely candidate for a book encouraging Christians to carefully and even prayerfully read the works of Homer, Virgil and the Greek tragedians. Surely the Christian reader seeking wisdom from the ancients will gravitate more toward Aeschylus and Sophocles, who are more interested in taboos and scapegoats, in divine destiny, and in the greater sacred drama than Euripides. Compared to Aeschylus and Sophocles, Euripides seems to be a rationalist, a skeptic, a freethinker; he could even be called a proto-secular humanist. And yet his is a voice that must be heard by Christians and non-Christians alike. Without him we cannot grasp the fullness of the golden age and, hence, the fullness of man himself.

PASSION PERVERTED

As I mentioned earlier, the story of Electra is the only one for which we have dramatic treatments by all three tragedians. In the magisterial version of Aeschylus, the murder of Clytemnestra and Aegisthus by Electra and Orestes is one episode in a vast, cosmic drama by which wrath and vengeance are transformed into justice and mercy. In Sophocles' version, the focus falls more on Electra's monumental grief and her intractable character. For both Aeschylus and Sophocles, Orestes is a messianic figure and his sister a creature of set purpose who gains our respect—if not quite our love—for her steadfastness and hope.

Not so in the distinctly antiheroic version of Euripides. In his *Electra*, the two children of the slain Agamemnon are anything but noble. In fact, these siblings come across as confused and cowardly upstarts: a rather nasty pair of maladjusted adolescents. Euripides seems to go out of his way to paint Clytemnestra and Aegisthus in a relatively positive light while portraying their slayers as rash, inhospitable and even impious. As a Shakespearian critic once quipped: how sick Hamlet appears despite his just cause; how healthy Claudius seems despite his crime. The same could be said of Electra-Orestes on the one hand and Clytemnestra-Aegisthus on the other.

As in Sophocles' version, Euripides' Electra is sexually repressed and obsessed with the illicit bedroom activity of her mother. Euripides, however, takes this aspect of her character in a direction that would no doubt have horrified Sophocles. In Euripides' telling, Electra has been married off to a farmer to ensure that she will not produce any noble offspring that might threaten Aegisthus's claim to the throne. The farmer, feeling unworthy to be married to such a highborn maiden, promises Electra that he will not despoil her of her virginity—and she agrees. By his skillful and carefully nuanced dialogue, Euripides manages to provoke in his audience a dual reaction to this strange marital pact: the farmer's offer to leave Electra untouched makes him appear noble and self-sacrificing; Electra's acceptance of the offer makes her seem selfish, frigid and unnatural. Even Orestes is shocked when he learns of the pact and at first feels outraged that the farmer should find his sister so unappealing!

Throughout the play, Electra, who ridicules her mother for the way she dominates her less noble husband, comes to dominate her own farmer spouse and treat him coldly and dismissively. When she seeks help from her tutor, an old and loyal friend of Agamemnon, she bosses him around and manipulates him to serve her own purposes. Orestes, for his part, is timid and conflicted, horrified by the deed he is driven to do. When he kills Aegisthus, he does so from behind in a manner devoid of heroism and nobility; when killing his mother, he is so ashamed that he throws his cloak over his face before stabbing her in the neck. While Electra gloats maliciously over the murders, Orestes feels neither euphoria nor a sense that he has righted the scales of justice. Though Euripides provides us with a deus ex machina in which Castor and Pollux, the deified brothers of Helen and Clytemnestra, appear above the stage and promise both a new husband for Electra and divine forgiveness and restoration for Orestes, we in the audience do not feel any sense of spiritual or intellectual clarification. Indeed, Euripides seems to be using the deus ex machina against itself: not as a way of acknowledging the unfathomable mysteries and sovereign power of the divine, but as a way of registering his despair at finding any higher meaning in a situation so wretched.

Where then are we to find the moral center of the play? Is there anything redeemable here, at least from the point of view of the Christian reader? Interestingly, that redemptive vision is not to be found in the "noble" protagonists but in the humble characters of the farmer and the old tutor. With his penchant for hearing the voice of the dispossessed, Euripides directs our attention away from the slayers and the slain to the faithful integrity of Electra's long-suffering husband and advisor. In a way, Euripides works here in the tradition of the *Odyssey* rather than the *Iliad*. The grand warriors and martyrs who march through the tragedies of Aeschylus and Sophocles remind us of Achilles and Hektor and Andromache. The less grand but more

human farmers, nurses and servants who appear in the plays of Euripides remind us of Eumaeus, that noble swineherd who wins our admiration in
Homer's more domestic epic. In Euripides, we are often encouraged to look
beyond the outside—beyond heredity and wealth, beauty and prowess—to
see an inner dignity and value that is often invisible to the world.

When Orestes first meets his sister's farmer husband, and before he is
himself revealed as the son of Agamemnon, he offers a lengthy speech in
which he warns Electra (and the audience) not to be deceived by external
appearances:

> Alas,
> we look for good on earth and cannot recognize it
> when met, since all our human heritage runs mongrel.
> At times I have seen descendants of the noblest family
> grow worthless though the cowards had courageous sons;
> inside the souls of wealthy men bleak famine lives
> while minds of stature struggle trapped in starving bodies.
> How then can man distinguish man, what test can he use?
> the test of wealth? that measure means poverty of mind;
> of poverty? the pauper owns one thing, the sickness
> of his condition, a compelling teacher of evil;
> by nerve in war? yet who, when a spear is cast across
> his face, will stand to witness his companion's courage?
> We can only toss our judgments random on the wind.
> This fellow here [the farmer] is no great man among the Argives,
> not dignified by family in the eyes of the world—
> he is a face in the crowd, and yet we choose him champion.
> Can you not come to understand, you empty-minded,
> opinion-stuffed people, a man is judged by grace
> among his fellows, manners are nobility's touchstone?
> Such men of manners can control our cities best,
> and homes, but the well-born sportsman, long on muscle, short
> on brains, is only good for a statue in the park,
> not even sterner in the shocks of war than weaker
> men, for courage is the gift of character. (367-90)[1]

---

[1]*Electra*, in *Euripides V*, vol. 9 of *The Complete Greek Tragedies*, ed. David Grene and Richmond Lattimore (Chicago: University of Chicago Press, 1959).

This passage is one of many from the ancient Greek world that reads as if it could have been written yesterday. It speaks to us directly, across the ages, reminding us that though fashions and governments and technologies change, the basic nature of man does not. Furthermore, this passage could easily have been spoken by the Jewish Solomon rather than the pagan Euripides; it might have been lifted from Ecclesiastes or the book of Proverbs. Indeed, it comes very close in spirit to one of the most memorable verses from the Old Testament, a verse that God speaks to the prophet Samuel to help him understand why he would choose the smallest and weakest son of Jesse to be the new king of Israel: "The Lord seeth not as man seeth; for man looketh on the outward appearance, but the Lord looketh on the heart" (1 Samuel 16:7).

Like Euripides, the God of the Bible has a penchant for hearing the voice of the dispossessed. Justice in the Old Testament is essentially defined as the fair and humane treatment of the widow, the orphan and the alien (see Deuteronomy 10:18, for example)—those who cannot fend for themselves. Of the three great tragedians of ancient Athens, only Euripides heard the silent cry for justice that rose from the lips of the powerless, the forsaken, the sojourner in the land. And because he heard it, he was able to pierce beyond the outward appearance to see the grace and nobility within. To the Jew, all non-Jews were lawless Gentiles; to the Greeks, most of their non-Greek neighbors were uncivilized barbarians. Euripides (like the book of Jonah in the Old Testament and the epistle to the Galatians in the New) helped his ethnocentric people look beyond such labels.

PASSION UNCONTROLLED

For all his skepticism and rationalism, Euripides possessed in miniature a virtue that we see perfected in Christ: the ability to look through to the heart. And nowhere does he look more deeply, more perceptively, more compassionately than in *Medea*. In this, Euripides' most audacious tragedy, we are catapulted into the mind of one of the greatest outsiders in all of literature.

As *Electra* begins with a fifty-line, scene-setting speech from the humble mouth of a farmer, so *Medea* begins with a similar speech from the equally humble mouth of a nurse. But while the farmer is dispassionate and resigned, the nurse is fiery and indignant. She begins by cursing the day when the Greek hero Jason sailed on the Argo to the eastern land of Colchis in search of the legendary golden fleece. It was then that her mistress, the princess Medea, fell madly in love with Jason and used her powers of witchcraft to ensure that Jason would win his prize. Although she knew she would be dismissed as a witch and a barbarian in Greece, Medea returned on the ship with Jason and bore him two children. Using her sorcery, she even deceived the daughters of Jason's Greek enemy into murdering their own father. The horror of her deed, which she felt compelled to do because of her love for Jason, has forced her to flee with her family to the southern city of Corinth, where Jason has pledged himself in marriage to the daughter of the king. Jason justifies his act by saying that his new marriage will win Medea's children a high status they would not otherwise have had as the offspring of a barbarian mother, but such excuses offer little solace to the slighted Medea. Although she begins the play by contemplating suicide, Medea ends by killing Jason's fiancée and her father through sorcery, stabbing her own children to death, and then flying off to Athens in a chariot drawn by dragons.

One would think that a mother who kills her own children would be presented as nothing less than a monster, yet Euripides constructs the plot and dialogue of his play so as to make us feel the most possible sympathy for Medea and the most possible contempt for Jason. I stated earlier that Euripides, as a "sentimental" dramatist, often dealt with the social and political issues of his day. One of those issues, which we encounter in the dialogues of Plato, concerned the ethical and pedagogical status of a popular group of highly paid teachers known as the Sophists. For a fee, these ancient spin doctors would teach their pupils the art of rhetoric, including the skill of making a weaker argument sound like the stronger. In the *Clouds*, a comedy written by the satirical playwright Aristophanes and performed in Athens about a decade after *Medea*, the Sophists are lampooned as moral relativists for whom truth and justice carry no absolute meaning and therefore can exert no real claims on behavior.

Throughout *Medea*, Jason, a great legendary hero whom Sophocles would surely have treated in the same high manner as his Ajax, Heracles

or Philoctetes, is presented by Euripides as a supreme sophist who con-
torts his words and logic to make his morally reprehensible behavior
seem not only proper but altruistic. He defends his ill treatment of
Medea by claiming that he owes her no debt of gratitude for helping him
win the golden fleece and defeat his enemies. It was Aphrodite, the goddess of love, who made her help him, and thus no reciprocity can be expected from Jason. On the contrary, he goes on to assert, it is Medea who
owes Jason a debt of gratitude. "Instead of living among barbarians," he
argues, "You [now] inhabit a Greek land and understand our ways, /
How to live by law instead of the sweet will of force" (536-38).[2] The
irony here would be funny if it were not so cruel. She is to be thankful
that she no longer lives in a barbarian land but in one run by laws, and
yet these very "laws" have stripped her of her rights and left her at the
mercy of men with no true sense of justice. Next to the Creon of Sophocles' *Antigone*, who sincerely believes he is doing what is best for the *polis*,
Jason appears cold, arbitrary and uncaring.

Medea, on the other hand, is allowed to argue her case with warmth,
conviction and fervor. In the midst of a society in which she as a woman
and foreigner has no status, she nevertheless gives voice to her struggles
and those of her equally dispossessed sisters. "We women," she cries out
earlier in the play,

are the most unfortunate creatures.
Firstly, with an excess of wealth it is required
For us to buy a husband and take for our bodies
A master; for not to take one is even worse.
And now the question is serious whether we take
A good or bad one; for there is no easy escape
For a woman, nor can she say no to her marriage.
She arrives among new modes of behavior and manners,
And needs prophetic power, unless she has learned at home,
How best to manage him who shares the bed with her. (231-40)

In a stunning reversal of Hesiod—who believed, like many ancient

---

[2]All citations are from *Medea* in *Euripides I*, vol. 5 of *The Complete Greek Tragedies*, ed. David Grene
and Richmond Lattimore (Chicago: University of Chicago Press, 1955).

Greek men, that marriage was at best a mixed blessing—Medea asserts that marriage is no bed of roses for women either. Too often the woman must suffer in silence. If she chooses her husband poorly, she will have no advocate to speak for her; if she chooses not to marry, she is left in a worse state. True, she does not have to fight in wars, but that does not mean her life is one of peace and safety. No, says Medea in a shocking line: "I would very much rather stand / Three times in the front of battle than bear one child" (250-51). If that were not revolutionary enough, Euripides has his chorus of Corinthian women voice the following complaint just moments before Jason enters the stage: "For not on us did Phoebus [Apollo], lord of music, / Bestow the lyre's divine / Power, for otherwise I should have sung an answer / To the other sex" (424-27). It is the men, the chorus is saying, who write the plays and the epics and the histories. Were women empowered to write their own books, to give their own interpretation of the events of their day, they would tell a very different story. In many ways, *Medea* (and several of Euripides' other plays) presents us with just such a "herstory."

Should we then label *Medea* a feminist play? Yes and no. If by feminism we mean the belief that women should be afforded rights to property, education and economic opportunity, given a say in how society and government are structured, and treated with respect and dignity by their male counterparts, then yes, *Medea* is very much a feminist play. However, if by feminism we mean the belief that men and women are the same, that masculinity and femininity are not essential aspects of our identities but constructs created by sociopolitical forces, then *Medea* is most certainly not a feminist play. Ironically, this latter form of feminism, which has strong roots in Marxism, often demeans and disenfranchises the essential feminine voice as much as sexism does. The sexist says that men and women are different but that masculine virtues are positive and normative while feminine ones are negative and even deviant. The Marxist feminist, on the other hand, says that men and women are the same but then goes on to judge all things by masculine measures.

It is this form of feminism that G. K. Chesterton objects to in *What's Wrong with the World* when he defines a feminist as "one who dislikes the chief feminine characteristics."[3] In this statement Chesterton is taking

Marxist feminists to task for being the true misogynists: haters not of women per se but of all that is feminine. While sexists ridicule the feminine as weaker and lesser, the feminists Chesterton critiques dismiss it as either unproductive or nonexistent. In either case, the upshot is that masculine always trumps feminine, for masculine and feminine, like love and truth and beauty, are real things whether or not the Marxist feminist—or the sophist—wishes to acknowledge them as such. In practical terms this means the rational is always privileged over the intuitive, the intellectual over the emotional, analysis over synthesis, active over passive, ideological over personal, competition over cooperation, law over nature, the claims of the *polis* over those of the family.

We will return to these binary pairs in the next chapter. For now, suffice it to say that the message of *Medea* is not that all differences between men and women should be eliminated, but that both should be allowed a voice in the *polis*. In the opening speech of the play, the nurse presents the time when Jason and Medea were united as the ideal state, when Medea was a true helpmeet to Jason and Jason honored her contributions and unique virtues: "This is indeed the greatest salvation of all— / For the wife not to stand apart from the husband" (14-15). But when the two cease to be what the Bible calls "one flesh," when (to use the language of Ephesians 5) Jason ceases to love sacrificially and Medea to submit, their opposing masculine and feminine natures become polarized and antagonistic. Jason becomes strangled by a cold and merciless rationalism even as Medea becomes consumed by an uncontrolled passion divorced from higher ethical standards. Their complementary unity is torn asunder, and the result is the destruction of the fruit of that lost union: their children.

Medea is one of the earliest extant plays of Euripides. In the years that followed he would take up different issues and causes, but he would never abandon his conviction that the poles of masculine and feminine, reason and passion must be held in a proper balance if the individual and the *polis* are to survive and thrive. Indeed, nearly twenty-five years later, as he lay in voluntary self-exile in Macedonia and contemplated his approaching death, Euripides would re-embody that conviction in a play

---

[3]G. K. Chesterton, *What's Wrong with the World* (San Francisco: Ignatius Press, 1994), p. 124.

that is not only his masterpiece, but that offers one of the most stunning and powerful intimations of Christianity to come out of the pagan world: the *Bacchae*.

15

EURIPIDES' *BACCHAE* AND *HIPPOLYTUS*

Apollonian versus Dionysiac

ART, NIETZSCHE ASSERTS BOLDLY IN *The Birth of Tragedy from the Spirit of Music* (1872), "owes its continuous evolution to the Apollonian-Dionysiac duality, even as the propagation of the species depends on the duality of the sexes, their constant conflict and periodic acts of reconciliation." Nietzsche links the masculine Apollonian (named for Apollo) to the plastic arts and to dreams: it is by nature rational, intellectual and stoic. The feminine Dionysiac (named for Dionysus), on the other hand, he links to music and to intoxication; it is intuitive, emotional and ecstatic. The former seeks a balance and tranquility that preserves individuality; the latter seeks a communal rapture in which the individual forgets himself completely. These "two creative tendencies," he argues, "developed alongside one another, usually in fierce opposition, each by its taunts forcing the other to more energetic production, both perpetuating in a discordant concord that agon which the term *art* but feebly denominates: until at last, by the thaumaturgy of a Hellenic act of will, the pair accepted the yoke of marriage and, in this condition, begot Attic [Athenian] tragedy, which exhibits the salient features of both parents."[1]

As Western thought has traditionally privileged the Apollonian over the Dionysiac, Nietzsche felt a strong need to defend the claims of Dionysus. In rich prose he celebrates the power of the Dionysiac to shatter boundaries, to reconcile both man and man and man and nature, and to achieve a mystical oneness. Nevertheless, Nietzsche's ultimate call is for a higher fusion of the Dionysiac and the Apollonian. He admits that the Dionysiac alone can lead to "brutal and grotesque" excesses. When pursued apart from the imposing presence of Apollo, it results in the "throwback of men to the condition of apes and tigers." However, when it is held in balance with the Apollonian, we "see entirely new rites celebrated: rites of universal redemption, or glorious transfiguration. Only now has it become possible to speak of nature's celebrating an aesthetic triumph."[2] Nietzsche located this triumph in the Attic tragedies of Aeschylus, Sophocles and Euripides, dramatic productions that were performed in honor of Dionysus but that bespeak a balance and perfection of form indicative of Apollo.

Through the sacred drama of incarnation-crucifixion-resurrection, the Apollonian aspects of the Mosaic Law (the Ten Commandments and the ethical laws concerning justice and right behavior) are reconciled with its more Dionysiac side (the Levitical laws involving ritual guilt, blood atonement and the sacrifice of animals) so as to achieve a universal redemption that is celebrated in the bloodless ritual of the Eucharist. In a manner analogous to this, Greek tragedy offered a communal ritual that drew together its audience of citizens in an aesthetic and thus bloodless reenactment of ancient taboos, tragic houses and human scapegoats. The catharsis we feel at the end of the greatest of the tragedies is inspired in part by our sense that a marriage has been formed between warring yet ultimately complementary opposites: justice and mercy (*Oresteia*), destiny and freedom *(Oedipus)*, state and family *(Antigone)*. At least that is the way we feel at the end of a tragedy by Aeschylus or Sophocles. It is not always the way we feel

---

[1]Nietzsche, *The Birth of Tragedy*, trans. Francis Golffing, in *Critical Theory Since Plato*, rev. ed., ed. Hazard Adams (New York: Harcourt Brace Jovanovich, 1992), p. 628.
[2]Ibid., p. 631.

at the end of a play by Euripides. Indeed, in Euripides' *Bacchae,* we feel the very opposite; rather than participate in a fusion of Apollonian and Diony-siac, we witness with horror what happens when these two forces become first antagonistic, then polarized, and finally destructive.

PASSION REPRESSED

The opening monologue of the *Bacchae* is spoken not by a humble farmer or nurse but by Dionysus himself, the god of wine. From his own lips we learn that he is the offspring of a mortal woman, Semele (daughter of Cad-mus, king of Thebes), and the divine Zeus. When Hera in a jealous rage destroyed the pregnant Semele, Zeus miraculously rescued the unborn in-fant and transported him to the East. For many years Dionysus dwelt in exile, but now he has returned to Thebes—"a god incognito, / disguised as man" (4-5)—to take revenge on his unbelieving aunts who denied their sister's claim to have been impregnated by Zeus.[3] In all the lands of Asia through which he has journeyed, Dionysus has been worshiped as a god, but when he arrives home, young King Pentheus, grandson of Cadmus and thus first cousin to Dionysus, along with his mother, Agave, and his aunts, refuses to accept his divine status or allow him to teach his ecstatic rites of song, dance and intoxication. The Christian that reads this opening mono-logue cannot help but be reminded that Jesus' brothers and sisters initially did not believe in him and even thought him mad (see John 7:5 and Mark 3:21). That is not to suggest that Dionysus and Christ should be equated with one another, but it does suggest that the Greeks may have caught a prophetic glimpse of a sad biblical truth: that when the long-awaited Mes-siah arrived, he would be misunderstood and rejected by his own (John 1:11). Though he brings joy and new hope, those closest to him refuse to accept it.

In many ways the central struggle of the *Bacchae* is a personal one—a civil war within the family of Cadmus—but it is also ideological. Pentheus is opposed to all that Dionysus represents. In the rites of Dionysus Pen-theus sees not freedom, joy or release from pain but impiety, irrationality

---

[3]All citations are from the *Bacchae* in *Euripides V,* vol. 9 of *The Complete Greek Tragedies,* ed. David Grene and Richmond Lattimore (Chicago: University of Chicago Press, 1959).

and bestiality; he fears that the very structure of the *polis* will be torn down by the "chaos" Dionysus has brought to Thebes. Pentheus, who combines the repressed sexuality of Sophocles' Electra with the sociopolitical rigidity of Creon (his future grandson), is scandalized by the physical and emotional excesses of Dionysus and fears that he will corrupt the women of Thebes. Prudish, judgmental and puritanical, Pentheus is unable to reconcile the claims of the body with those of the spirit and harbors a deep mistrust of female sexuality. Whereas Pentheus embodies what the Greeks called *nomos* ("law" or "custom"), Dionysus embodies *phusis* ("nature"). The former sees restraint and reason as necessary checks on the excesses of human nature; the latter sees revelry and ecstasy as necessary for freeing and restoring human nature.

Over the last century, Protestant Christianity, while avoiding the extremes of Euripides' play, has seen some division between the Apollonian and the Dionysiac—a heavy focus on systematic theology and expository Bible preaching versus an insistence on the centrality of charismatic worship and the free exercise of such spiritual gifts as tongues and prophecy. When sound, Bible-centered doctrine and Spirit-led worship are brought together in the same congregation, the results can be powerful indeed; when one seeks to exclude the other, a church can fall prey either to rigid legalism or heterodox emotionalism. On the liturgical side, imagine what would happen if the seasons of fast and feast, Lent and Carnival (Mardi Gras), were to totally reject the claims of the other rather than working in unison to prepare the soul for Easter. There have been times in church history when believers have gone too far in the direction either of asceticism or antinomianism, but thankfully the body of Christ as a whole has been able, with the guidance of the Holy Spirit, to navigate between these extremes. That is because Christ fuses within himself both the Apollonian and the Dionysiac. As the god Dionysus is but a shadow pointing to only one aspect of Christ—his role as messianic deliverer and bringer of hope, freedom and spiritual ecstasy—he necessarily causes a division within Thebes and the family of Cadmus that leads in the end to bloodshed and destruction.

Thus, while the young Pentheus resists the "madness" of Dionysus, his old grandfather Cadmus and the blind prophet Tiresias immediately embrace the rituals of the god of wine. Just before Pentheus makes his entrance onto the stage, we see these two wise elders of Thebes dressed in the effeminate robes and ivy crowns of the Bacchae (the followers of Dionysus, or Bacchus); with almost childlike abandon they shake their heads and move their feet to the beat of a primal dance. They are grotesque, but they feel neither shame nor guilt. "Did the god declare / that just the young or just the old should dance?" asks Tiresias. "No, he desires his honor from all mankind. / He wants no one excluded from his worship" (206-9). Their age has taught these two elders that there is a season for everything: a time for rules, rigidity and hierarchy and a time to lose oneself in the communal, democratizing dance.

Pentheus does not share their acquiescence. When he first sees Cadmus and Tiresias, he is disgusted by their behavior and scolds them for making a mockery of themselves and Thebes. In what seems a clear reference to the Eleusinian mysteries, Tiresias lessons the rash young man by speaking to him of the powers of the earth as they are embodied in the bread of Demeter and the wine of Dionysus. When filled with the liquid gift of Dionysus, says Tiresias,

> suffering mankind forgets its grief; from it
> comes sleep; with it oblivion of the troubles
> of the day. There is no other medicine
> for misery. And when we pour libations
> to the gods, we pour the god of wine himself
> that through his intercession man may win
> the favor of heaven. (280-86)

The Christian who reads such a passage cannot help but pause and wonder. This exiled god from the East who is born of a divine-human coupling, who is rejected by his family, and who brings joy and restoration to a grieving world is here not only linked to the elements of bread and wine but is said to be present in the wine and to intercede for us with heaven. The gift he offers is free, but it is rejected by a legalistic ruler who finds his ways to be permissive, blasphemous and destructive of law and custom.

In the scenes that follow, Dionysus, who appears "incarnationally" in the form of his own messenger, extends to Pentheus numerous chances to repent and accept him. Even after Pentheus puts his followers into prison and Dionysus frees them by first breaking their chains and then sending an earthquake to tear open the prison (see Acts 12:1-19; 16:22-40), the patient god still extends his hand in friendship. Later in the play Pentheus learns of an incident in which a group of peaceful Bacchae were provoked by inter-lopers who attempted to spy on their secret rituals. A skirmish ensued in which Dionysus's female revelers defeated spear-bearing village men even though they carried only ivy-twined staffs. Pentheus swears that he will call out his army and attack the Bacchae, whereupon Dionysus gives him a final warning: "If I were you / I would offer him [Dionysus] a sacrifice, not rage / and kick against necessity, a man defying / god" (793-96). The actual met-aphor used in Greek is "kick against the goads" or "kick against the pricks"—exactly the same metaphor Christ uses when he reveals himself to Saul of Tarsus on the road to Damascus (Acts 26:14). Both Pentheus and Saul are like stubborn, intractable oxen whose master attempts to beat them on with a goad—a long stick with a pointy end. In a futile act of resistance, the ox kicks back against the goad, cutting open its hooves and making its unavoidable work even more difficult and painful.

Unfortunately, unlike St. Paul, Pentheus refuses to cease his persecution of Dionysus and his followers, so the god is forced to enact his judgment. In a moment of deep psychological insight, Euripides has Dionysus turn to the raging Pentheus as he is calling out his troops and ask him seduc-tively if he would like to see the scantily clad and uninhibited Bacchae in their revels. Pentheus, like a twisted, pharisaical censor who spends inor-dinate time viewing the pornography he would abolish, gives in to his sup-pressed voyeurism and agrees. Once he does so, he begins to lose his ra-tional judgment. Dionysus convinces him to dress in the effeminate garb of the Bacchae and march through the center of town. Having sufficiently humiliated the deluded king before his people, Dionysus sets him high in a tree where he can spy on the Bacchae. But Pentheus's forbidden thrill is short-lived. The godlike voice of Dionysus calls out to the Bacchae, who are led by Agave and her sisters, that they are being spied on, and they shake Pentheus down from the tree and tear him to pieces. Deceived by Dionysus into thinking that Pentheus is a mountain lion, Agave rips off her son's head and mounts it proudly on her staff.

Agave carries the head back to the palace where she is greeted by her father Cadmus. Cadmus instructs her to look up into the sky (the realm of Apollo), and her madness slowly ebbs away, leaving her to mourn over what she has done to her own child. As the play draws to a close, Dionysus, now in the form of a god from the machine, appears above the stage and justifies his cruel actions; he then prophesies to Cadmus the further suffering he must yet endure. Cadmus stoically accepts his tragic fate and that of his family, but there is little sense here, as there is at the end of the *Oresteia* or *Oedipus*, that a higher, overarching destiny is in control. We are as unsatisfied by this deus ex machina as we are by the one that ends Euripides' *Electra*. Rather, we cannot help but conclude that the actions of Dionysus have been as cruel and excessive as those of Pentheus.

But, I would argue, that is the very point of the play. The Apollonian and the Dionysiac must be kept in balance—in the play, in the *polis*, in the human psyche—or they will tear each other apart. Room must be made for reason and intuition, *nomos* and *phusis*, the masculine and the feminine. As in *Medea*, when logic parts company with passion, the former becomes as cold as the grip of death and the latter as hot as the fires of hell. We must acknowledge (as the Marxist feminist does not) the unique and essential differences between masculine and feminine and then proclaim (as the sexist will not) that both are of equal value and worth.

And there is more: the part Euripides could not know, the remedy his society did not yet possess. The *Bacchae* should be essential reading for Christians, not because it is a Christian play but because it is a pre-Christian play that calls out for a fuller revelation of truth and mercy. Dionysus, for all his links to Christ, is a violent, egocentric savior who does not know how to forgive or to suffer with the humans he claims to care for. He cannot bring either reconciliation or redemption, for he is not himself whole—neither fully godlike in compassion nor fully human in empathy. At the end of the play, Cadmus, while accepting the decree of Dionysus, tells him that his "sentence is too harsh" and that the gods "should be exempt from human passion" (1345, 1347). Cadmus does not mean that the gods should be impassive but that they should be able to overcome the excesses of human passion, to be true judges and mediators of the volatile extremes that tear humanity apart. But again, the pre-Christian world of Euripides can have but the faintest notion of such a savior.

In many ways Dionysus is both the most interesting and disturbing of the "pagan Christs" to appear in the literature of ancient Greece. He alternately thrills us as a bringer of good news and repels us as a bringer of madness and gratuitous violence. And yet, oddly, the violence that follows in Dionysus's wake may itself be a pagan intimation of Christian truths to come. A sort of combination of Achilles and Odysseus, Dionysus embodies a divine wrath that results in a fiery Day of the Lord that destroys the stiff-necked Pentheus and his fellow Thebans as swiftly and apocalyptically as Odysseus destroys the evil suitors. In the last chapter of the Old Testament, Malachi, looking ahead to the Day of the Lord, prophesies that when the Sun of Righteousness (the Messiah) comes, he shall simultaneously burn up those who are proud and wicked and bring healing to those who fear his name (Malachi 4:1-2). Like the sun, Christ's power both gives life and takes it away, both renews and destroys. In the *Bacchae* of Euripides we catch a glimpse of that coming joy—and terror.

PASSION DENIED

In *Women of Trachis*, Sophocles relates the tragic end of the great hero and beast-slayer Heracles; in *Hippolytus*, Euripides relates the equally tragic end of an equally great hero and beast-slayer, Theseus. As stated earlier, Heracles and Theseus were responsible for "cleaning up the roads" of ancient Greece and allowing civilization to take root in a land once terrorized by monsters. Alas, once Heracles had completed his labors and brought an end to the old bestial rule, he was himself killed by the mingled blood and venom of two beasts—Nessus and the Hydra—that he had slain long before. Theseus, on the other hand, who had slain the dreaded Minotaur, was left to end his life in sorrow after he in an ignorant rage summoned a monstrous bull from the sea to kill his only son. Here is the tale as dramatized by Euripides.

While warring with the Amazons, Theseus had taken a mistress who had born him an illegitimate son named Hippolytus. Later he married Phaedra, daughter of King Minos of Crete, with whom he hoped to have legitimate children to succeed him. Meanwhile Hippolytus, perhaps blaming Aphrodite for his illegitimate status, takes a vow of chastity and becomes a devotee of Artemis, virginal goddess of the hunt. Enraged by Hippolytus's contempt for her, Aphrodite causes Phaedra to conceive an unholy lust for her stepson, a tragically apt curse since Phaedra's mother had given birth to the very Minotaur killed by Theseus after consummating an equally unholy lust for a bull. Egged on by her earthy and sophistical nurse, Phaedra reveals her passion for Hippolytus. The nurse, thinking to help her tormented mistress, tells Hippolytus, who responds by heaping contempt not only on Phaedra but on all womankind. In a fit of anger and shame Phaedra hangs herself, leaving a suicide note in which she accuses Hippolytus of raping her. Like Potiphar in the Joseph story (Genesis 39), Theseus believes the false testimony of his wife and calls down the curse that summons the bull from the sea. Not surprisingly, the play ends with a deus ex machina in which Artemis assures Theseus of his son's innocence. The two are reconciled before Hippolytus's death, and Artemis leaves them with the dubious consolation that she will destroy one of Aphrodite's devotees: a fitting end since the play begins with a monologue by Aphrodite laying out her plans to destroy Hippolytus.

Even this brief synopsis reveals the play to be fully Euripidean in focus and scope. As so often in his dramas, we have a deus ex machina that offers no real reconciliation or catharsis, spoken by a god who seems unconcerned with human misery. At the center of the play we have a dispossessed hero— Hippolytus's illegitimate status makes him as much a powerless outcast as Medea—to whom Euripides gives a compelling voice. We have as well the polarization of Apollonian and Dionysiac; Hippolytus, like Pentheus, succumbs to prudery and disgust for the physical and the feminine, while Phaedra yields to an irrational, Medea-like passion that allows love and lust to trump all other duties. In the beginning of the play, one of Hippolytus's servants pleads with him to "loosen up" and offer a prayer to Aphrodite, but he stubbornly refuses. Phaedra too is given the chance to conceal her lust and refuse to indulge it, but she is convinced that her lust is natural and must be indulged lest it kill her. In an odd twist, the sophistical arguments of the nurse lead Phaedra to embrace an extreme (lawless, illicit) version of the Dionysiac in the same way that Jason's sophistical arguments lead him to embrace an equally extreme (heartless, merciless) version of the Apollonian. Both Hippolytus and Phaedra are far more noble and heroic than either

Jason-Medea or Pentheus-Dionysus—they are almost Sophoclean—yet they still exhibit the deep psychological flaws of the typical Euripidean hero. Hippolytus is a self-satisfied prig who thinks himself more pure and holy than the typical mortal; Phaedra allows herself an excess of self-pity and renders herself weaker than she in fact is. Could they learn from each other, they might lessen the flaws and refine the virtues of the other, but throughout the play they are kept apart: neither meets nor speaks directly with the other. They are isolated and estranged.

Of course even if they were to meet, they would perhaps be unable to communicate. The play (and Euripides' pre-Christian society) not only affords them no meeting ground, but it lacks a touchstone against which to measure their opposing claims. Theseus himself impotently notes the lack of such a touchstone when his son pleads innocent to the charge leveled against him in Phaedra's suicide note. "If [only] there were," cries Theseus,

> some token now, some mark to make the division
> clear between friend and friend, the true and the false!
> All men should have two voices, one the just voice,
> and one as chance would have it. In this way
> the treacherous scheming voice would be confuted
> by the just, and we should never be deceived. (924-30)[4]

In the absence of such a mark to allow us to distinguish true from false, friend from foe, right from wrong, we are left "all at sea"—a metaphor that recurs often in the play. The gods, flawed and petty as they are, cannot provide the needed standard, and the higher fate and necessity that Aeschylus and Sophocles celebrate in their plays are too shadowy to provide a clear yardstick.

Interestingly, this futile call for a fixed, divine measuring rod surfaces often in the plays of Euripides. In *Electra,* as we saw in the previous chapter, Orestes asks, "How then can man distinguish man, what test can he use?" and answers his own question by conceding that we "can only toss our judgments random on the wind" (373, 379). More despairingly, Medea voices her complaint to the gods in this way:

---

[4]All citations are from *Hippolytus* in *Euripides I*, vol. 5 of *The Complete Greek Tragedies*, ed. David Grene and Richmond Lattimore (Chicago: University of Chicago Press, 1955).

O God, you have given to mortals a sure method
Of telling the gold that is pure from the counterfeit;
Why is there no mark engraved upon men's bodies,
By which we could know the true ones from the false ones? (516-19)

It is the absence of such a distinguishing mark that leads to the tragedy we encounter not only in the plays of Euripides but of Aeschylus and Sophocles as well. When in the signature deus ex machina of Euripides' plays the gods appear and sort out the mess, their divine revelations rarely offer anything on which to build a higher system for measuring right and wrong (though the deus ex machina at the end of Sophocles' *Philoctetes* points dimly in that direction, as does the establishment of an Athenian "Supreme Court" at the end of Aeschylus's *Oresteia*). The appearances of Dionysus in the *Bacchae* come closest to the intimate divine encounter necessary for realizing such a system, yet even here Dionysus's arbitrary and merciless character prevents him from embodying a true standard.

In the dialogues of Plato (whose teacher, Socrates, was only ten years Euripides' junior) our broken world of change, decay and death—what he terms the "world of becoming"—is set over against an ideal, transcendent, unchanging world—the "world of being"—where dwell the eternal, invisible forms. In the world of becoming there exists a variety of trees, chairs and truths; in the world of being dwell the perfect and original Tree, Chair and Truth. Everything in our world is ultimately a shadow or imitation of those forms. The Platonic philosopher seeks to lift his vision above the changing forms of our world to the eternal forms that dwell above in unsullied purity. And yet even when this is achieved, the division between becoming and being tends to remain. The physical world is surpassed rather than being inhabited and transformed by the invisible forms.

As a poet rather than a philosopher, Euripides cries out for something more concrete: namely, for a gleam from the world of being to manifest itself in the world of becoming. The touchstone he seeks in his plays must embody a universal, unchanging truth, but if that truth is to save his heroes and heroines from destruction, it must make itself visible and tangible. The mark his characters yearn for can help them only if it can be seen or heard or touched. God, of course, provided the Jews with just such a measuring rod in the Law of Moses and in the proclamations of the prophets: the former a divine standard imprinted in stone and lived out in the community, the latter a divine word mediated through a human voice. Had Euripides been granted access to the Law and the Prophets (that is, the Old Testament), it would have provided him with the necessary touchstone.

Well, not quite. Beneath Euripides' cry for "some token . . . some mark," there lies a yearning for an intimacy that the Law and Prophets alone cannot satisfy. Only in the incarnation of God in Christ does there come into the world a full and intimate divine-human touchstone; only when the divine Word takes on flesh (John 1:14) does it become possible to know God and what he desires of us. It would take the tragic, once-and-for-all enactment of the ultimate divine-human scapegoat slaughtered on the stage of the world and then raised again in a perfect deus ex machina before Theseus's mark could be engraved indelibly in the Word, in the sacred community of the church and in the human heart.

During the deus ex machina of Hippolytus, Artemis, noticing that her devotee is about to breathe his last, tells the dying Hippolytus that she must now leave him, for she "must not look upon the dead. / [Her] eyes must not be polluted by the last / gaspings for breath" (1437-39). How great the difference between her refusal to be sullied by death and the mercy of Christ who himself suffered the throes of death on our behalf! Apart from such a radical divine mercy, unafraid and unashamed to sully its purity with the dirt and pain of our broken world, the remedies sought by Euripides and his fellow tragedians remain but stabs in the dark: yearnings and gropings for that "true Light, which lighteth every man" (John 1:9).

PART THREE

Virgil

16

THE SACRED HISTORY OF ROME

DOES GOD WORK THROUGH PAGAN KINGS and nations that do not know him? To the casual reader of the Old Testament, the Bible may seem silent on this question. A closer reading, however, will reveal that the Bible does indeed offer an answer—a resounding "yes."

In the second chapter of the book of Daniel, Nebuchadnezzar, the mighty monarch of the Babylonian Empire, has a dream that troubles him greatly. In his dream, he sees a giant statue made of four metals: gold, silver, bronze and iron. The giant seems impervious until a rock, uncut by human hands, falls on the feet of the statue and causes it to shatter into dust. But the stone remains and grows into a huge mountain that fills the earth. Only Daniel, inspired by God, can interpret the pagan monarch's dream. The four metals, he tells Nebuchadnezzar, are four great kingdoms that will succeed one another over the coming centuries. During the rule of the fourth, a fifth and final kingdom will be established by God, one that will never end. The first kingdom is Babylon. The three succeeding empires have proven to be the Persian (founded by Cyrus), the Greek (founded by Alexander) and the Roman. True to the prophecy, it was during the reign of the first Roman emperor, Caesar Augustus, that the foundations for God's eternal kingdom were established. Indeed, though Protestants like myself might downplay this, it was in the capital of the fourth empire that God set up a new kind of kingdom—the church, which would in its own way be more glorious and enduring than Babylon, Persia, Greece or Rome. Nebuchadnezzar's dream is a breathtaking vision and prophecy, and it is made even more breathtaking by the fact that the Spirit chose to convey it through the troubled dreams of a pagan king: a king who would later be humbled by this unknown God of his dreams and forced to hail Yahweh as supreme (Daniel 4:34-37).

Fast-forward a half century to Cyrus the Great, another pagan king whom God used in an even more amazing way. In keeping with a prophecy made by Isaiah, God impelled Cyrus to allow the exiled Jews to return to Jerusalem and rebuild the temple: an act that would lead the Jewish prophet to refer to Cyrus by the sacred name of "Messiah" (Isaiah 45:1). Fast-forward another two centuries and we come to Alexander, whose conquest of the known world caused Hellenistic language and culture to spread throughout the Mediterranean (thus the Old Testament was translated into Greek about 250 B.C., and the New Testament was written in Greek). It was this shared language and culture, allied with the global efficiency and order imposed by Rome, that allowed the gospel of Christ to spread so quickly throughout the Western and Near Eastern world. In its own way, each of the four "metals" helped prepare the diverse cultures of the Mediterranean for the coming of the long-promised Messiah. Indeed, I have often wondered if Paul did not have this partly in mind when he wrote: "But when the fullness of the time was come, God sent forth his Son" (Galatians 4:4).

Yes, for those who have eyes to see, the hand of God can be read in the histories of all the pagan nations of the past. And yet of all these nations, Rome's history seems most miraculous, most watched over by the providence of Yahweh. Accordingly, let us trace the "sacred" history of Rome from its mythical beginnings to the birth of Christ. By so doing, we will see the mystery of God's providence and set the stage for the greatest proto-Christian poet, Virgil, who "read" Rome's history in a way not dissimilar from how many biblical writers "read" the history of Israel.

THE RISE OF THE ROMAN REPUBLIC

According to an ancient Roman legend that long predated Virgil, the founder of Rome was not an Italian but a Trojan named Aeneas. When Troy is destroyed by the Greeks, Aeneas, son of the mortal Anchises and the immortal Venus, flees the city with his father and son Iulus. Guided by divine prophecies, he sails to Italy. Along the way, he falls in love with Dido, queen of Carthage, but forsakes her to found Rome. After much fighting, he wins control of a portion of Italy, marries an Italian princess, and founds a dynasty. Iulus becomes the first king of Alba Longa, a region south of Rome, and is followed by several generations of kings.

About 800 B.C., one of his descendants ousts his brother and appoints his niece a vestal virgin, but she is impregnated by Mars and gives birth to Romulus and Remus. The usurper sets the twin boys adrift on the river Tiber, but their boat floats downstream to the future site of Rome where they are suckled by a she-wolf and then raised by a herdsman. They eventually grow up, discover their true heritage, and return to Alba Longa to restore their grandfather to his throne. This completed, they head back to "Rome" to establish their own kingdoms. Each brother selects one of the seven hills of Rome (Romulus chooses the Palatine, Remus the Aventine) and begins to construct his city. Romulus, more cautious than his brother, begins his labors by constructing a low wall. Amused by the spectacle, Remus playfully runs up the Palatine and leaps over his brother's wall in a single bound. Enraged, Romulus seizes his brother and drives a dagger into his heart. "Thus," he cries, "shall die all who attempt to overleap my walls." Legend has it that Romulus laid the foundations for the city that would bear his name in 753 B.C., but it was a city founded on civil strife and the blood of fratricide. Like Cain (Genesis 4), that other ancient kin-slayer, Romulus would go on to live as an outlaw. Indeed, legend adds that Romulus built up the population of Rome by first inviting male fugitives and rogues to be citizens, and then supplying them with wives by abducting the daughters of a neighboring tribe, the Sabines.

For the next two centuries Rome is ruled by a succession of kings, some of whom rule justly but most of whom prove to be tyrants. However, when the evil son of the last evil king of Rome, Tarquin the Proud, rapes the noblewoman Lucretia, a citizen named Brutus rises up and with great oratorical skill convinces the Roman people to expel Tarquin and all future kings. The date Roman historians ascribed to this event, which gave birth to the Roman Republic, is 509 B.C., a significant date since it was the same year that Athens threw off the last of her tyrants, thus laying the foundation for Athenian democracy, the Greek defeat of Persia and the birth of the golden age. Though the story of the rape of Lucretia is probably legendary, the date appears to be historically accurate, for it was about this time that the Romans expelled the last of the Etruscan kings and established themselves as the dominant power in northern Italy.

The early Republic, ruled by an aristocratic senate and two annually elected consuls, was initially weak and often attacked by the exiled Tarquin and other opportunistic tyrants, such as the Etruscan Lars Porsenna. Rome survived by sheer willpower and the sacrifices of the republican heroes, whose tales of courage and selflessness were told as bedtime stories to generations of Roman boys. There was Brutus himself who, when he learned that his two sons had been plotting with Tarquin, oversaw their summary execution. There was Gaius Mucius who, when captured in an attempt to assassinate Lars Porsenna, voluntarily burned off his own right hand to prove to the tyrant that he would do nothing to betray his beloved Republic. There was Horatius Cocles who single-handedly held a bridge against the forces of Porsenna and then leapt in full armor into the Tiber. There were mighty generals like Cincinnatus and Camillus, who saved Rome from her enemies but when offered absolute power by the people refused to become kings. And there were the legendary martyrs like Marcus Curtius and Decius Mus, who gave themselves as willing scapegoats to save Rome from a curse or ensure her victories in war.

Through the patriotism and heroism of her citizens and the effectiveness of her republican institutions, Rome slowly but inevitably expanded until, by the middle of the third century, she had gained control of all Italy and cast her eyes toward Greece and the wider Mediterranean. As so often was the case in Rome's military history (or at least as the Romans themselves liked to believe), the next phase of Roman expansion was initiated by a call for help from Roman allies in Sicily. The Sicilians had long feared the growing might and aggression of Carthage, a city on the north coast of Africa that controlled a vast trading empire. Over the next century, Rome fought a series of brutal and bloody wars with Carthage. When they were over, Carthage and her empire were destroyed, and Rome, who also defeated her remaining Greek enemies in 146 B.C., emerged as the undisputed mistress of the Mediterranean world. Although Rome was the victor in all three wars with Carthage, she came very close to losing the second. This near defeat was orchestrated by the military genius of Hannibal, a Carthaginian general who in a bold move marched his troops over the Alps so as to attack Rome from the north. For fifteen years Hannibal ravaged the terrified lands and peoples of Italy and even encamped his army around the gates of Rome. For centuries afterward, his name was used to frighten naughty Roman children.

Though Carthage was located in modern-day Tunisia, the Carthaginians were not Africans but Phoenicians; they hailed geographically from the area we now call Lebanon. Because the Romans referred to Phoenicia as Punis, the battles they fought with Carthage are known to us as the Punic Wars. It is a detail that holds more than merely academic interest. As G. K. Chesterton points out in his Christian précis of human history, *The Everlasting Man* (1925), the Phoenicians were among the most ruthless and depraved nations of the ancient world. It was the Phoenicians who sacrificed their own children to Baal (the name Hannibal means "the glory of Baal") and who sought to corrupt the Israelites with their worship. Jezebel was a princess of Phoenicia, and it was against her priests of Baal that Elijah won his great spiritual victory atop Mount Carmel (1 Kings 18:16-46). Their chief cities were at Tyre and Sidon, cities that Jesus himself invokes as bywords of wickedness comparable to Sodom (Matthew 11:20-24). Indeed, when Ezekiel prophesies against the king of Tyre, he uses language that makes it clear that behind the Phoenician king lies the power of Satan himself (Ezekiel 28:12-19).

In *The Everlasting Man*, Chesterton presents the Punic Wars as nothing less than a war between the good pagans (Rome) and the bad pagans (Carthage). Though some Christians might balk at the idea of levels of paganism (are we not either believers or unbelievers, regenerate or unregenerate?), I agree with Chesterton on this point. If you were to give a student a map of the world with no country names printed on it but with each country shaded a different color, and then you asked him to place his finger on Brazil, there would be only one possible right answer. Some wrong answers, however, would be closer to the truth than others: if the student pointed to Argentina, he would have come much closer to the geographical truth than if he had pointed to France or Egypt or India. Just so, when compared to other pagan nations, Rome was far more pious, more concerned with honor, truth and virtue. Chesterton, like Dante before him, saw in Rome the highest achievement of man apart from grace. True, he admits, Carthage was more sophisticated than Rome (as the Philistines were more sophisticated than the Jews), but they were also, quite literally, demonic. "These highly civilized people," Chesterton writes, "really met together to invoke the blessing of heaven on their empire by throwing hundreds of their infants into a large furnace."[1] Consumed by materialistic greed, the cold-hearted, calculating merchant princes of Carthage were the filthy capitalists of the ancient world. Their idolatry, writes Chesterton, was purely practical: all that mattered were results. If the devil could guarantee a sufficient bottom line, they were happy to do business with him.

The story of Rome's near-defeat at the hands of Hannibal in the second Punic war is, for Chesterton, both the story of Troy and the story of the cross: victory out of defeat. We might add that it is also the story of the fall of man and of the Jews in Egypt. When all seems lost, a remnant escapes and leads the way to greater glory. Moderns balk a bit, says Chesterton, at Rome's decision to raze Carthage to the ground, but her decision is not so different from God's command to Joshua to place Jericho "under the ban": to destroy it utterly, lest the people become corrupted by its evil. As Yahweh used the pagan Cyrus to send the exiled Jews back home, so he used the pagan Roman Republic to eradicate the bad paganism of Carthage.

FROM REPUBLIC TO EMPIRE

Having defeated all her external enemies by 146 B.C., it was only a matter of time before the Roman Republic would succumb to internal strife. For the next century Rome fell prey to a seemingly unending cycle of civil wars that began in the senate when two liberal-minded aristocrats, Tiberius and

---

[1]G. K. Chesterton, *The Everlasting Man* (Garden City, N.Y.: Image, 1955), p. 145.

Gaius Gracchus, attempted to institute land reforms that would aid the poor and were promptly assassinated for their troubles. Squabbles in the senate soon extended to social wars in Italy over issues of suffrage, citizenship and land reform. Next, Rome was plagued by a succession of strong military men—most notably, Marius and Sulla—who controlled their own private mercenary troops and paid for them by seizing the lands of anyone they could claim was a supporter of their rival, a practice known as proscription. And if that were not enough, Rome was later threatened by a massive slave revolt led by Spartacus. In 60 B.C. the senate, desperate to establish a truce between the warring strong men, decided to form an agreement known as the first triumvirate, by which power would be shared between Rome's two greatest generals, Pompey and Julius Caesar, and her richest aristocrat, Crassus, who quickly fell out of the picture. For a decade, while Pompey and Caesar were fighting along the eastern and western borders of the empire, the agreement worked. However, when Caesar returned in 49 B.C. from his triumphs in Gaul and decided to cross the river Rubicon (thus entering Roman territory) with his troops armed and ready for battle, civil war broke out again.

Caesar defeated Pompey's army and chased him into Egypt. There Caesar helped to oust the young Pharaoh Ptolemy in favor of his more ambitious sister, Cleopatra, with whom he had an affair and fathered a child. Caesar returned to Rome in triumph and began to style himself as a monarch, but the senators, led by Brutus and Cassius and fearing that Caesar would destroy the Republic, assassinated him on the Ides of March in 44 B.C. Over the next two years Caesar's strongest general, Marc Antony, and his adopted son Octavian tracked down the regicidal senators and killed them. Antony and Octavian, along with another rich man named Lepidus, formed themselves into a second triumvirate and for a decade were able to maintain peace. Had history continued in the expected manner, the stronger and more charismatic Antony would have wrested control from the weaker Octavian and established himself as the ruler of Rome. But that was not to be. Like Caesar before him, Antony ventured into Egypt, where he fell passionately in love with Cleopatra—and with the more flamboyant and decadent ways of the East. He returned to Rome for a few years, marrying and fathering several children with Octavian's sister Octavia (ideal-

ized by later Romans as the perfect wife), but the lure of Cleopatra and the
East were too strong. Antony returned to the arms of Cleopatra, whereupon Octavian censured him before the senate as a would-be Eastern po-
tentate who had abandoned Rome and her virtues. A final and decisive
civil war broke out that ended with a naval victory for Octavian at Actium
in 31 B.C. The defeated lovers both committed suicide—Antony by falling
on his sword, Cleopatra by holding an asp to her breast—and Octavian
emerged as the sole ruler of the Mediterranean world. In 27 B.C., he for-
mally changed his name to Caesar Augustus and ruled until A.D. 14 as the
first emperor of the Roman Empire.

Lucky for Rome (and the future history of Western civilization), Augustus, who had used every form of deceit and brutality to win the crown,
transformed himself into a just and enlightened emperor. Forsaking the
ostentatious lifestyles of the tyrants of the East, Augustus ruled Rome so-
berly and efficiently, instituting much-needed social, political and legal reforms, initiating an aesthetic program that would make Rome the cultural
center of the world, and enforcing a "family values" package that would attempt to revive the more pious practices of the revered heroes of the Roman Republic. Most wondrous of all, Augustus brought to Rome and her
empire what she longed for most: peace. It was Caesar Augustus who be-
queathed to the West the longest continuous reign of peace it had ever
known and would ever know again: the Pax Romana.

Just as Athens' defeat of Persia ushered in the golden age of Athens, so
Augustus's defeat of Antony at Actium ushered in the golden age of Rome.
The greatest flower of that age was the poet Virgil, who converted the history of Rome into an epic, sacred tale that begins with the fall of Troy and
ends gloriously with the empire of Augustus. Virgil, born in 70 B.C., grew
up during a tumultuous time in Roman history; at one point he almost lost
his entire patrimony in the proscription wars of Marius and Sulla. From
Virgil's point of view, Actium meant the end of the civil wars and the triumph of universal peace. If for G. K. Chesterton the Punic Wars were
God-ordained struggles that ensured the final defeat of the bad pagans (a
struggle that began with the judges and kings of Israel), and if for Moses
the exodus marked the end of a cycle begun five hundred years earlier when
God called Abraham out of Ur, then the Battle of Actium marked for Vir-

gil an equally divine event toward which all of history had been moving since Aeneas left Troy.

Like the writers of the Bible, the pagan Virgil held an eschatological vision of history in which the end not only explained but justified the suffering that preceded it. Indeed, in the light of that glorious end, even the sins and errors of the past could be seen as good things. Thus did the Latin fathers of the church speak of the fall of man as a *felix culpa* (or "happy guilt"), for it led to the incarnation; in the same way, they spoke of the day of crucifixion as Good Friday, for it was the necessary prerequisite to the resurrection. Even so, as Virgil gazed backward on Roman history from the exalted vantage point of Actium, he saw in every death, every defeat, every painful sacrifice and tragic misstep the seeds of glory that would come. It is a vision he would enshrine for all time in his own poetic chronicle of the sacred history of Rome: the *Aeneid*.

THE MAKING OF A ROMAN EPIC

AS THE FATHER OF WESTERN LITERATURE, Homer left his heirs a daunting legacy. How does one surpass, or even imitate, the grandeur and perfection of the *Iliad* and the *Odyssey?* For seven hundred years, the poets of Greece and Rome struggled to fulfill this task, most of them opting to abandon the epic and pursue other literary genres. When Virgil, however, was commissioned by the emperor Caesar Augustus to write a Homeric-style epic to celebrate the values and glory of Rome, he couldn't very well refuse. Mustering all his creativity and extensive learning, Virgil reviewed all that had come before him in hopes of finding a method for transforming Homer's stately Greek masterpiece into a Latin epic that would aesthetically, historically, philosophically and theologically embody the twin legacies of Western literature and the Roman experiment. The method he finally adopted—the Virgilian solution—remains one of the greatest poetic triumphs of all time. It also provided a method and a hermeneutic by which Christians from Augustine to Aquinas, Dante to Milton could integrate the works of Virgil and other "virtuous pagans" into the fuller revelation of Christ.

FROM HOMER TO VIRGIL

As products of a scientific age, we moderns often find it difficult to conceive of anything in non-evolutionary terms. Because "newer is better" is generally the rule for health and medicine, transportation and communication, biology and technology, we often take for granted that it is true for all other endeavors as well. It is not. Only a fool (or an academic!) would accept that modern art or philosophy or theology, simply because it is modern, is superior to the art, philosophy and theology of the past. Indeed, in a monumental slap in the face to this mindset, the Western literary canon begins with what are arguably its two greatest creations: twin epics that can be neither surpassed nor "improved." The *Iliad* and the *Odyssey*, though located in the late thirteenth century B.C., ultimately exist in an absolute heroic past that transcends simple chronology: Sophocles, Virgil, Dante, Shakespeare, Pope, Shelley and T. S. Eliot are all equally near and equally far from Homer's aesthetic microcosms. The citizens of the golden ages of Athens and Rome are just as distant from, and just as intimate with, Achilles and Odysseus as we who live in the twenty-first century. There is in the works of Homer a purity that cannot be recreated in a sophisticated, self-conscious age. We can only look back in awe and try to do something like Homer: which is, in fact, precisely what the poets between Homer and Virgil did.

Homer's first great "non-imitative imitator" is his likely contemporary Hesiod, who consciously turns away from the epic sweep of the *Iliad* to fashion a briefer and somewhat less ambitious type of poetry. While preserving Homer's high rhetoric, Hesiod narrows his focus to the origin of the gods in *Theogony* and the life of the farmer in *Works and Days*. In the former, he concerns himself with etiology; in the latter, he shifts to something closer to science. The former, like Genesis, offers narrative infused with theology; the latter, like Proverbs, is more practical and earthy. After the death of Hesiod, Greek literature stagnated for two centuries, and the legacy of Homer passed down through a long line of opportunistic imitators who wrote long, dull "historical" epics to flatter rich patrons. Like modern tricksters who will, for a fee, provide you with an "authentic" coat of arms for your family, these money grubbers fashioned false genealogies to link their grateful patrons to heroes like Achilles, Heracles or Jason.

Eventually, however, Greece reclaimed her true literary patrimony and let her imagination soar once again. In the early fifth century B.C., just before Athens defeated the Persians and entered her golden age, a poet rose up who shared Homer's glorification of the warrior in all his masculine beauty and heroism but who forsook Homer's epic sweep. His name was Pindar, and in the wake of earlier poets like Archilochus, Stesichorus and Sappho, he perfected what aesthetic critics refer to as lyric poetry. Shorter, more musical, more free-flowing than the epic poetry of Homer, Pindar's lyrics explore human fame and immortality through a series of odes that celebrate Olympic athletes and offer praise to the gods who inspire them. In their passion, sincerity, and depth and range of emotion, Pindar's *Odes* are the closest Greek equivalent to the Psalms of David. They demonstrate that poetry can glorify man's struggles and triumphs without "robbing" God of the glory due him.

Perhaps taking their cue from Hesiod and Pindar, the great writers of the golden age also developed other genres that reworked the high themes of Homer from a number of different aesthetic perspectives. We have already explored how the tragedies of Aeschylus, Sophocles and Euripides offer a new spin on the events, themes and heroes of Homer; while Aeschylus steps back to contemplate the forces of history and fate, Sophocles moves closer, focusing on character and the passions that drive men and women to ruin. Euripides meanwhile presents the Greek heroes as more brutal and less noble and the gods as more distant, inscrutable and vengeful. Peering deeply into the intricacies of human psychology, he plumbs the twisted passions of overly prudish men and overly passionate women. In all three tragedians, the vision is darker and more ominous than that of Homer; their recurring theme is not war or homecoming, but the fall of a great house that destroys itself from within.

There were, however, two other golden age prose writers who fully shared Homer's interest in war. Each felt that his age had participated in a military struggle whose scope was as epic as that of the Trojan War, and each desired to chronicle that struggle in a work as noble and serious as the *Iliad*. The first of these writers was Herodotus, and his chosen conflict was the Persian War. For Herodotus, this conflict was more than a skirmish between opposing armies: it was nothing less than a titanic struggle between

East and West. However, while Homer saw an equally heroic ideal in his eastern Trojans and western Greeks, Herodotus saw the distinction as a choice between tyranny and democracy, slavery and freedom, barbarism and civilization. Nevertheless, Herodotus learned much from Homer. As Homer devotes equal time to exploring the Greek and Trojan camps, Herodotus presents a full overview not only of Greek culture and politics, but of the rites and rituals of Babylon, Egypt, Persia and the other people groups that made up the Persian Empire. By so doing, Herodotus succeeded in inventing simultaneously the disciplines of history and comparative anthropology; he also managed to present on an epic scale what the Greek victory against Persia "meant" to the future of Western civilization. The stakes, Herodotus shows us, were high indeed.

Herodotus's younger contemporary Thucydides, on the other hand, found his Homeric struggle in a war not between East and West, but between two different political and social structures. Just as Rome's defeat of the Carthaginians led all too quickly into a period of civil war, so Greece's defeat of Persia gave way to the Peloponnesian War, an internal struggle between the democratic Athenians and the oligarchical, even fascistic Spartans. Far more detailed and academic than Herodotus's *Histories*, Thucydides' *Peloponnesian War* offers not a work of comparative anthropology but a treatise in political science. It is interested less in narrative (Herodotus is the superior storyteller) than in the close analysis of propaganda, political justification and realpolitik. Thucydides is a man of the world who understands the often underhanded motives that propel history and military decisions. Still, Thucydides also learned from Homer. For all of its academic rigor and occasional dryness, Thucydides' work comes alive because of his decision to convey the issues of the war through a series of speeches by key Athenian and Spartan generals.

Though Thucydides' work breaks off before the end of the war, the war itself did come to an end, with a total victory for Sparta and a humiliating defeat for Athens. It was a defeat that would stymie Greek literature for a century and a half and eventually shift the center of Hellenic culture. When the seed of Homer took root again, it was not in Athens, or even in Greece, but in Alexandria, Egypt, one of the cities founded by Alexander the Great. Here in the first "college town" of the ancient world, scholars from across the Mediterranean gathered to share their knowledge and study the legacy of the past. Employing the newly invented skills of editing and textual analysis, these Alexandrian scholars performed the first academic study of Homer's works and produced the first "critical editions" of the *Iliad* and the *Odyssey*.

For the Alexandrians, Homer was the be-all and end-all of literature; they praised, honored and emulated him for his genius and his skill. And yet of all writers, these ancient *literati* were least able to imitate Homer, for they were as self-conscious and sophisticated as Homer was direct, unmediated and artless. As a result, when they set their hand to the task, they created a poetry that was artificial, allusive and mannered. There was Callimachus, whose *Aitia* follows in the tradition of Hesiod's etiological *Theogony* but which focuses, like Pindar, more on emotional detail. There was Apollonius of Rhodes, who wrote a mini, four-book treatment of Jason's quest for the golden fleece called the *Argonautica*, which is psychologically rich but a bit plodding. Unlike Homer's Achilles and Odysseus, Apollonius's Jason is a conflicted and static character who is Hamlet-like in his inability to make up his mind. The centerpiece of the epic (and its most memorable sequence) is the section in which Medea falls in love with Jason and decides to help him: an episode that Apollonius handles with delicacy and insight. Finally, there was Theocritus, who wrote a series of lyrics known as the *Pastorals:* nostalgic, melancholy poems that carry their sophisticated readers back to a beautiful but artificial world of shepherds who live close to the land and spend their days playing pipes and singing.

Meanwhile in Italy, the Romans were embroiled in the Punic Wars, and they too looked to Homer for poetic and epic inspiration. Until the time of Virgil and even beyond, most Roman artists, whether sculptors, poets or craftsmen, felt inferior to the Greeks and sought desperately to imitate them. Two of the first to do so were Naevius and Ennius, for whom we have fragments rather than complete works. The former, in his *Bellum Punicum* of the late third century B.C., sought to do for the Punic Wars what Homer had done for the Trojan War. The latter, in his *Annales* of the early second century B.C., attempted to retell the fuller history of Rome. Alas, both works are vast, unwieldy and dully chronological; they lack the epic unity, power, concentration and intensity of imagination found in Homer.

They were followed in the first century B.C. by Cicero, whose epics have rhetorical force but are really veiled political pamphlets.

And then came the golden age of Caesar Augustus, an age that was as sophisticated and self-conscious as that of the Alexandrians. Eager and filled with hopes of eternal fame, a coterie of young writers formed around the court of Augustus and gained the patronage of the rich, generous Maecenas. They included Livy, who offered in his 142 books of Roman history a breathtaking panorama that stretches from Aeneas to Augustus, Horace, who wrote stately odes and verse epistles that celebrated civic virtues and poetic decorum, and Ovid, who took a sophisticated, urban, erotic look at modern and mythological lovers. Augustus praised them all (though he later turned against the naughty Ovid who upset his "family values" package), but none of them could write the poem he really wanted: a Homeric epic to celebrate his newfound empire. That task would eventually fall to Virgil, but at first Virgil vehemently resisted Augustus's pleas. He felt inadequate to the task and refused to be another Naevius, Ennius or Cicero. Instead, Virgil spent many years crafting ten aesthetically perfect *Eclogues* (or *Bucolics*) in imitation of the Alexandrian *Pastorals* of Theocritus, and a four-book "farming epic" titled the *Georgics* in imitation of Hesiod's *Works and Days*. Augustus hailed both works, but he persisted with his pleas for an epic. In the end Virgil accepted, but he vowed to himself that he would not put his name to it unless his epic could: (1) combine the purity and power of Homer with the sophistication of the Alexandrians, (2) possess the unity and decorum called for by Aristotle and Horace, (3) celebrate Roman history without becoming propaganda or a dull chronicle, and (4) perform a grand fusion of Homer and the best qualities of post-Homeric literature. To even the greatest poet this would have seemed an impossible task, but Virgil miraculously pulled it off. Here's how he did it.

THE VIRGILIAN SOLUTION

Though both Naevius and Ennius had begun their epics with Aeneas, they both left him quickly behind in favor of a chronological approach. Virgil's great brainstorm was to set his entire epic in the absolute heroic past of Homer and then employ a battery of narrative devices to allow allusions to future events. That is to say, the *Aeneid*, though it occurs simultaneously with the *Odyssey,* concerns itself wholly with the full sacred history of Rome: a history that reaches us through prophecies, visions, engravings, genealogies and even a trip to the underworld. By carefully manipulating this twofold structure, in which a millennium of Roman history is contained in a narrative covering less than a decade, Virgil accomplished two vital goals: to maintain the mythic force of his tale throughout the work and to provide his epic with a rich etiological substructure. Because of this "double vision," Virgil could present the heroic journey of Aeneas in such a way as to locate in that journey the true origins of a number of Roman events, practices and beliefs. Thus, while the virtues Aeneas must learn if he is to survive are the same virtues that made Rome great, his tragic affair with Dido, the queen of Carthage, is presented as the root cause for the Punic Wars—rather as the biblical rivalry between Isaac and Ishmael may be seen as the root cause of the modern strife between Jews and Arabs.

Having established these etiological links between the legendary past and the historical present, Virgil could use those links to infuse his epic with an aesthetically justified form of propaganda. On the simplest level, Virgil used his epic to do artistically what the bad imitators of Homer had done so crudely: flatter his rich patrons by linking them to ancient heroes. Just as many of the names that appear in the *Aeneid* were really contemporary Roman names, so many of the rituals practiced in the epic were those favored by Augustus himself. On a deeper level, Virgil used this aspect of his epic as a forum for reinterpreting Roman history along the lines of Herodotus (the struggles between Rome and her enemies, whether past or present, are really struggles between West and East, order and chaos, civilization and barbarism) and Thucydides (Rome's rise to power, for all its sweeping grandeur, also involved heavy doses of political expediency, underhanded tactics, and realpolitik). Whereas we who live on the other side of the Vietnam War and Watergate tend to view propaganda as negative and disingenuous, Virgil used it to open the eyes of his readers to deeper meanings, to those unseen, divine forces that propel history along its appointed grooves.

And this takes us back to Virgil's eschatological view of history, which he shared unknowingly with the writers of the Old Testament. Like Moses or Samuel or Isaiah, Virgil learned through surveying the victories and setbacks of his people that history is neither haphazard nor arbitrary; to the contrary it moves forward, as an Aristotelian plot, in accordance with necessity, probability and inevitability. History is going somewhere; it seeks what the Greeks called *telos*—a purposeful end. For Virgil, of course, that *telos* was the Battle of Actium, which ended the civil wars and brought Augustus to the throne. Just as nothing can stop Aeneas from reaching his destined end, so nothing can stop Rome from reaching her *telos* in the empire of Augustus. And with that eschatological vision and faith comes an equally firm belief in typology. Like eschatology, typology (the belief that present events and people are prefigured in earlier ones) also appears frequently in the Bible: Elijah, who roams the wilderness dressed in sackcloth and challenges the political powers of his day, is a type of John the Baptist; the near sacrifice of Isaac by his father Abraham is a type of God's actual sacrifice of his son at Calvary; the brazen serpent prefigures the crucifixion (see Numbers 21:4-9; John 3:14-15). In the same way, as we shall see in the succeeding chapters, Aeneas is presented again and again as a type or prefiguring of Augustus: a literary device that allows Virgil either to praise or criticize his emperor by praising or criticizing the actions and choices of his hero.

Which leads us finally to what must have been Virgil's most difficult aesthetic choice: his depiction of Aeneas. Though psychologically richer than either Achilles or Odysseus, Aeneas is, like Apollonius's Jason, a far weaker and less charismatic figure. He is, in fact, a new kind of hero: one who possesses the strength of a Homeric warrior but who is ultimately the subject of historical-cosmic forces that he can neither control nor fully understand. In that sense, he might make a modern reader think more of King Arthur than of Beowulf, more the idealistic leader led astray by his own passions and those of his people than the more self-assured but primitive slayer of Grendel. More to the point, he is less like Homer's heroes, whom the gods help because they are strong, and more like those of the Bible, who are strong because God helps them. He is, in fact, very much like Saint Paul, who never asked to be commissioned by God, who eventually left Asia Minor and found his way to Rome, who had to endure a long and painful "education" by means of which he was transformed from a member of a small, isolated people to a citizen of a boundless, universal kingdom whose reign shall never end.

18

Virgil's *Aeneid* I

The Fall of Troy

BOTH THE *ILIAD* AND THE *ODYSSEY* begin with a brief prologue in which Homer lays forth his epic theme. In the former, that theme is the wrath of Achilles (*wrath* is the first word in Greek); in the latter (where the first word in Greek is *man*), Homer's theme centers more on the resourcefulness of a single man and his struggles to maintain his identity and resist the temptation to folly. The *Aeneid*, in contrast, begins not with a man or with one of the qualities of a man, but with the word *arms*, or *warfare*. Our focus in this epic, the prologue suggests, will be less personal. Yes, there will be a hero who will go on a perilous sea voyage (like Odysseus) and fight in a great war (like Achilles), but the real focus will be elsewhere. Thus Virgil ends his prologue, "So hard and huge / A task it was to found the Roman people" (I.48-49).[1] Indeed, as if to drive home the importance of that founding over the personality of its founder, Virgil holds off nam-

---

[1] All references in this chapter and those that follow will be by the book and line numbers as they appear in the *Aeneid*, trans. Robert Fitzgerald (New York: Vintage Books, 1984). Fitzgerald's line numbers do not correspond with those of the original Latin; however, he does provide the cumulative Latin line numbers at the bottom of each page.

ing Aeneas until well into the first book of his epic. Even more startling, when Aeneas does finally appear by name, he is not given a dramatic "stage entrance" but is seen in the midst of a chaotic storm over which he has no control.

The storm that threatens to destroy Aeneas and his crew has been caused by Juno (Hera), the wife of Jupiter (Zeus). Juno, the prologue tells us, hates Aeneas, partly because he is of the same despised Trojan race as Paris (who had snubbed her when he gave the golden apple to Aphrodite/ Venus, the mother of Aeneas), and partly because Juno is the patron goddess of Carthage, which she knows Rome is destined to destroy—if Aeneas can manage to establish its foundations. As the storm rages, writes Virgil, "Every sign / Portended a quick death for mariners. / Aeneas on the instant felt his knees / Go numb and slack, and stretched his hands to heaven" (I.129-32). In this state of despair, Aeneas addresses his men in words that closely imitate a speech that Odysseus makes to himself when his raft almost capsizes; in both cases, the speeches are despairing and suicidal, but the fact that Aeneas makes his before his men makes him far less heroic. With the help of Jupiter, Aeneas lands his ships on the shore of Carthage, but even now he continues to be afraid, and he delivers a second speech to his men, one that is also patterned closely after a passage from the *Odyssey.* This time, Aeneas appears more hopeful, but the contrast between his speech and that of Odysseus is still strongly marked. In the Homeric version, Odysseus calls on his men to trust in him to get them out of danger; in the Virgilian version, Aeneas tells his men to look ahead and trust in the promise of a new Troy.

But that is not the only difference between the speeches of Aeneas and Odysseus. When Aeneas gives his second speech to his men, Virgil makes it clear that he is not telling his men what is really on his heart: "So ran [Aeneas's] speech. Burdened and sick at heart, / He feigned hope in his look, and inwardly / Contained his anguish" (I.284-85). Virgil is not accusing Aeneas of dishonesty but linking his hero to the politicians of his day. The speech that Aeneas delivers, while imitative of Homer, is equally modeled on the rhetorical speeches one might have heard in the Roman forum or senate. Odysseus is free to speak as he pleases, but Aeneas, a "proto-Roman," must be both a public and private man. No matter how frightened he may feel on the inside, it is his duty to use his rhetorical gifts to calm the fears of his men.

THE GOOD END

Though the story of Aeneas and his journey to Rome begins with the fall of Troy, Virgil does not begin his tale with that event. Rather, like Homer, he begins his epic in medias res, after Aeneas has already spent seven years at sea searching for the land that has been promised him. As we have seen, Virgil's choice to begin his epic at this point has the disturbing but intentional effect of stripping Aeneas of his conventional heroic prerogatives. In fact, to return to a point I made earlier, it places him in closer company with the heroes of the Pentateuch than with those of Homer: with Abraham, who shows deceitful cowardice when he pretends that his wife is his sister (Genesis 12:10-20); with Jacob, who shows guilty cowardice when he is about to meet his brother Esau (Genesis 33:1-4); with Moses, who shows rash cowardice when he flees from Egypt after killing an Egyptian and faithless cowardice when he tries to excuse himself from God's call (Exodus 2:11-15; 3—4). Still Aeneas's flaws do not disrupt or deconstruct the story, for just as the choices of Abraham, Jacob and Moses are circumscribed within a greater sacred history, so Aeneas's flawed choices are made within the framework of an overarching, divine plan.

After Aeneas lands on Carthage and bids his men to trust in fate, Venus (like Thetis in the *Iliad*) flies to Jupiter to petition his aid for her unlucky son. In the *Iliad*, Thetis's prayer sets in motion the entire epic; here Venus's prayer sets in motion something far grander. Like Zeus in the *Iliad*, Jupiter lays out the parameters for what is to follow in the epic; however, he then leaps past the end of the *Aeneid* to foretell the future glory of Rome. Jupiter's words are, in their own way, as glorious and breathtaking as God's promise to Abraham that his descendants would outnumber the stars in the sky and the sand on the shore and that through him all the nations would be blessed (Genesis 22:15-18). Leaping forward three centuries, Jupiter foretells the birth of Romulus and Remus and their suckling by a she-wolf. It is Romulus, he promises Venus, who "will take the leadership, build walls of Mars, / And call by his own name his people Romans. / For these I set no limits, world or time, / But make the gift of empire without end" (I.372-75). Once established, Rome will continue to grow in might until she conquers all the lands of Greece (thus reversing Troy's defeat) and "circumscribe[s] / Empire with Ocean" (I.385-86). He then ends with a vision of the coming Pax Romana that recalls the biblical images of that final millennial kingdom when the lion will lie down with the lamb; in that far-off day, Jupiter promises, the fratricides (Romulus and Remus) will be reconciled and "grim with iron frames, the Gates of War / Will then be shut: inside, unholy Furor . . . / Will grind his teeth and howl with bloodied mouth" (I.394-98).

With this prophecy ringing in our ears, we are led back to Aeneas, who, while scouting out the city to see if its inhabitants are friendly, receives— or, rather, we the readers receive through him—his first lesson in eschatology and typology. In the center of town he comes upon a grove sacred to the Carthaginians; it was here, we learn, that Queen Dido, forced to flee Phoenicia after the murder of her husband, found the sign from Juno that indicated she was to build her new city in that spot. And that sign, Virgil tells us, was a "proud warhorse's head: this meant for Carthage / Prowess in war and ease of life through ages" (I.603-4). Though Aeneas seems blind to the irony, we the readers cannot help but note the strangeness of a horse symbolizing the founding of a city, since it was a horse—the Trojan Horse—that led to the downfall of Troy. And yet, Virgil's point is precisely that this is not a strange thing. When viewed eschatologically (from the perspective of the good end), the destruction and founding of a city are linked events. The Jews under Joseph had to descend into Egypt and eventually into slavery before they could, under Moses and Joshua, ascend out of bondage and reclaim that very Holy Land from which they had originally set out. Without the fall, there cannot be the rise; without the descent, there can be no ascent. Just as the fall of man when viewed eschatologically is seen as a good thing, a *felix culpa*, for it leads to the incarnation and then to the New Jerusalem, so the fall of Troy is an eschatologically hopeful event for it starts a historical process that leads to the founding of Rome by Romulus and culminates in the establishment of the mighty Roman Empire of Caesar Augustus.

The *Aeneid*, like the Old Testament, forces us to continually gaze forward in anticipation of a greater end. And yet throughout the *Aeneid* there exists a strong competing desire to look backward nostalgically to a lost past. A melancholy mood suffuses much of the epic that critics have referred to as the "Virgilian sadness," a reluctance to let go, to forget, to move on. Near the sacred grove where Dido found the warhorse's head, Aeneas comes upon a great temple to Juno; on its walls he finds engraved in stone the story of the Trojan War. Aeneas scans the wall and reads on it all the tragic events that led to the fall of his city, even as we, the readers, take in all the scenes familiar to us from Homer's *Iliad.* Indeed, as Aeneas hungrily absorbs the images, we sense that there is another onlooker: the poet Virgil, who is taking this opportunity to review the legacy of Homer before moving on to create his own epic. It is a time of silent reflection for poet, hero and reader alike, a pause that prepares us emotionally and aesthetically for the next two books of the *Aeneid,* during which Aeneas (like Odysseus at the court of the Phaeacians) will relate his sad past to the hospitable Queen Dido.

THE GHOSTS IN THE MACHINE

Though he alludes to it briefly in the *Odyssey,* and though the tale was well known in the ancient world, Homer never tells the full and tragic story of the fall of Troy. That telling would be left to Virgil, who would shape the ancient legend of the Trojan Horse into one of the most harrowing and moving narratives in all of literature. In the tenth year of the war, Odysseus (whom Virgil, following the Greek tragedians rather than Homer, depicts as a Machiavellian villain) instructs the Greeks to build a giant horse of wood with a hollow belly wide enough to house a company of warriors. The Greeks drag the horse before the walls of Troy, then return to their ships and pretend to sail back home. Odysseus (*Ulysses* in Latin) hopes of course that the Trojans will take the horse into their city, but they do so only after Ulysses unleashes his backup plan: a double agent named Sinon who appeals to the Trojans for sanctuary, claiming that Ulysses has betrayed him and turned his fellow Greeks against him. The Trojans naively pity him, for, Virgil tells us through the mouth of Aeneas, they are "unable to conceive such a performance" (II.144). Like Adam before the fall, the Trojans are innocent, unlearned in the ways of guile and deceit. Their eyes will soon be opened.

As the Trojans, heeding Sinon's deceptive advice, drag the horse into the city and begin to celebrate the end of the war, Aeneas is sleeping peacefully in his bed: it is the last peaceful night he will know. He does not hear the click when the trap door opens and the concealed Greeks exit the wooden belly, nor does he hear the gate opening in the night to let in the waiting Greek army. What he hears instead is a sound of moaning as the ghost of Hektor, torn and bloody as if it had been dragged again behind Achilles' chariot, appears to him in a dream and warns him to flee the city, which even now is being burned by the Greeks:

> Ai! Give up and go, child of the goddess,
> Save yourself, out of these flames. The enemy
> Holds the city walls, and from her height
> Troy falls in ruin. Fatherland and Priam
> Have their due; if by one hand our towers
> Could be defended, by this hand, my own,
> They would have been. Her holy things, her gods
> Of hearth and household Troy commends to you.
> Accept them as companions of your days;
> Go find for them the great walls that one day
> You'll dedicate, when you have roamed the sea. (II.387-97)

When Hektor commissions Aeneas to take with him the "gods / Of hearth and household," he speaks anachronistically. It was the Romans, not the Trojans, who worshiped such gods, whom the Romans called "Lares" and "Penates." Virgil is establishing an etiological link between Troy and Rome that will provide Roman religious practices with a legendary and heroic basis. Here, Virgil suggests, is the true origin of Rome's most sacred rituals.

Hektor's commission to the frightened Aeneas is both urgent and non-negotiable. One expects Aeneas to pack his bags and flee the city at once. But he does not. On the contrary, he tells Dido, "To arm was my first maddened impulse—not / That anyone had a fighting chance in arms" (II.421-22). Indeed, as Troy collapses around him, Aeneas delays leaving again and again. To understand why, we need to recall the microcosm of the *Iliad* and those virtues—bravery, honor, prowess on the battlefield—so esteemed in that microcosm. It was in just such a microcosm that Aeneas was raised, and his first desire is to do precisely what Hektor would have done were the situation reversed: die with his city like a captain who goes down with his ship. But that option is not left to Aeneas, for he now exists in an eschatological microcosm, one that is focused on the end. As a result, he must learn new strategies and cultivate new virtues. The world of Virgil's *Aeneid* rewards patience, faith and steadfastness over reckless courage and two-dimensional prowess; it calls for personal sacrifice in the service of a hope that cannot be seen, for a reeducation born through pain, for the loss of everything but a shadowy future glory to be inherited by one's distant progeny.

It would be easier, far easier, for Aeneas to perish in the flames, but the gods have other plans for him. Like St. Paul, he must become something other than he was so that he might fulfill a mission he never dreamed of doing. The transition will be painful and confusing. As Aeneas wanders through the burning streets and witnesses the murder not only of his countrymen but of good King Priam, he finds himself face to face with Helen of Troy. Tormented by the horror around him and desperate to find a reason, a cause, a justification for what is happening, the normally gentle Aeneas lifts his sword to kill the defenseless Greek woman. He knows it will do no good, but he hopes it will at least bring some relief to slay the purported cause of the war. Before he can strike, however, his mother Venus appears to him in a vision and stays his hand: "You must not hold [Helen], / That hated face, the cause of this, nor Paris. / The harsh will of the gods it is, the gods, / That overthrows the splendor of this place / And brings Troy from her height into the dust" (II.790-94). Something is going on here that is larger than Paris or Helen, something Aeneas cannot see with his earthly eyes.

"Look over there," she tells her confused and despairing son, "I'll tear away the cloud / That curtains you, and films your mortal sight, / The fog around you" (II.795-97). And when Aeneas looks again, he sees a vision that will stay with him for the rest of his life. Where he saw before an army of Greek soldiers tearing down the walls and gates of Troy, he now sees the looming figures of titanic gods prying up stones with their massive hands and gigantic weapons. What Aeneas sees in this prophetic flash is what I like to call the "ghosts in the machine," the hidden forces that propel history toward its appointed end. Though the vision confuses Aeneas, as it would anyone not accustomed to seeing such "ghosts" in person, it calms him and brings him to his senses. For a brief, suspended moment he has peered into the inner workings of destiny, and it has renewed his faith.

When I, as a Christian, read this powerful scene, I cannot help but be reminded of the prophetic visions granted to such men as Isaiah, Ezekiel and John. No doubt these prophets (unaccustomed to gazing directly into the face of eternity) found it difficult, if not impossible, to understand what they saw. Still, the images were vivid enough to remain in their minds and to make their way into their prophetic books. Like Aeneas, the biblical prophets are vouchsafed a vision they cannot fully understand, but which fills them with hope. But there the similarity ends. Whereas Virgil's gods, though immortal, appear to be locked within time, the God of the Bible transcends both space and time. Further, while the gods of Virgil use such visions to manipulate, the visions Yahweh grants enhance and signify the covenantal love between God and his people.

His vision ended, Aeneas rushes to his father's house and tells him they must leave. But Anchises, like Aeneas, is a product of the microcosm of the *Iliad,* and he staunchly refuses. Again Aeneas loses his resolve and prepares to leap into battle—until once again the gods send a divine portent to convince father and son alike to leave. Aeneas lifts the aged Anchises onto his shoulders, takes his son Iulus in hand, and heads toward a breach in the wall. This image, of the dutiful Aeneas simultaneously leading his son and bearing the weight of his father, became something of an icon in the Rome of Augustus: an eternal sign of the central Roman virtue of duty (*pietas* in Latin).

Having reached the wall, Aeneas looks around for his wife, Creusa, who was supposed to meet him there, but she is nowhere to be seen. The reluctant hero rushes back into the burning city to find his wife. Vainly he calls out into the night, risking death at the hands of any Greek soldier who might hear his cries. "I filled the streets with calling," Aeneas recalls, "in my grief / Time after time I groaned and called Creusa, / Frantic, in endless quest from door to door. / Then to my vision her sad wraith appeared— / Creusa's ghost, larger than life before me" (II.999-1003). It is the third and final "ghost" the gods send Aeneas to ensure his escape from

Troy; with each visitation, the apparition increases in intimacy: first friend, then mother, then wife. It is not easy to live in an eschatological world when the promised end lies so far away. So it was for the prophets of old who "enquired and searched diligently" that they might know the time and the hour when the awaited Christ would come, knowing full well that it was not for themselves but their descendants that they labored (1 Peter 1:10-12).

In one of those sad, sad ironies that must ever accompany a fallen world whose hope lies in the *felix culpa*, it is Aeneas's own wife who must bid him to leave her and Troy behind; it is she too who must prophesy that Aeneas shall find not only a new land but a new queen as well. When she has finished her prophecy and bids her last farewell, Aeneas reaches out to embrace her: "Three times / I tried to put my arms around her neck, / Three times enfolded nothing, as the wraith / Slipped through my fingers, bodiless as wind, / or like a flitting dream" (II.1028-32). Virgil is imitating an episode from the *Iliad* when Achilles tries in vain to embrace the ghost of Patroclus, but the pathos here is far stronger. Aeneas is losing more than a friend: he is being forced to let go of his past, to relinquish all he knows and loves. With slow steps he returns to the wall, but when he arrives, the spot is teeming with a great crowd of "men and women / Gathered for exile, young—pitiful people / Coming from every quarter, minds made up, / with their belongings, for whatever lands / I'd lead them to by sea" (II.1036-40). Poor duty-bound Aeneas; he is not even given time to grieve.

19

VIRGIL'S *AENEID* II
Aeneas and Dido

IN HIS TWENTY-FOUR-BOOK *ODYSSEY*, Homer devotes four books—one-sixth of his entire epic—to Odysseus's first-person flashback narrative; in his twelve-book *Aeneid*, Virgil preserves this epic ratio by devoting two books to Aeneas's first-person narrative. The first of those two books, as we saw in the previous chapter, recounts the tragic fall of Troy. The second, Book III, covers Aeneas's wanderings as he crisscrosses the Mediterranean in search of his destiny. Ironically, throughout most of his wanderings, Aeneas follows the same path as Odysseus; he even passes by some of the same locales. For the duration of Book III, Virgil's proto-Roman hero inhabits not only the same mythic time but the same mythic space as Homer's Greek hero. But alas, Aeneas, like Virgil himself, must ever tread one step behind his famous Greek forebear. In many ways, Book III is the most derivative book of the *Aeneid;* like so much of Roman art and literature, it closely imitates its Greek predecessor. And yet even here, Virgil's inspired, even prophetic vision allows him to transcend both Homer's great poem and the Hellenic culture that sprang from it like Athena from the head of Zeus.

Near the end of Book III, Aeneas lands on the island of the Cyclopes, where he is met by a wild-looking Greek who supplicates Aeneas to take him away on his ship. The Greek turns out to be a member of Ulysses' crew who was left behind when Ulysses escaped from the island. Neither the man nor his terrible fate is mentioned in Homer; the story is invented by Virgil to make a powerful point about Aeneas and his Roman virtues. Although Aeneas has every reason to leave the Greek behind on the island (he is after all a compatriot of the hated Ulysses, he who masterminded the Trojan Horse), he pities the man and carries him safely to their next port of call. If we recall that in the *Odyssey* Odysseus is the only member of his crew to make it to Ithaca alive, we will quickly see what Virgil is doing here. The Roman Aeneas, this episode tells us, has such a great sense of duty, such *pietas,* that he succeeds in doing what Odysseus himself could not do: save the lives of the Greek sailors entrusted to him. And the episode teaches us something else as well. It reminds us that Aeneas is a qualitatively different hero than Odysseus. The individualistic Odysseus need only ensure his own safe return to Ithaca to fulfill his epic goal; if Aeneas does the same, if he alone makes it to Italy, he will have failed his mission. The burden on Aeneas is far greater and far heavier: he is responsible not just for himself but for an entire people. The fate of an empire rests on his shoulders.

FALSE HOMECOMINGS

That is not to say, of course, that Aeneas transforms overnight into the founding father he is destined to become. Indeed, the recurring theme of Book III is Aeneas's perpetual reluctance to press on in search of that shadowy western land promised him by the gods. Again and again, Virgil's impatient founder attempts to cut short his voyage and to build his new city on the first available island. At one point, Aeneas receives a prophecy that he must seek out his own mother, a prophecy he promptly misinterprets. Although one of Aeneas's ancestors had come from Italy (hence the prophecy to seek out his mother), Aeneas prefers to heed the misguided advice of his father and to set sail for the closer and more familiar shores of Crete, from which a more recent ancestor had come. On one level Aeneas's mistake is understandable, but Virgil uses it to expose Aeneas's willingness to make such a mistake if it means an end to his wanderings. Indeed, so eager is Aeneas to build his new city that the very moment he lands on Crete, he begins to establish laws and till the fields. He does not pause to consult the gods, for he is afraid they will tell him that Crete is not his destination.

But Aeneas (like the biblical Jonah) cannot hide from the gods or his fate. Even as he issues his laws, a plague falls on his new settlement, killing the crops and sapping the men of their strength. With great reluctance, Aeneas sets sail again. And so it goes throughout Book III, with Aeneas seizing every opportunity to pull his ships ashore and found his colony. In chapter fifteen we compared Pentheus and Saul of Tarsus, both of whom are admonished by a god (Dionysus/Christ) for "kicking against the pricks." Like these two stubborn heroes, Aeneas too resists the divine call, making his journey longer and more bitter by so doing. Perhaps the most difficult moment for the weary Aeneas is when he lands on the western coast of Greece and discovers a Trojan colony led by Helenus, a son of Priam, and Hektor's widow, Andromache, whom Helenus has taken as wife. On this foreign shore they have built a Troy in miniature, complete with a small-scale replica of the river Xanthos and the Scaean Gate. When he sees this, Aeneas is filled with envy, for this is exactly what he desires to do: rebuild Troy in a new land. Sick for his lost home and vanished way of life, Aeneas is unable to conceive that the gods want him to found not a resuscitated Troy but a new and greater Troy that will rule the whole Mediterranean world through which Aeneas now wanders. The desire of the God of the Bible is not that his people return to Eden, but that they move on to the New Jerusalem. Jupiter desires the same for his Trojans.

Well, let me qualify that last statement. Jupiter's desire for his Trojans is not the same thing as God's desire for his bride but a pagan intimation of that desire. Virgil seems to have glimpsed in the process of telling his epic tale that God does have a purpose for us, but we cannot achieve our purpose unless we are willing to participate in God's divine plan, unless we are willing to sacrifice our own immediate desires and trust in his promises. The pagan poet seems to have glimpsed as well that God's greater plan was to work through a somewhat reluctant patriarch (Aeneas, Abraham), who would lay the foundations for a single nation (the Jews, the Romans), through whom all of the world would be blessed. Indeed, we can say of Aeneas what the Bible says of Abraham: that he was a stranger in a strange land. Still, the differences between the *Aeneid* and the Bible are as striking as the similarities.

What we miss in the Roman epic is any sense of true intimacy between Jupiter and his people, any sense that Jupiter might participate in the sacrifice he calls Aeneas to make. To put this another way, though Virgil did see that the gods might intervene in the flow of human history, he was unable to see or even dream that the Lord of the gods could so love and desire communion with his people that he would leave his heavenly throne to enter human history. For all the guidance that Jupiter and Venus give Aeneas, the Trojan must in the end suffer alone. Aeneas, like the biblical patriarchs, is in search of a promised city, but the city promised to Aeneas will remain secular and earthbound. In contrast, the promised land toward which all of the Bible points is the New Jerusalem, where God will dwell directly with his people. Like the deistic God of the eighteenth century, Jupiter seeks only to nudge his mortals toward a secular utopia.

As Aeneas sails in search of that utopia, he faces the same temptation Odysseus faced: the temptation of the false homecoming. Odysseus's struggle, however, is far less difficult than that of Aeneas. Homer's hero has a home and family to return to; Virgil's hero, even if he does finish his mission and make it to Italy, will have only begun his struggle. Aeneas's arrival in Italy promises no family reunions; it means only that Aeneas can begin to lay the foundations of the home of Rome's future citizens. It is understandable then that when Aeneas lands on Carthage and Dido offers him the opportunity to remain and to rule Carthage jointly, he leaps at the opportunity. Like Dido, Aeneas has lost both his spouse and his country and is eager to build a new home. Indeed, when Aeneas first arrives on Carthage and sees Dido's people building walls and theaters, planting crops, and enacting laws, he exclaims: "How fortunate these are / Whose city walls are rising here and now" (I.595-96). The gods would not allow him to stay with Helenus and Andromache in their mini-Troy, but surely now they will allow him to stay in Carthage and build an empire with Dido.

Aeneas and Dido turn out to be male and female counterparts of one another—soul mates, really—and they quickly fall in love. And yet their love is not fully their own: the affair is being orchestrated behind the scenes by two goddesses, Venus and Juno, with their own scheming plans. In constructing the fatal romance that first unites and then drives apart Aeneas and Dido, Virgil looks back to the *Argonautica* of Apollonius of Rhodes, in which a similar divinely orchestrated love affair springs up between the royal Medea and the seafaring Jason. As in Apollonius, the woman is most driven wild by passion and finds herself unable to think of anything but the godlike captain. So strong is that passion, in fact, that it causes both women to betray someone they love: in the case of Medea, her father; in the case of Dido, her dead husband Sychaeus, before whose ashes she had taken a voluntary vow that she would never remarry. Day and night Dido burns with desire for the embraces of Aeneas. At first she refuses to indulge her desire, promising herself that she will stay true to her vow, but her sister (like the earthy nurse in *Hippolytus*) convinces her that such vows do not matter to the dead.

Eventually Dido gives way to her passion and neglects building and administering her new city. During a hunting expedition, the lovesick queen and her smitten Trojan become separated from the party and find themselves in a cave. There, in the presence of "Primal Earth herself and Nuptial Juno" (IV.229), the two are married in a primitive ceremony without the "benefit of clergy." It is a passionate, almost operatic moment, but Virgil says of their impulsive vow that it "was the first cause of death, and first / Of sorrow" (IV.233-34). In the eschatological universe of the *Aeneid,* a bad event like the fall of Troy can give way to a good end; just so, what seems like a good event—the marriage of Aeneas and Dido—can lead to disaster.

PIETAS VERSUS FUROR

The *Aeneid* is a Roman epic, and as such it embodies a specifically Roman value system: one that codifies right and wrong as a series of opposing pairs. Thus while the Romans of both the Republic and the Empire highly valued the virtues of civilization, order and unity, they hated and feared the corresponding vices of barbarism, chaos and fragmentation. Strongly masculine in outlook, the Romans (like the Pentheus and Jason of Euripides) favored reason over passion, law *(nomos)* over nature *(phusis)*, duty to the state over duty to the family, the Apollonian over the Dionysiac. They exalted the distant, more stoic gods such as Jupiter, Apollo and Minerva/Athena, and they looked with suspicion on primitive, chthonic deities like Dionysus and the Furies. Things that consumed and destroyed—fire, storm, lust—were the enemy of the perpetual Roman urge to build and arrange and systematize. For the Roman, things that threatened unity and the fulfillment of vows and obligations—things like romantic love, individual self-expression, or the desire for wealth and finery—were to be rejected out of hand. Private had to yield to public, the needs of the one to the needs of the many, the desire for personal happiness to the demands of the *polis.* When a Christian today hears the words "piety" and "virtue," he is most likely to conceive of them in passive, feminine terms; to the pagan Romans, *pietas* and *virtus* meant, respectively, "duty" and "manliness" (*vir* in Latin means "man"). Decius Mus showed perfect *pietas* when he sacrificed his life for the Roman army; Gaius Mucius embodied *virtus* when he thrust his hand into the fire. In eternal opposition to *pietas* and *virtus* stood what the Romans called *furor,* the irresistible fury and unquenchable passion that tears civilization apart.

Though we as modern, romantic readers tend to view the affair of Dido and Aeneas in mostly positive terms, the Romans would have seen in it the destructive face of *furor.* It starts as a fever within Dido that cannot be cured, progresses to a fire that burns away her vow to Sychaeus, and rages into a storm that brings all building in Carthage to a dead halt. Even worse, once they sanctify their "marriage," Aeneas begins to dress in Eastern (Phoenician) finery, and the two parade their love publicly throughout Carthage—"careless of their good name" (IV.301), says Virgil, with Roman scorn in his voice. In no time at all, rumor, gossip and slander fill the air, and the news of Aeneas's marriage finds its way to the ear of Jupiter. Infuriated that Aeneas should forsake his divine mission to seek out personal happiness, Jupiter calls on Mercury to deliver a stern message to the backslidden Aeneas: "No son like this did his enchanting mother / Promise to us, nor such did she deliver / Twice from peril at the hands of Greeks. / He was to be the ruler of Italy . . . / And bring the whole world under law's dominion" (IV.309-15). Aeneas, Jupiter insists, was not saved out of the ashes of Troy to be the plaything of an Eastern queen; he was to be the linchpin on which the next thousand years would hang. He was selected by heaven not to rule a local kingdom, but to found a universal empire. It is as unthinkable for him to abandon his call and rule with Dido as it would have been for Moses, having led the Israelites out of slavery, to marry a Canaanite princess and adopt her language, culture and religion.

Mercury soars on his winged slippers toward Carthage, passing on his way "Giant Atlas, balancing the sky / Upon his peak—his pine forested head / In vapor cowled, beaten by wind and rain" (IV.338-40). Atlas is both a Titan who holds up the sky and Mount Atlas, which stands on the tip of Africa across the straits from Gibraltar. In a sense, he is the perfect Roman, an individual who has sacrificed personal joy and happiness to serve that cosmic empire we call the universe: a sacrifice that has caused so much of his humanity to be effaced that he is as much mountain as man. In a moment, Mercury will call on Aeneas to make a similar sacrifice, to become something almost made of stone that the plans of Jupiter might be fulfilled. That Atlas also happens to be the great-great-great-great-great-great-grandfather of Aeneas makes Virgil's subtle, understated comparison even more poignant. When Aeneas receives the message, he agrees that he must leave as soon as possible and tells his men to prepare the ships for departure. The decision is difficult for Aeneas, for his love for Dido is real and deep; however, having made his decision to leave, he finds that he lacks the courage to tell Dido of his plans. Instead, he keeps his departure a secret while he seeks to find "the right occasion" (IV.400) to tell her. Unfortunately, what Aeneas seems to mean by the "right occasion" is the moment his ship actually pulls out of the dock!

Needless to say, Dido soon learns of Aeneas's plans to abandon her—"for who deceives a woman in love?" (IV.404)—and confronts her cowardly and unfaithful lover. Aeneas, though his heart is breaking, beats down his feelings and addresses Dido coldly and informally. He claims that he never meant to injure her and even has the audacity to remind her that they were never "officially" married. He tries to explain that his departure has been forced on him by the gods, but as he does so, he does not weep or sigh or even look at her. When he finishes his speech, Dido erupts in a rage of fury and accuses him of being inhuman: "Some rough Cauca-

sian cliff / Begot you on flint. Hyrcanian tigresses / Tendered their teats to
you" (IV.505-7). She cannot believe that this heartless, stone-faced man
who stands before her is the same man who pledged his love to her. Slowly,
terribly, her once-passionate love for Aeneas transforms into bitter hatred,
and the queen who days earlier had resembled the loyal, innocent, love-
smitten Medea of Apollonius of Rhodes metamorphoses into the vengeful
and destructive Medea of Euripides. Virgil compares her to one of the
Bacchae who are "driven wild" (IV.411) and flee the *polis* to revel on the
mountains. Like the Clytemnestra of Aeschylus, she becomes possessed,
almost literally, by the Furies, a dark and sinister embodiment of all those
chaotic and chthonic forces that cause civilizations to topple.

Throughout the whole affair, the Roman Virgil is fully on the side of
Aeneas. Or is he? Though it is clear that Aeneas is in the right (his "marriage" to Dido was certainly not a marriage but an impulsive indulgence in
lust), it is also clear that he is in the wrong. True, he has no choice but to
leave Carthage, but there is no reason for him to leave the way he does. The
true tragedy of Book IV is that Aeneas is not, at heart, a double for Euripides' Jason; he does love Dido and desperately wants to remain with her,
but his self-doubt and fear of intimacy cause him to become overly masculine—which is to say, overly Roman. It is not so much his leaving as his
sudden and total capitulation to an extreme, unyielding form of Roman *pietas* that pushes Dido into the arms of an equally extreme form of *furor*.
Had Aeneas allowed Dido to see how much his departure was ripping him
apart, had he let her down slowly and gently, had he perhaps given her the
option to accompany him to Italy, she might not have reacted with such
hatred and rage. Again, the Roman Virgil is on Aeneas's side, and he is
well aware of the destructive potential of (feminine) emotion unchecked
by (masculine) reason, but Virgil the poet works too hard at evoking our
pity for the distraught Dido to allow his reader, especially his contemporary Roman reader, to offer unqualified praise to Aeneas and utter rejection
and scorn to Dido. That is why, I would argue, when Aeneas "plays the Roman" in his farewell speech to Dido, his decision proceeds not out of his
strengths or virtues but out of his weakness of character.

Still, however we interpret the faults and virtues Aeneas displays in this
scene, one thing is certain: the upshot of Aeneas's bitter breakup with Dido

is to forever polarize *pietas* and *furor*, West and East, the Apollonian and the Dionysiac. That polarization is not just personal, nor is it merely theoretical; rather, it is both global and historical. In her mania, Dido calls down curses not only on Aeneas but on all of his descendants:

> No pact must be between our peoples; No,
> But rise up from my bones, avenging spirit!
> Harry with fire and sword the Dardan countrymen
> Now, or hereafter, at whatever time
> The strength will be afforded. Coast with coast
> In conflict, I implore, and sea with sea,
> And arms with arms: may they contend in war,
> Themselves and all the children of their children! (IV.868-75)

Here, in this terrifying, almost demonic speech, Virgil synthesizes the many strands and layers of his great poem: etiology and propaganda, eschatology and typology. The tragic affair of Dido and Aeneas is not just a tale from a bygone era, but the historical cause, the spiritual-emotional origin, and the moral-ethical explanation for the Punic Wars. The curse of the Cyclops Polyphemus in the *Odyssey* is completed and expiated by the end of the epic, but Dido's curse will reverberate for a millennium until the avenging spirit she calls down on Aeneas takes form in the person of Hannibal—of whom Dido is herself a type.

But the layers of meaning go even deeper. Dido's curse is closely patterned on the speech the wrathful Achilles makes in the *Iliad* after Hektor begs him to take a vow that neither will defile the corpse of the other if he kills his opponent. Achilles' response, like that of Dido, is that no pacts or oaths can exist between them, only perpetual and unyielding enmity. In the final book of the *Iliad*, there is, of course, a reconciliation between Achilles and the father of Hektor, and yet the potency of Achilles' curse still reverberates. When less than a year later the Greeks defeat Troy, they not only loot it but raze it to the ground. In 146 B.C., when Rome defeated Carthage for the third and final time, she would prove just as brutal as the Greeks.

Dido's curse, as much as any passage in the *Aeneid*, pays tribute to the multiple layers of meaning that lend such richness to Virgil's epic and make it at once a strongly derivative and breathtakingly original work. Yet

Virgil is not done. After issuing her curse, Dido consummates her Bacchic fury by stabbing herself to death while lying on the marriage bed she once shared with Sychaeus (an image that recalls the suicides of Jocasta, Deianira and Phaedra). As she does the deed, she speaks these words: "I die unavenged . . . but let me die, / This way, this way, a blessed relief to go / Into the undergloom" (IV.915-17). In the original Latin, "this way, this way" is *sic, sic,* a sibilant sound that mimics the hissing of a snake. Dido, we suddenly realize, is not just a type of Hannibal but of another passionate Eastern queen who would commit suicide, not with a knife but a snake. An Egyptian queen whose love affair with a Roman warrior would come as close to destroying Rome as did the Carthaginian armies of Hannibal. Though linked eschatologically to the Punic Wars, Dido is simultaneously a prefiguring of Cleopatra. But if Dido is Cleopatra, then who is Aeneas? Is he Marc Antony or Octavian (Caesar Augustus)? The answer is that he is both. In the first half of Book IV, when he decides to abandon his mission to join Dido, he is Antony; when he decides to forsake Dido in favor of Rome, he transfigures into Augustus. By the power of typology, Virgil converts a two-person struggle into a political love triangle.

By becoming Augustus, Aeneas emerges from the triangle as victor, but Virgil, who mixes his Roman propaganda with a strong critique of Augustan realpolitik, allows Dido as well a unique type of triumph. Dido dies, Virgil tells us, "not at her fated span / Nor as she merited, but before her time" (IV.963-64). That is to say, she achieves through her tragic suicide something that Aeneas, for all his courage and *pietas,* will never be able to accomplish. Dido and Dido alone breaks free from the predetermined eschatological course of history in which Aeneas will forever be trapped. While rebuking Aeneas for the coldness of his breakup speech, Dido rebukes as well the "serene immortals" (IV.525) who have orchestrated her doom. These stoic "masculine" gods seem to care nothing for love or joy or passion; to them, men and women are pawns in a cosmic chess game. Dido knows she cannot defeat them, but by ending her own life, she succeeds at least for a moment in scattering the pieces and overturning the board.

20

VIRGIL'S *AENEID* III

To Hell and Back

JUST AS AENEAS'S WIFE CREUSA DIES AT the end of Book II and his lover Dido dies at the end of Book IV, so his father Anchises dies at the end of Book III. Aeneas buries his father on Sicily and shortly thereafter is caught in the storm that shipwrecks him on the shore of Carthage. When Aeneas leaves Carthage one year later (significantly, Aeneas spends the same amount of time with Dido as Odysseus does with Circe) and sails north for Italy, he decides to stop on Sicily to honor the one-year anniversary of his father's death. The ritual he chooses to pay that honor, an athletic competition in which his men take part, closely imitates a famous passage in Homer. In *Iliad* XXIII, Homer devotes over six hundred lines of poetry to a blow-by-blow description of the funeral games the Greeks engage in to celebrate the prowess of the dead Patroclus (as Homer most likely composed the *Iliad* a generation or so after the founding of the Olympics in 776 B.C., it is quite possible that he modeled Book XXIII after a real Olympic competition). Book V of the *Aeneid*, that is to say, is as strongly derivative of Homer as Book III; yet here too Virgil's genius allows him to transcend mere imitation.

By using the games to honor Aeneas's father rather than one of his friends (and Virgil does give us a double for Patroclus in whose memory Aeneas might have celebrated games), the Roman Virgil emphasizes the *pietas* of his hero and his devotion to his ancestors (Roman religion, like the traditional religions of China and Japan, was founded in great part on ancestor worship). In addition, by placing the games where he does, Virgil provides the love-torn Aeneas with a strongly masculine society into which he can temporarily retreat. Indeed, while the male members of Aeneas's crew honor Anchises' memory by demonstrating their *virtus* on the athletic field, the female members of his crew remain by the ships where they indulge in excessive weeping and wailing to express their own grief for the dead patriarch. As in Book IV, Virgil here both praises and critiques Aeneas's exclusive embrace of the masculine at the expense of the feminine. For Rome to become what she is destined to become, it is necessary that more weight be accorded the masculine virtues, and yet both in Books IV and V, when Aeneas pushes so far in that direction that he loses sight of the complementary feminine virtues, disaster strikes. In the former case, Aeneas's refusal to honor or even acknowledge Dido's emotional, feminine needs leads literally to her suicide and eschatologically to the Punic Wars. In the latter, the strict male-female segregation in which Aeneas indulges leads to a crisis that compromises and almost destroys Aeneas's divine mission.

ONE SHALL BE LOST

When Juno, whose hatred of Troy (and Rome) still rages within her, looks down from Olympus and sees the women weeping by the ships, she conceives a plot to frustrate the prophecies of her husband. Whereas Zeus's messenger in the *Iliad* is primarily Iris, the rainbow, and his messenger in the *Odyssey* is primarily Hermes, Virgil makes use of both in his epic. In Book IV, when Jupiter wants to rip Aeneas away from the passionate Dido, he sends the male Mercury to rouse the slothful Trojan. In Book V, when Juno wants to upset Roman *pietas*, she sends the female Iris to rouse up a wave of *furor* that will swallow Jupiter's sacred plan for Rome. Alighting by the ships, Iris takes on the form of a Trojan woman and calls on the mourners to abandon their weary and endless journey. Claiming to have been visited in a dream by Cassandra, a female prophetess who is the sister of the male prophet Helenus, the disguised Iris urges the weeping women to set fire to the ships and thus prevent Aeneas from taking them away to yet another foreign shore. In a fit of Bacchic fury not unlike that of Dido, the women do as Iris bids them, and thick billows of black smoke soon rise skyward from the shore.

Aeneas and his son are the first to see the smoke and rush to the ships. Unable to put out the raging fires, Aeneas sends up a desperate prayer to Jupiter, who causes a sudden storm of rain to put out the blaze. Despite Jupiter's intervention, half of the ships are destroyed, and Aeneas must make the difficult decision to leave half his crew behind on Sicily. Ironically, this nearly fatal episode, caused in great part by Aeneas's refusal, or at least inability, to hear the voices of his female shipmates, is a danger that the far less rigidly masculine Odysseus need never face. Odysseus carries only men on board his black ships. Aeneas, who is a different kind of hero than Odysseus, must preserve the lives of men, women and children and then lay the foundations for an empire that will draw all things into a greater unity: an empire that will give way to a church that will proclaim (if not always practice) the essential and positive complementarity of the sexes and their equal dignity and worth in the eyes of God.

As the fires die down, the ghost of Anchises appears to Aeneas and instructs him to sail to the underworld, where he must come to visit him before sailing on to Italy. Meanwhile, as Aeneas prepares for the journey, Neptune (Poseidon) and Venus discuss the fate of Aeneas. Neptune reminds Venus that he once before saved Aeneas during the Trojan War and prophesied that he would survive to carry on the legacy of his people; he then promises her that Aeneas will also survive his ordeal in Hades. Still, a price will be paid to ensure Aeneas's safe return: "One shall be lost, / But only one to look for, lost at sea: / One life given for many" (V.1064-66). Virgil expresses here the Roman concept of *devotio* (sacrificial devotion) that would later be embodied in the voluntary deaths of such heroes as Decius Mus and Marcus Curtius. In the *Aeneid,* the "one life" that must be given turns out to be that of Palinurus, a close friend of Aeneas and the helmsman of his ship. His death is recounted at the very end of Book V, as those of Creusa, Anchises and Dido are told in the final lines of Books II

III and IV. One by one, all those who are most dear to Aeneas are ripped away, until all he has left are his shadowy visions of future glory. It is only fitting then that Aeneas, who must suffer the loss of everyone he loves, should ultimately be forced to face his own figurative death by descending into Hades.

In the *Odyssey*, Odysseus's descent into the underworld is preceded (and, it appears, ritually paid for) by the accidental death of one of his men, Elpenor, whose shade he later encounters in Hades. In imitating Homer, Virgil also has Aeneas meet up with Palinurus's shade near the beginning of his descent; however, Virgil's meeting is longer and far more significant. Palinurus (like Elpenor) begs his captain to give him a proper burial so that he can find rest in the afterlife. Odysseus quickly promises to fulfill Elpenor's request, but Aeneas is prevented from doing likewise. After Palinurus speaks, Aeneas's guide (the mysterious Sibyl) cuts in and tells Palinurus that he must "abandon hope by prayer to make the gods / Change their decrees" (VI.506-7). The Sibyl then comforts the grieving shade by promising him that future generations will find his body, build him a tomb, and name the nearby cape after him. "The Sibyl's words," Virgil tells us, "relieved him, and the pain / Was for a while dispelled from his sad heart, / Pleased at the place-name" (VI.513-15). Throughout this brief exchange Aeneas remains silent, and yet it is vital that he overhear the Sibyl's promise to Palinurus. Like his deceased helmsman, Aeneas too has only the future promise of glory (of a "place-name") to help him endure the terrible losses he must suffer over the course of the *Aeneid*.

Indeed, a numbing sense of loss hangs over all of Book VI, a sense that greets us at the very outset when Aeneas and his men land on the coast of Cumae and pass through the doors of the temple of Apollo, where his prophetess the Sibyl dwells. On the doors of the temple, they see engraved the tragic tale of Daedalus and Icarus, how King Minos of Crete had imprisoned them and how they had escaped on wings fashioned by Daedalus. The engraving does not, however, include Icarus's fatal fall, for the artist is Daedalus, who found himself unable to depict the death of his son: "Twice," says Virgil with great sympathy, "your father had tried to shape your fall / In gold, but twice his hands dropped" (VI.49-50). The Greek artist is unable to express a grief that is inexpressible, yet this is precisely what the Roman poet attempts to do in his epic: to sing both the glory of Rome and the losses that made that glory possible. In the episode that follows, Aeneas, instructed by the Sibyl, plucks the magical golden bough that will allow him safe passage through the underworld. With joy he returns to his crew, only to find that another young man, Misenus, has died in his absence, seemingly as a scapegoat for the bough. Later, after Aeneas leaves Cumae, his old nurse dies as well, another victim to pay for Aeneas's journey. Neptune, it seems, was wrong: not one but three (four if we include Icarus) shall be lost.

With the Sibyl to lead him and the golden bough to protect him, Aeneas makes his way through the mouth of Hades and into the dark regions below. At one point in his descent, he comes upon the fields of mourning where dwell the shades of "those whom pitiless love consumed / With cruel wasting" (VI.596-97). Among these sad ghosts he spies Dido and pauses to address her. In sharp contrast to his breakup speech, Aeneas now weeps and speaks tenderly to her, though he continues to blame the gods and fate for his decision. He hopes that Dido will speak to him, but instead she begins to move back into the shadows. "Wait a little," Aeneas cries in desperation, "Do not leave my sight. / Am I someone to flee from?" (VI.625-26). But Dido remains silent and fixes her gaze on the ground, "her face no more affected than if she were / Immobile granite or Marpesian stone. / At length she flung away from him and fled, / His enemy still" (VI.632-35). In Book IV, Dido accuses Aeneas of being as hard as a Caucasian cliff; this time around, it is she who has become as hard and inflexible as stone. Beware, Virgil seems to be warning Augustus: if you treat others with cruelty, they will treat you likewise when the situation is reversed. Yes, Rome must be strong, as Aeneas must be strong, but she must avoid policies that will convert her foes into implacable and eternal enemies. For if she does, she will suffer what is perhaps the greatest loss of all: isolation from companionship and love.

The sad, final meeting of Aeneas and Dido ends with Dido receding into a "shadowy grove / Where he whose bride she once had been, Sychaeus, / Joined in her sorrows and returned her love" (VI.635-37). Sychaeus is no Roman; he has forgiven Dido for breaking her vow and has taken her back into his heart. As the reunited lovers go off into the grove,

Aeneas gazes "after her in tears, / Shaken by her ill fate and pitying her" (VI.638-39). And yet, we feel, perhaps Aeneas should pity himself. Dido (like Antony and Cleopatra) has lost her kingdom but won her heart; Aeneas (like Augustus) will win his kingdom but at the loss of his heart. Which, the *Aeneid* forces us to ask, is the greater loss? It is the masculine, Roman way to choose *fama* ("fame") over *amor* ("love"), and the weight of the *Aeneid* certainly falls in that direction. Nevertheless, Virgil will give a voice to the feminine, to that which ever chooses *amor* over *fama*, to that which says it is not worth it, even if only one should be lost along the way.

THE MARCH OF ROMAN HISTORY

When Odysseus descends into the underworld, he sees only gloom, misery and pain. Aeneas, in contrast, eventually makes his way past scenes of sorrow and torment to reach the Elysian fields where his father Anchises dwells in bliss. Though Homer mentions the Elysian fields briefly in the *Odyssey*, he does not locate them in Hades but at the world's end. Virgil, following other ancient writers (most notably Plato), locates the abode of the blessed in a region of the underworld where the souls of the righteous sing, dance and wrestle on a wide expanse of green grass. Here dwell all those who have gained *fama* by performing deeds on earth that will ensure their eternal memory. Aeneas and the Sibyl make their way slowly across the grass until they come to a lush valley. There they find Anchises surveying a group of human souls who are destined to return to the earth in the form of Anchises' own descendants.

In another grand fusion of etiology and propaganda, eschatology and typology, Virgil here suggests that the future glory of Rome is not only written prophetically in the stars but is spiritually "stored up" in the underworld. The seeds of a historical Roman harvest to come are already present, literally, in a mythic Hades. In Book IV, Virgil identifies Dido as a type of Cleopatra; in this episode, Virgil moves beyond typology to suggest that Cleopatra might in fact be the reincarnation of Dido. Any notion of the transmigration of souls is, of course, incompatible with the Scriptures, and yet Jesus himself pushes the typological envelope when he explains to his disciples that Elijah had returned as prophesied in the person of John the Baptist (Matthew 17:10-13). Among the many reasons that the early and medieval church saw Virgil as a proto-Christian was his stunning insight into the deeper forces that propel history and his sense that history could be linear (having a beginning, middle and end) while still expressing and fulfilling itself through historical repetitions and epicycles. In Virgil as in the Bible, history is both meaningful in itself and capable of giving meaning to what might otherwise seem a chaotic or arbitrary series of events.

As Anchises watches the souls of his descendants parade by him, he (or, better, Virgil) seizes the opportunity to recount the future history of Rome. As Jupiter does in Book I when he assures Venus of his high plans for Aeneas and his progeny, Anchises covers most of the highlights of Roman history (see chapter sixteen). Although not surprisingly he lavishes his greatest praise on Caesar Augustus and his golden age, the real thrust of his history lesson is to illustrate both the virtues of patriotism and duty, and the dangers of civil strife and fratricide. His speech rises to a mighty crescendo as he reminds all future Romans (that is, Virgil's contemporaries) that their true art is not to be sculpture or rhetoric or astrology—arts in which the Greeks surpassed the Romans—but the art of just rule. The arts of Rome, he concludes, are to be these: "To pacify, to impose the rule of law, / To spare the conquered, battle down the proud" (VI.1153-54). Incredibly (and, to my mind at least, providentially) Virgil here echoes the Magnificat of Mary: "[God] hath shewed strength with his arm; he hath scattered the proud in the imagination of their hearts. He hath put down the mighty from their seats, and exalted them of low degree" (Luke 1:51-52). Rome is not to be the bully of the Mediterranean but a force for unity and good. She is to dispense justice rather than brute force, civilized order rather than crushing conformity.

His secular sermon over, Anchises points out the future soul of Marcellus—son of Augustus's sister Octavia (not by Antony but an earlier spouse) and husband of his daughter Julia—who Augustus hoped would succeed him. Anchises prophesies Marcellus's tragic death and offers his own tender, heartfelt eulogy. Tradition has it that Virgil read Book VI aloud to Caesar Augustus and his court; when he got to the death of Marcellus, it is said that Octavia fainted in grief. And so, in an unexpected twist that allows him to simultaneously praise and critique Augustus and his empire,

Virgil transforms the great march of Roman history into a funeral proces-
sion for Marcellus. Perhaps, he suggests, the price of Roman history is too
great; perhaps it is not worth the loss of such fine young men as Icarus,
Palinurus, Misenus and Marcellus.

Earlier, when Virgil describes Aeneas's plucking of the golden bough
(which, the Sibyl had told him, would break off easily in his hand if he
were the chosen one), he mentions that the bough clings "greedily"
(VI.298) to the tree, as though resisting the pull of Aeneas. With this
doubt as to Aeneas's "chosen-ness" still ringing in our ears, Virgil ends
Book VI by sending Aeneas back to the surface not through the gate of
horn, by which true shades come and go, but by the gate of ivory, through
which false dreams are sent. The matter of the bough and the two gates has
puzzled critics since ancient times: has Aeneas—and thus Augustus, of
whom Aeneas is a type—truly been chosen? Is the history of Rome a
march of glory or a false dream? To such questions the *Aeneid* gives no simple answer; Virgil would have us wrestle with him.

21

VIRGIL'S *AENEID* IV

Just War?

WHEN AENEAS DESCENDS INTO THE underworld, his old Trojan identity dies with him; when he returns to the world of the living, it is no longer as a prince of Troy but as a Roman soldier and proto-emperor. So runs the traditional reading, and it is clear that Virgil means us, at least in part, to interpret the shift from the first half of his epic to the second in such a manner. Aeneas is our hero, and Rome and her virtues are good things. Still, Virgil persists in dramatizing the terrible cost that must be paid to ensure the foundations of Rome. And he refuses to assert clearly and categorically that the outcome is worth the cost. Palinurus and Misenus (and Icarus and Marcellus) are merely forerunners of a whole slate of young men who are mowed down in the battles that run throughout the final six books of the *Aeneid*. Ultimately, the only young man who survives is Iulus, Aeneas's son; indeed, Virgil seems to suggest that many of the young men who die are scapegoats to ensure Iulus's survival. As before, far more than one must be lost.

If I may submit a somewhat tentative analogy, Virgil may have viewed the empire of Augustus the way some modern Christians view Constantine's decision to Christianize the Roman Empire. It is surely a good thing that God used the often brutal Constantine to end Rome's persecution of Christianity and pave the way for the Roman Catholic Church; we may even, if we wish, view Constantine as a sort of Christian version of Caesar Augustus. And yet, many today have argued, by institutionalizing the faith and drawing it into the corridors of power, Constantinianism tempted Christian leaders to become as oppressive as their previous persecutors. Nevertheless, very few of those troubled by the negative repercussions of Constantinianism would wish to return the church to her pre-Constantine status as a persecuted minority. Just so, Virgil, though he may have pined for the virtues of the old Roman Republic, surely had no desire to return Rome to her pre-Actium days of bloody civil strife. No, despite his critiques of Augustus, Virgil is finally more like Dante, who critiqued the excesses of Rome while remaining a devout Catholic, than Martin Luther, who broke from Rome altogether. Virgil is a critic from within.

FROM EDEN TO THE NEW JERUSALEM

If Books I to VI are closely patterned on the journeys of Odysseus, then Books VII to XII, which concern themselves with the wars Aeneas must fight to win control of Italy, are more derivative of the *Iliad*. Virgil, in fact, structures the second half of his epic around a love triangle meant to point back typologically to the Paris-Helen-Menelaus triangle that initiated the Trojan War. When Aeneas arrives in northern Italy, the land is ruled by a just king named Latinus, whose daughter Lavinia has been promised in marriage to a neighboring prince, the brave and noble Turnus. At first all seems to go well. Latinus recognizes that Aeneas's coming has been divinely authorized and pledges that his daughter will be given to Aeneas; it even seems that Turnus will accept the marriage as having been destined by the gods. However, as in Book V when she riles up the Trojan women to burn the ships, Juno intervenes and sends one of the Furies to drive mad both Latinus's wife, Amata, and Turnus. As a result, Amata (like Dido) becomes crazed and rages through the countryside in a fit of *furor*. She calls the Italian women to join her in forsaking their homes and exchanging their *pietas* as wives and mothers for a life of Bacchic revelry. She even raises up a torch and pledges her daughter to Turnus in a primitive, unsanctioned ceremony that recalls Aeneas and Dido's "marriage" in the cave. Turnus joins her in her resistance, and, like Menelaus, calls on his fellow Italians to avenge Aeneas's abduction of Lavinia.

Rome, it seems, will not be built so easily. Though by all rights the *Aeneid* should end midway through Book VI with the wedding of Aeneas and Lavinia, the *furor* aroused in Amata and Turnus will lead to a series of battles that will lay waste much of the countryside and leave countless Trojans and Italians dead. If the tragic affair of Aeneas and Dido will prove to be the eschatological cause of the Punic Wars between Rome and Carthage, then the wars between Aeneas and Turnus and their respective allies will be the eschatological origin of the civil wars that tore apart Rome for a century (146 to 31 B.C.). Virgil hints at the latter connection early on in Book VII through the mouth of the enraged wife of Jupiter. Juno knows she cannot stop Jupiter's plans, but she does have the power "to pile delay / Upon delay" (VII.430-31). As Dido calls for eternal enmity between her people and those of Aeneas, so Juno calls for a breach between Latinus and Aeneas: "Let father and son-in-law / Unite at that cost to their own! In blood, / Trojan and Latin, comes your dowry, girl [Lavinia]" (VII.433-35). In this powerfully compact passage, Virgil combines elements from both the past and the future. In speaking of Lavinia's dowry of blood, Virgil calls to mind the imagery of the *Oresteia*, where Aeschylus presents us with a number of blood weddings: Paris and Helen, Agamemnon and Clytemnestra, Achilles and Iphigenia. With his reference to father and son-in-law, however, Virgil draws his reader forward to the first century B.C., when Pompey (who was married to Julius Caesar's daughter, Julia) fought a brutal civil war with his father-in-law that left countless Roman soldiers dead and catapulted Rome into civil war.

Past, present and future are all marked by violence, deceit and bloodshed. There is no straight and peaceful path from Troy to Rome; what victory there is rises out of defeat. In fact, it is Turnus's declaration of war on Aeneas that causes the Trojan to receive his first sight of the city that will become Rome. In desperate need of Italian allies, Aeneas (like Romulus and Remus three centuries later) is carried along the river Tiber to the future site of Rome. There he is taken in by good King Evander who, like Aeneas, is a direct descendant of Atlas. Evander tells the inquisitive Aeneas that Italy once lived in a golden age of pastoral innocence, during which time Saturn (the father of Jupiter) and his fellow Titans lived on the earth with men. Sadly, Italy had since fallen from her age of gold, though during Virgil's day the Romans yearly celebrated the Saturnalia, a raucous, Mardi Gras-like festival of joy and plenty. The Saturnalia was held near the winter solstice, a fact that influenced the church's decision to choose December 25 as the birthday of Christ.[1] Like the Greeks, who also firmly believed they had once lived in a golden age, the Italians yearned for a return of the reign of Saturn, and the church fathers, who knew well the pagan classics, understood that the coming of the Messianic child had both mythically and historically heralded the eventual return of edenic bliss. But it would be a bliss lived out not in a pastoral garden but in a renewed and perfected city: the New Jerusalem. Of course, Virgil tells the same sacred tale. An edenic Italy, along with an edenic Troy, is lost for a time, suffers pain, loss and war, and then is reborn in the perfected city of Rome, capital of a secular New Jerusalem that brings back to earth the lost age of gold.

It is imperative that Aeneas not lose faith in that coming golden age, that he not give in to total despair as he watches civil strife devour both his own men and the men of Italy. In order to strengthen that faith and hold back despair, Aeneas is given a gift by his mother that points simultaneously back to Homer and forward to Augustus. In the *Iliad,* Achilles is given a magnificent suit of armor made by Hephaestus, the god of the forge. Included in the armor is a shield that Homer describes in great detail, for on that shield Hephaestus engraves in bold symbols the eternal choice between war and peace, chaos and civilization, revenge and justice. Aeneas too is given a shield; however, in Virgil's reworking, the shield becomes a repository not of choice per se, but of that glorious end that will give meaning and purpose to the choices, good and bad, that we make on our way toward that future. As in Homer, the shield is forged by Hephaestus (Vulcan), and the one who requests it is the mother of the hero (Thetis, Venus), but this time around, the mother also happens to be the wife of the craftsman. What that means, if I may be blunt, is that Virgil's Vulcan is

---

[1]For a different, and fascinating, interpretation of the dating of Christmas, see William J. Tighe, "Calculating Christmas," *Touchstone* 16, no. 10 (December 2003): 12-14.

asked to make a suit of armor to protect the bastard son of his unfaithful wife! And yet so good a Roman is he, so filled with self-sacrificial *pietas*, that he does as he is asked.

Along with Jupiter's prophecy in Book I and Anchises' secular sermon in Book VI, Virgil's description of the shield (VIII.848-986) marks the third passage in the *Aeneid* in which the history of Rome is recounted in detail. Significantly, at the center of the shield, Vulcan does not engrave Romulus's founding of Rome or the defeat of Hannibal, but the Battle of Actium:

> Vivid in the center were the bronze-beaked
> Ships and the fight at sea off Actium.
> Here you could see Leucata all alive
> With ships maneuvering, sea glowing gold,
> Augustus Caesar leading into battle
> Italians, with both senators and people,
> Household gods and great gods . . .
> Then came Antonius with barbaric wealth
> And a diversity of arms, victorious
> From races of the Dawnlands and Red Sea,
> Leading the power of the East, of Egypt,
> Even of distant Bactra of the steppes.
> And in his wake the Egyptian consort came
> So shamefully . . . a frenzy out of Egypt,
> Never turning her head as yet to see
> Twin snakes of death behind, while monster-forms
> Of gods of every race, and the dog-god
> Anubis barking, held their weapons up
> Against our Neptune, Venus, and Minerva.
> (VIII.912-18; 926-32; 943-48)

In his epic-historical telling of the Persian War, Herodotus distinguished carefully between the Western Greeks, who were unified, civilized, freedom-loving and pious, and the Eastern Persians, who were disunified, barbaric, tyrannical and blasphemous. Virgil embodies a similar cultural dichotomy in his richly symbolic depiction of Actium. Though Caesar Augustus was still called Octavian at the time of Actium,

Virgil here uses his later title to assert that it is at this very moment that the soldier-politician Octavian metamorphoses into the messianic Augustus. On the shield, the future emperor is the glue that unifies not only senators and people, but the more provincial Lares and Penates, which Virgil has Aeneas anachronistically carry out of Troy, and the more universal, cosmopolitan gods of Olympus that link the new grandeur of Rome with the old glory of Greece. Set against him is the barbaric and ostentatious Antony, who leads a mongrel, Babel-like crew and who is joined in illicit passion with Cleopatra (whom Virgil never names). The Eastern forces pay homage to hideous and bestial monster-gods, while Augustus fights in the name of the gods of civilization and order. Actium, Virgil's iconic image is telling us, is more than a battle between two potential emperors; it is a clash of civilizations in which the one must totally defeat the other.

Just as the Jews of the Old Testament were commanded by God to annihilate the "bad" pagan tribes of Canaan lest they corrupt Israel, so here Jupiter uses Augustus to eliminate both the armies and the "worldview" of Antony and Cleopatra. Of course, Rome's destruction of Carthage resulted in a similar elimination of the "bad" pagans, but at Actium the threat was greater, for it came perilously close to corrupting Rome from within. All of this—physical and moral struggle alike—is engraved on the shield, and as Aeneas gazes on it, he feels both wonder and joy. Like Isaiah, Ezekiel and John, Aeneas does not know what the prophetic pictures mean, but they fill him with a sense of hope and promise. Book VIII closes with Aeneas lifting up the shield, and thus "taking up / Upon his shoulders all the destined acts / And fame of his descendants" (VIII.990-92). Unlike Achilles, who carries with him into battle the burden of human choice, Aeneas carries upon his arm the full weight of the future.

DELAY UPON DELAY

Virgil's earliest Latin critics were well aware that *Roma* (Rome) written backwards spelled *Amor*, a significant anagram since Romans like Julius Caesar made much of the fact that they were descended both from war (Mars, the father of Romulus) and love (Venus, the mother of Aeneas). Indeed, though Aeneas follows Greek tradition in identifying Venus as the wife of Vulcan, the Romans more often depicted Venus as married to Mars. Early critical consensus had it that Virgil had used this anagram as a structural device for his epic: Books I to IV, which climax in the tragic affair of Aeneas and Dido, embody *Amor*, while Books V to VIII, which include Anchises' secular sermon, the shield and Aeneas's visit to the future site of Rome, embody *Roma*. What then of Books IX to XII? For the last third of the *Aeneid*, the critics believed, Virgil used another anagram: *Mora* ("delay"). Though the exalted finale of Book VIII gives us hope that Aeneas will charge into battle carrying his prophetic shield and quickly restore unity to Italy, we get instead four very long books of delay that stretch out Juno's curse in Book VII to the point of utter exhaustion and frustration.

Every time we think that peace has been achieved, war breaks out again. Virgil even factors into the ever-renewed conflict a typological replay of a second Homeric triangle. Not only do Aeneas and Turnus, along with Lavinia, replay the triangle of Paris, Menelaus and Helen (and simultaneously Agamemnon, Achilles and Briseis), the two warriors, along with a soldier named Pallas, also replay the triangle of Achilles, Hektor and Patroclus. In addition to supplying Aeneas with troops, Evander entrusts him with the life of his son Pallas. Though Aeneas quickly comes to care for the young warrior, their friendship is not as deep as that between Achilles and Patroclus; rather, the true bond that ties the two men is that of *pietas:* the duty Aeneas owes to Evander to protect his son from harm. As the *Aeneid* is bound both to the future history of Rome and the past legacy of Homer, Virgil must eventually allow Pallas to be killed by Turnus, and Turnus to be killed in turn by Aeneas.

But the Roman poet does something with his Homeric allusion that Homer could not have done. As the later poet, Virgil is able not only to link his hero to three successive characters in the *Iliad*—Paris, Agamemnon and Achilles—but to suggest a troubling shift from the first to the second to the third. As a type of Paris, Aeneas retains his link to Troy and the noble Hektor, Paris's brother. When he shifts slightly into a type of Agamemnon, he loses his Trojan status but is still defined over against Turnus, who himself shifts into a type of Achilles (Turnus, in fact, boldly identifies himself as a second Achilles at one point). When, however, Aeneas morphs into Achilles himself, the greatest and fiercest enemy of Troy, and

leaves Turnus to assume the typological role of Hektor, he loses much of
our sympathy and much of his own identity. He has become the enemy, has
embodied that unstoppable wrath *(furor)* of Achilles that ripped the life
out of Hektor and thus Troy. This sad, grueling transformation is developed slowly over the last six books, and then is replayed in miniature over
the course of Book XII.

Near the start of Virgil's final book, Aeneas, though he has been deeply
injured by Turnus and his Italian troops, makes a generous, high-minded
oath that he will "not make Italians underlings / To Trojans . . . [but will
allow] both nations, both unconquered, both / Subject to equal laws, commit themselves / To an eternal union" (XII.255-59). Aeneas will, it seems,
live up to Anchises' Magnificat-like charge that he spare the conquered by
extending what the Romans called *clementia* ("clemency") to his enemies.
But it is not to be. War breaks out again, and when Aeneas lifts his right
hand to calm his own troops, an arrow flies out of nowhere and strikes him
down, though it does not kill him. Virgil never identifies the would-be as-
sassin, though he surely had in mind the three unsuccessful assassination
attempts that had been made on Augustus; he might have remembered as
well that some of the senators who plotted to kill Julius Caesar had been
recipients of Caesar's *clementia* (as King Saul had been a recipient of
David's clemency). The movement of history often defies a clear series of
causal events; the arrow that strikes down Aeneas is dramatized by Virgil
as a silent, faceless stab against fate and destiny. It cannot be explained or
justified, only endured—like the two massacres of innocent children perpetrated by Pharaoh and Herod, which nevertheless failed to kill Moses or
Jesus.

Once healed of his wounds, Aeneas dons his armor and prepares to reenter the battle, pausing only to say farewell to his son. The scene is meant
to recall Hektor's farewell to his wife and son in the *Iliad,* but Virgil makes
a subtle change. Unlike Hektor, Aeneas does not remove his helmet before
hugging his boy; rather, he embraces him "with steel" and brushes his lips
"through his vizor" (XII.593-94). Aeneas is slowly surrendering his Hek-
tor-like gentleness and humanity to become the kind of soulless killing
machine that Achilles becomes in *Iliad* XX to XXII. So furious, in fact, do
Aeneas and his fellow warriors become that Virgil himself, in a rare mo-

ment of authorial intrusion, cries out: "Was it thy pleasure, Jupiter, that peoples / Afterward to live in lasting peace / Should rend each other in so black a storm?" (XII.684-86). Despite the prophecies, the oaths and the ghosts in the machine, *furor* draws both armies into a whirlpool of destruction. Aeneas, while still swearing that he fights against his will, goes so far as to set fire to the capital of Latinus's kingdom. It is now the Trojan Aeneas and not the brutal Achilles or deceitful Ulysses who sets fire to a defenseless city filled with innocent women and children.

In the end, as it must be, Aeneas and Turnus face each other for a one-on-one duel. For a while, Juno protects Turnus by sending his deified sister, Juturna, to assist him in the battle; but Jupiter, grown weary of Juno's meddling and the needless bloodshed it is causing, finally intervenes and prevents her from further delaying Aeneas's conquest of Italy. Juno gives in to her husband's command, but asks of him one favor: the Trojan victors must not be allowed to eradicate the culture and traditions of the native Italians. Jupiter agrees, promising that the Trojans will "mingle and be submerged, incorporated. / Rituals and observances of theirs / I'll add, but make them Latin, one in speech" (XII.1134-36). It is a breathtaking moment, and a powerfully mature one. Over the course of the New Testament, we slowly watch as Israel, God's chosen people, becomes incorporated into the church, the bride of Christ, preserving some of her distinctives yet yielding her name and former identity. Here we watch a similar process as Jupiter fashions a new Latin-Roman bride out of the fusion of Trojan and Italian. The feminine has been appeased—or, better, masculine and feminine have each asserted their different but complementary concerns—and it has led to a union not unlike that of Jew and Gentile.

Could we end at this heightened and idealizing moment, all would be well. But Virgil does not end here. In order to chase away Juturna and allow Aeneas to defeat Turnus, Virgil has Jupiter call out of the ground a hideous, chthonic fiend, a "spawn / Of Night" (XII.1164-65) who strongly resembles the Fury that Juno called up to enflame Amata and Turnus. This hell-born demon, one of two who attend at the very throne of Jupiter, does the bidding of her master; however, unlike Juno's Fury (who is put back into Hades at VII.766-72), Jupiter's Fury is never put back in her underground prison. Instead, the *Aeneid* implies, she is still at large in Augustus's

Rome. Could Virgil be suggesting that the Pax Romana was not so "Pax" as his emperor claimed?

Still, one last ray of hope remains. In the closing lines of the *Aeneid*, as Aeneas prepares to kill his vanquished enemy, Turnus appeals to him for *clementia*, and Aeneas grants it. That is, until he notices that Turnus is wearing an engraved swordbelt that Turnus had taken from the corpse of Pallas (as Hektor had stripped Achilles' armor off the body of Patroclus). When he sees the swordbelt, Aeneas loses all thought of sparing the conquered, and perceiving Turnus as his "enemy still" (XII.1287; see VI.635), "[sinks] his blade in fury in Turnus' chest" (XII.1295). The verb Virgil uses for "sink" is the same verb used to describe the "founding" of a city; it recalls how Romulus founded his fratricidal sword in the body of Remus. Although the typological link between Aeneas and Romulus could be interpreted here to embody the hope of the *felix culpa*, Virgil's staging of the scene offers little hope of a lasting Pax Romana between Rome and her enemies, both foreign and domestic. Indeed, as if to drive home the precariousness of peace in a world of *furor* and civil strife, Virgil abruptly and disturbingly ends his epic at this lowest of points, when his hero—a type of Augustus—has given himself over to wrath. It is as if Homer had ended the *Iliad* with the death of Hektor rather than with the reconciliation of Achilles and Priam. Virgil, it seems, is issuing to his contemporary Roman audience (and his emperor) a stern warning: that the sword once drawn cannot easily by resheathed. But he may also be prophesying unknowingly to his later, unintended Christian audience that the "good" pagans of Rome could only go so far in their messianic role. The time was coming— and was now at hand—when the true Jupiter would reveal to the world his own eternal Pax Romana.

CONCLUSION

The Myth Made Fact

THOUGH MOST READERS ARE AWARE that C. S. Lewis, arguably the greatest Christian apologist of the twentieth century, was a former atheist, many do not know that his conversion occurred in two distinct stages. Before embracing Christ as the only begotten Son of God, Lewis spent two intermediate years as a theist, believing in the existence of God but still rejecting the doctrines of the trinity and the incarnation. Among the events and influences that led Lewis to make the leap from theism to Christianity, the most important was a long evening talk he had with a close friend, a devout Roman Catholic named J. R. R. Tolkien (author of *The Lord of the Rings*). As they walked along the grounds of Magdalen College in Oxford, Lewis confided in Tolkien that his knowledge of mythology (which was extensive) prevented him from accepting the gospel narrative as true. After all, the mythologies of the world were filled with stories of gods who came to earth, took on human form, died violent deaths, and returned again to life: Adonis, Osiris, Tammuz, Mithras, Balder and so on. Was not Christianity just another such myth, albeit a more sophisticated one? In response, Tolkien acknowledged the prevalence of god-men in pagan myths and legends, but then went on to suggest a different way of interpreting this phenomenon. What if, Tolkien challenged his skeptical friend, the reason that the story of Christ sounded so similar to the pagan tales of dying and rising gods was because Jesus was the myth that came true?

Tolkien's challenge revolutionized Lewis's way of viewing mythology, and not many days would pass before he would surrender his life to Christ, the historical God-man. No longer a stumbling block, the ancient Greek, Roman and Norse tales that Lewis so loved would become one of the mainstays and bulwarks of his new faith. Rather than dismiss the miraculous elements of Christmas and Easter as having no more historical validity than the scapegoat tales of Oedipus or Prometheus (as many moderns do), or reject the myths themselves as either irrelevant to faith or lies of the devil meant to deceive (as many Christians do), Lewis came to view the myths as glimpses, road signs, pointers to a greater truth that was someday to be revealed literally and historically in a specific time and place. To quote Lewis himself:

> The heart of Christianity is a myth which is also a fact. The old myth of the Dying God, without ceasing to be myth, comes down from the heaven of legend and imagination to the earth of history. It happens—at a particular date, in a particular place, followed by definable historical consequences. We pass from a Balder or an Osiris, dying nobody knows when or where, to a historical Person crucified (it is all in order) under Pontius Pilate. By becoming fact it does not cease to be myth: that is the miracle. . . . God is more than a god, not less: Christ is more than Balder, not less. We must not be ashamed of the mythical radiance resting on our theology. We must not be nervous about "parallels" and "Pagan Christs": they ought to be there—it would be a stumbling block if they weren't.[1]

For Lewis, it is just as vital that we proclaim and accept the full historicity of the Christian gospel as it is that we celebrate and experience its full mythic power. Yes, Lewis asserts, Christ is more than Balder (or Achilles or Hercules or Dionysus) in the sense that his death and resurrection occurred in real time and had real consequences. But we must not allow his

---

[1]C. S. Lewis, "Myth Became Fact," in *God in the Dock*, ed. Walter Hooper (Grand Rapids: Eerdmans, 1970), pp. 66-67.

status as the historical dying god to rob him of his mythic splendor. Christ should speak not only to our rational, logical side, but to our sense of wonder and awe as well.

If Christianity is true, then the God who created both us and the universe chose to reveal himself through a sacred story that resembles more the imaginative works of epic poets and tragedians than the rational meditations of philosophers and theologians. The historical enactment of the Passion did not render the old pagan tales unclean; on the contrary, it had the reverse effect of baptizing and purifying them. The coming of the Jewish Messiah made clean the lawless, nonkosher Gentiles (see Acts 10); may it not have made clean as well their deepest mythic yearnings? The relationship between Mary and the baby Jesus has made potentially sacred the relationship between every mother and child both B.C. and A.D.; in a like manner, the gospel story spreads its light both forward and backward to uplift and ennoble all stories that speak of sacrifice and reconciliation, of messianic promise and eschatological hope. It was through the Psalms and the Prophets, which were written in poetry, as well as the "epic" tales of the Old Testament—Abraham's long, circuitous journey, Joseph and his brothers, the Passover and Exodus—that Yahweh prepared the hearts and minds of his people for the incarnation of the Christ. Is it so unbelievable that he should have used the greatest poets, storytellers and "prophets" of antiquity to prepare the hearts of the pagans?

Indeed, as these pagans were without the Law and cut off from the special revelation given to the biblical writers, how else could God have reached them? Yes, God certainly spoke to them through the natural world (see Acts 14:15-17; Romans 1:18-20), but how was he to reach them at the deeper levels of their being? According to Lewis, before the full revelation of Christ, God communicated with men in three basic ways: through their consciences, through his historical struggles with a single, chosen race of people, and through what Lewis calls "good dreams: I mean those queer stories scattered all through the heathen religions about a god who dies and comes to life again and, by his death, has somehow given new life to men."[2] It has been the burden and joy of this book both to examine and

---

[2]C. S. Lewis, *Mere Christianity* (New York: HarperCollins, 2001), p. 50.

celebrate some of these "good dreams" as they were distilled and reshaped by the finest poets of Greece and Rome. I have, of course, widened the scope of those good dreams to include tales and characters that embody pre-Christian themes and yearnings not directly related to the dying and rising scapegoat; however, I have tried to keep true to the belief shared by Lewis, Tolkien, Dante, Newman and many others that the light of God's revelation shines (if dimly and intermittently) through the literary masterpieces of antiquity.

And what of today? Do we who live on this side of Calvary still need good dreams? I would say that we do, that we need them even more, for the secular, rationalistic, post-Enlightenment world in which we live has dissected, demythologized, and denied many of our most cherished myths. To make matters worse, Christians are often the first to distance themselves from that which is mythic, not (as they try to convince themselves) because they are believers, but because they have absorbed, generally unconsciously, the modern world's suspicion of fairy stories. Yet the hunger remains, a hunger that has, I believe, sent many young people rushing into the arms of the neopagan New Age in search of a lost sense of the numinous and the sacred. Despite 250 years of Enlightenment rationalism, they still yearn, and if they yearn, then they can be wooed back—perhaps not directly to Christ, but at least to a pre-Christian mindset that will open the door for a later embrace of the historical God-man. Lewis's Chronicles of Narnia and Tolkien's *Lord of the Rings* (both on page and screen) have carried on this wooing with great success. Childhood precedes adulthood as the seed the tree: just so, the pagan mind, whether B.C. or A.D., cannot perceive God face to face until it has first peered dimly into the dark, mysterious glass of myth.

BIBLIOGRAPHICAL ESSAY

I MUST ACKNOWLEDGE RIGHT OFF THE bat that there is already an excellent book offering a Christian look at Homer, Virgil and the Greek tragedians: *Heroes of the City of Man: A Christian Guide to Select Ancient Literature* by Peter J. Leithart (Canon, 1999). If you have enjoyed reading my book, you should enjoy this one as well; though Leithart covers most of the same primary texts, our approaches complement rather than overlap one another. Leithart looks more with the eye of a theologian and Bible scholar (he is particularly adept at uncovering the chiastic structures of ancient literature), while my perspective is more that of an English professor and literary theorist. Leithart focuses more on background and narrative structure; I focus more on characters, themes and symbols. Finally, though Leithart and I would no doubt agree on most points, his work is a bit more reluctant than my own to embrace the ancients as full pre-Christian writers from whom Christians can learn truths that will deepen and enrich their faith.

For those wishing to beef up on their Greco-Roman mythology, the best four reference books are Edith Hamilton's *Mythology* (Mentor), Bulfinch's *Mythology*, Michael Grant's *Myths of the Greeks and Romans* (Mentor), and Robert Graves's *The Greek Myths* (Penguin; two volumes). Hamilton's is probably the most accessible of the four; Graves's is the most detailed and scholarly. Two other excellent references that are worth having on your shelf are Betty Radice's *Who's Who in the Ancient World* (Penguin) and Benet's *Reader's Encyclopedia* (the fourth edition is edited by Bruce Murphy for HarperCollins).

Still, though these reference works are all helpful, it is my hope that this book will inspire you to go directly to the primary sources, to the original and very accessible tellings of these classic tales. In addition to Homer, Virgil and the tragedians, the best primary sources are the *Homeric Hymns*, Hesiod's *Theogony* and *Works and Days*, Plato's *Symposium*, *Phaedo* and *Republic X*, Pindar's *Odes*, Apollonius of Rhodes's *Voyage of the Argo (Argonautica)*, *The Library of Apollodorus*, Ovid's *Metamorphoses*, Apuleius's *The Golden Ass* and Quintus Smyrnaeus's *The Fall of Troy*. Remember: Greek mythology is not a systematic thing; each poet tells the myth in a way that will further his own thematic purposes. That is to say, there are from our modern, "scientific" point of view lots of "contradictions" in the wide and varied field of Greek mythology: chronologies, motivations, place names, character relationships and so on differ from poet to poet. Like the diverse stories surrounding the age and exploits of Arthur and his knights, the tales of Greek mythology are the raw material that inspired the poets of Greece and Rome to explore the essential questions and issues of humanity.

PART ONE: HOMER

My favorite translation for the *Iliad*, and the one from which I quote in this book, remains that of Richmond Lattimore (University of Chicago Press), though the translation by Robert Fagles (Penguin) is also excellent and a bit easier to understand; you can even purchase a series of audiotapes in which British Shakespearean actor Derek Jacobi reads aloud Fagles's *Iliad*. I prefer to use the prose translation of the *Odyssey* by E. V. Rieu (updated by his son, D. C. H. Rieu; Penguin, 1991). If you want a verse translation, the ones by Robert Fitzgerald, Richmond Lattimore and Robert Fagles are all excellent.

A good way to get yourself in the mood for reading Homer is to purchase Michael Wood's *In Search of the Trojan War* (University of California Press, 1998); based on Wood's own PBS series, this gives the most compact and accessible overview of issues related to Homer and his epics. I have also greatly enjoyed the chapters on Homer in Thomas Cahill's *Sailing the Wine-Dark Sea: Why the Greeks Matter* (Doubleday, 2003) and Glenn C. Arbery's *Why Literature Matters* (ISI Books, 2001); Arbery does a particularly good job discussing Achilles' semidivine status and the nature of his wrath. Perhaps the best introduction to the *Iliad* itself is Lattimore's long introduction to his own translation. For a line-by-line analysis of Lattimore's translation of the *Odyssey*, consult Peter V. Jones's *Homer's Odyssey: A Companion to the Translation of Richmond Lattimore* (Southern Illinois University Press, 1988). There are also two companions to Lattimore's *Iliad* available: one by Malcolm Willcock (University of Chicago Press, 1976) and another by Norman Postlethwaite (University of Exeter Press, 2000). Bernard Knox has also written good notes to accompany Fagles's translations of Homer. One of my favorite studies of Homer is Seth Shein's *The Mortal Hero* (University of California Press, 1985); it was Shein who first drew my attention to the fact that the Greek gods (unlike Yahweh) help heroes who are already strong. My understanding of the role of *aidos* and *nemesis* in Homer is strongly indebted to Gilbert Murray's *The Rise of the Greek Epic* (Oxford: Oxford University Press, 1960).

I would especially encourage the non-specialist to pick up a copy of the *Norton Critical Edition of the Odyssey*, which, in addition to the fully annotated text, includes numerous essays that offer useful background information and a number of different perspectives on Homer in general and the *Odyssey* in particular. The *Norton Anthology of World Literature*, Volume I (any edition will do) offers generous selections from Homer and Virgil and several tragedies that are all well annotated. I have found Howard W. Clarke's *The Art of the Odyssey* (Bristol Classical Press, 1989) to be a particularly good read, and there are fine chapters on Homer and the tragedians in *Ancient Greek Literature*, edited by K. J. Dover (Oxford University Press, 1997) and C. M. Bowra's *Ancient Greek Literature* (Oxford University Press, 1960). For a multitude of perspectives, the reader might wish to consult the *Cambridge Companion to Homer*, edited by Robert Fowler. I must also acknowledge here a personal debt I owe to Professor H. D. Cameron, who led the Great Books Honors Program at the University of Michigan while I was there getting my Ph.D. I was one of the teaching assistants for his class in 1990, and his lectures helped inspire and organize many of my reflections on Homer and Virgil.[1]

For readers who are up to the challenge, Robert Lamberton's *Homer the Theologian: Neoplatonist Allegorical Reading and the Growth of the Epic Tradition* (University of California Press, 1986) offers a wide-ranging study of how Homer was read allegorically both by pagan Neoplatonists and by Classical and medieval Christians.

An additional resource are the many excellent audio and video lecture series produced by the Teaching Company (1-800-TEACH12; www.teach12.com). Elizabeth Vandiver has put together fine courses not only on the *Iliad* and *Odyssey*, but on the *Aeneid*, *Greek Mythology* and *Greek Tragedy*. I myself have produced a series (*Plato to Postmodernism: Understanding the Essence of Literature and the Role of the Author*) that offers two lectures on Aristotle's *Poetics*.

PART TWO: THE GREEK TRAGEDIANS

In all but one case, I have chosen to quote the Greek tragedies as they appear in *The Complete Greek Tragedies*, edited by David Grene and Richmond Lattimore for University of Chicago Press. Part of the reason for my choice was practical; these editions of the plays include line numbers that are very closely keyed to the original Greek. However, I also find that the translations have a stark and timeless quality that captures much of the grandeur and eternality of the plays. Although the translation of Aeschylus's *Oresteia* by Lattimore is superb, I chose to quote from Fagles's translation in chapter ten because it renders the choral lyrics in a more accessible manner. Still, I heartily recommend Lattimore's translation. I should also mention that Penguin Classics has published a set of books that include the full tragic canon and that are well worth reading. They are often a bit

---

[1] I would also like to add here a special thank you and acknowledgment to Anthony Esolen and Louise Cowan, both of whom read this book in manuscript form and offered me invaluable advice on how to strengthen and expand some of its arguments. Finally, I would like to acknowledge the assistance of my fine editor, Joel Scandrett.

more fluid and colloquial than the ones published by Chicago and will probably offer a smoother read for those unacquainted with the tragedies. It would not be a bad thing to have both the Chicago and Penguin editions on your shelf. I would also highly recommend *Ten Play by Euripides*, translated by Moses Hadas and John McLean (Bantam Reissue, 1984). This book includes all four Euripides plays discussed in chapters fourteen and fifteen, along with six others; the translations are well executed and good for performance. *Critical Theory Since Plato*, edited by Hazard Adams, revised edition (HBJ, 1992) includes the full text of Aristotle's *Poetics* along with other key works in the history of literary criticism.

To my mind, the two books that offer the best and clearest overview of the subject are H. C. Baldry's *The Greek Tragic Theatre* (Norton, 1971; also see his *Ancient Greek Literature in its Living Context*) and Peter D. Arnott's *An Introduction to the Greek Theatre* (Indiana University Press, 1967; Arnott has also written several other good books on Greek theater). Richmond Lattimore's *Story Patterns in Greek Tragedy* (University of Michigan Press, 1964) offers a helpful survey of the various plot structures that underlie Athenian drama. A great one-volume resource is the *Norton Critical Edition of Oedipus Tyrannus*, which, in addition to the annotated text, offers two hundred pages of assorted critical essays. If one remains aware of its clear Marxist bias, George Thomson's *Aeschylus and Athens* (Universal Library, 1968) has insightful chapters on the playwright and his plays; if one is aware of its Enlightenment bias, much is to be gained from Gilbert Murray's *Euripides and His Age* (Oxford University Press, 1965).

PART THREE: VIRGIL

My preferred translation of the *Aeneid* remains the one by Robert Fitzgerald (Vintage); it has epic drive and is a pleasure to read. It also includes an excellent glossary of names and a good postscript by Fitzgerald. The translation by Allen Mandelbaum (Bantam) is slightly more accurate than the one by Fitzgerald, but I find it a tad dull compared to Fitzgerald's more rousing style. Virgil's *Fourth Eclogue* can be found in the Penguin edition of Virgil's *Georgics and Eclogues*. The former poet laureate of Britain, C. Day Lewis, has also done a splendid translation of these works (Anchor, 1964).

To understand both the grand sweep and the lesser details of the history of Rome, the best friend of the lay reader is Michael Grant, who has published numerous works on various aspects of Roman history that have been frequently reissued; I would suggest three of his books in particular: *The History of Rome*, *The World of Rome* and *The Fall of the Roman Empire*. Another good overview can be found in Donald R. Dudley's *The Civilization of Rome* (Signet, 1960). Also make sure to read G. K. Chesterton's *The Everlasting Man* (Ignatius, 1993) for his Christian interpretation of Roman history.

However, the best way to get to know Rome from the inside (as Virgil himself would have known it) is to read her own great historians, some of whom were Greek and others of whom were Italian. Here are some of the books that I would suggest (all available in inexpensive Penguin paperbacks): for the foundations of Rome from Romulus to the Republic, read Livy's *The Early History of Rome*; for the Punic Wars, read Polybius's *The Rise of the Roman Empire*; for the heyday and fall of the Roman Republic, read Plutarch's *Makers of Rome and Fall of the Roman Empire*; for Julius Caesar's military campaign in France, read Caesar's *The Conquest of Gaul*; for an intimate look at the civil strife of the late Republic, see Cicero's *Selected Works*; for a Rome-behind-closed-doors look at all the emperors from Julius Caesar to Domitian, read Suetonius's *The Twelve Caesars*; for an in-depth study of the early Empire, including Nero's persecution of the Christians, read Tacitus's *The Annals of Imperial Rome*. This list by no means exhausts the primary sources, but it is a good place to start; let Livy and Plutarch be your initial guides, and then move on to Polybius and Cicero.

One of the best books on Virgil and his poetry is Brooks Otis's *Virgil: A Study in Civilized Poetry* (University of Oklahoma Press, 1995); chapter seventeen of this book owes a debt to the second chapter of this fine study. A good, standard analysis of the *Aeneid* is to be found in Richard Heinze's *Virgil's Epic Technique* (now available in paperback from Duckworth, 2004). A good study of the divine structure of the *Aeneid* is Denis Feeney's *The Gods in Epic* (Oxford University Press, 1993). For a darker but still balanced reading of the *Aeneid*, see Michael Putnam's *The Poetry of the Aeneid* (Cornell University Press, 1989). For a multitude of perspectives, consult the *Cambridge Companion to Virgil*, edited by Charles Martindale. Another helpful resource is *Reading Vergil's Aeneid: An Interpretive Guide*, edited by Christine Perkell (University of Oklahoma Press, 1999). This book evolved out of a 1994 NEH-sponsored summer institute on the *Aeneid* held at Emory University and directed masterfully by Perkell; I was myself a participant in this institute and benefited greatly from it. Indeed, some of my insights on Virgil's critique of Augustus, his use of the gods, and his handling of the funeral games for Anchises are indebted in part to the fine lectures given by, respectively, Putnam, Feeney and Joseph Farrell.

For readers who are up to the challenge, Domenico Comparetti's *Vergil in the Middle Ages* (translated by E. F. M. Benecke; Princeton University Press, 1997) offers a classic, detailed study of how Virgil was read and "Christianized" throughout the Middle Ages.

Index